A New History of Spani

A New History of Spanish Writing
1939 to the 1990s

Chris Perriam, Michael Thompson,
Susan Frenk, and Vanessa Knights

OXFORD
UNIVERSITY PRESS

OXFORD
UNIVERSITY PRESS

Great Clarendon Street, Oxford OX2 6DP
Oxford University Press is a department of the University of Oxford.
It furthers the University's objective of excellence in research, scholarship,
and education by publishing worldwide in
Oxford New York
Athens Auckland Bangkok Bogotá Buenos Aires Calcutta
Cape Town Chennai Dar es Salaam Delhi Florence Hong Kong Istanbul
Karachi Kuala Lumpur Madrid Melbourne Mexico City Mumbai
Nairobi Paris São Paulo Singapore Taipei Tokyo Toronto Warsaw
with associated companies in Berlin Ibadan

Oxford is a registered trade mark of Oxford University Press
in the UK and certain other countries

Published in the United States
by Oxford University Press Inc., New York

© Chris Perriam, Michael Thompson, Susan, Frenk, and Vanessa Knights 2000

The moral rights of the authors have been asserted
Database right Oxford University Press (maker)

First published 2000

All rights reserved. No part of this publication may be reproduced,
stored in a retrieval system, or transmitted, in any form or by any means,
without the prior permission in writing of Oxford University Press,
or as expressly permitted by law, or under terms agreed with the appropriate
reprographics rights organizations. Enquiries concerning reproduction
outside the scope of the above should be sent to the Rights Department,
Oxford University Press, at the address above

You must not circulate this book in any other binding or cover
and you must impose this same condition on any acquirer

British Library Cataloguing in Publication Data
Data available

Library of Congress Cataloging in Publication Data
Data available

ISBN–0–19–871516–1
ISBN–0–19–871517–X (Pbk.)

1 3 5 7 9 10 8 6 4 2

Typeset in Sabon
by Cambrian Typesetters, Frimley, Surrey

Printed in Great Britain
on acid-free paper by
Biddles Ltd.
Guildford and King's Lynn

Preface

Spain's peculiarly dramatic history since the end of its Civil War has given rise to a series of major responses by imaginative writers. Some texts are vibrant, some battling with despair; some are already among the canonical texts of European and world literature, others—responding with just as much force to historical circumstance—have kept away or been kept away from the categories of literary writing. This *New History* looks at 'Spanish literature' in the period 1939 to the 1990s, but also at frontier genres, such as the journalistic essay, and at texts so loosely—or recently—connected with the notion of literature that we have chosen to leave the word 'literature' out of our title and to avoid rehearsals in our narrative of caveats and redefinitions.

The book is aimed at all students of Spanish culture, and we hope that we have also been able effectively to suggest one or two new ways into the subject for those who teach it. The latter will find what is always found in studies such as this—omissions they would rather had not been made: for that we offer the usual apologies, and the explanation which follows.

In discussing canonical texts we have made more space than is usual for comment and analysis; similarly, in wishing properly to contextualize literary writing we have made time to pause on forms of writing not treated at any length in the standard histories. We also depart from these histories by favouring not a chronological narrative but a thematic approach in which we have attempted to deal as much with abstract issues (silence, for example) as with the apparently straightforward ones (the family, or realism). The reader will find that substantial periods of time are covered within individual chapters and even, where appropriate, sections; and that the same periods may be returned to from another perspective elsewhere: in this way we hope to show how the issues treated feed into one another in ways more complex than the simply sequential. Writing and writers are considered, then, not just as products of social change, but as participants in multiple networks of construction and deconstruction of ideologies and identities.

However, Chapter 1 performs the equally necessary task of taking the reader through the period from start to finish, cross-matching historical and literary (or textualized) events and trends in a relatively straightforward way, and assuming provisionally that this makes 'sense', at least as a starting point. Authors or topics which receive substantial treatment elsewhere in the text are marked with an asterisk: cross-references can be found by using the index. The index restricts itself to topics, writers, magazines, and journals, specific texts can be located through their authors. All quotations and titles of imaginative works are translated; technical terms, abbreviations, and nomenclatures are explained in the text, and when in Spanish are, again, translated.

We have had, for lack of expertise and out of commitment to our remit, to focus on Castilian-language writing and do not, in the main, cover the writings of the other languages of Spain in the hope that the excellent full-length studies now coming out of Spain will find English-language equivalents to supplement the smaller-scale, though substantial, scholarly work being done in Australia, Britain, Canada, New Zealand, and the USA.

C.G.P.
M.P.T.
S.F.F.
V.N.M.K.

Contents

Notes on Contributors   xi

1. FIRST PERSPECTIVES: SPAIN FROM 1939 TO THE 1990s   1
   1.1. Introduction   1
   1.2. Springtime for Franco: From 1939 to the early 1950s   1
   1.3. Making the Dictatorship Work: Change in the 1950s   13
   1.4. Cracks and Fissures: 1962–1975   15
   1.5. Changes: 1975–1996   20

2. REWRITING HISTORY
   2.1. Eternal Spain: The Mythology of Empire   25
   2.2. Educational Texts: Indoctrinating the Young   27
   2.3. Poetry of the 1940s: Victory, 'Rootedness', Uncertainty   31
   2.4. Drama: Restaging the Past   36
   2.5. Prose Writing in the 1940s   38

3. RECLAIMING HISTORY
   3.1. Essays in New History   44
   3.2. Poetry: Becoming Committed   45
   3.3. Drama: History in Motion   47
   3.4. Representing Ordinary Histories: Ramón José Sender and Ignacio Aldecoa   57
   3.5. Deconstructing History   62

4.	KEEPING IT IN THE FAMILY	68
	4.1. Constructing the Model	68
	4.2. Deconstructing the Model	73
	4.3. Family Dramas	77
	4.4. Women Writing the Family	86
	4.5. Modernization and the Family	90
5.	POWER AND DISEMPOWERMENT	96
	5.1. Gendered Discourses of Power	96
	5.2. Church and State	105
	5.3. Answering Back	108
	5.4. Against the PSOE	114
6.	LANGUAGES OF SILENCE	118
	6.1. Keeping it Quiet	118
	6.2. Poetry of Exile and Absence	125
7.	GETTING A SENSE OF REALITY	135
	7.1. Power and Reality	135
	7.2. Versions of Realism	135
	7.3. From Realism to Anti-Realism?	143
	7.4. Escapisms and Realisms in the Theatre	149
	7.5. New Realism in Poetry	157
8.	NEW WRITING: NEW SPAIN?	163
	8.1. Problems of Categorization	163
	8.2. Experience and Experimentalism: Juan Goytisolo and Juan Benet	168
	8.3. A Return to Realism	175
	8.4. Wild Fantasies	177
	8.5. Poetic Rewrites	179
	8.6. 'New' Theatre: Abolishing the Pyrenees	184

9.	LANGUAGES OF PLEASURE	188
	9.1. The Persistence of Romance	188
	9.2. Eroticism and Sexual Liberation	193
	9.3. Pleasure in Poetry	200
	9.4. Commercial Erotica	204
10.	THROUGH THE KALEIDOSCOPE	208
	10.1. From One Nation to Many	208
	10.2. Old and New Voices	213
	10.3. Women's Voices?	214
	10.4. Generation X: Who am I?	216
	10.5. Resexing the Nation	219

References 222

Index of Names and Topics 235

Notes on Contributors

SUE FRENK is Lecturer in Spanish at the University of Durham. Her teaching and research interests lie in modern narrative, gender, and literary theory and she has published on Isabel Allende, Carlos Fuentes, and women in Central America.

VANESSA KNIGHTS is Lecturer in Spanish at the University of Newcastle and a member of the University's Centre for Gender and Women's Studies. Her teaching interests are in contemporary Hispanic literary and cultural studies and she has published on Spanish feminisms, contemporary women writers and science fiction, Carmen Martín Gaite, and Rosa Montero. She is author of *The Search for Identity in the Narrative of Rosa Montero* (Edwin Mellen Press, 1999). She is currently researching Latin American popular music.

CHRIS PERRIAM is Professor of Hispanic Studies at the University of Newcastle and a member of the University's Centre for Gender and Women's Studies. His teaching and research interests are in contemporary Spanish fiction and cinema, twentieth-century poetry in Spanish, and Cultural and Gay/Queer Studies. He is author of *Desire and Dissent: An Introduction to Luis Antonio de Villena* (Berg Publishers, 1995) and is currently writing on issues of masculinity and representation in Spanish cinema of the 1980s and 1990s.

MICHAEL THOMPSON is Lecturer in Spanish at the University of Durham. He has published on and edited the work of several contemporary Spanish playwrights and is editor of *Fire, Blood and the Alphabet: One hundred years of Lorca* (Durham Modern Language Series, 1999). His main research interest is in historical theatre, and he is currently writing on Rodríguez Méndez's history plays.

1
First Perspectives: Spain from 1939 to the 1990s

1.1. INTRODUCTION

The intention of this first chapter is to provide a brief chronological overview of the years between the end of the Spanish Civil War and the late 1990s, setting a context within which the specific issues that form the focus of the following chapters will be considered. Substantial coverage in English of the social and cultural history of the period can be found in Carr (1980: 155–81), Carr and Fusi (1981), Preston (1986, 1993), Shubert (1990: 206–64), Hooper (1995), and Graham and Labanyi (1995). Concise general accounts in English published recently are Grugel and Rees (1997) and Romero Salvadó (1999). Numerous studies in Spanish have been published since 1975: Equipo Reseña (1977), Blanco Aguinaga, Rodríguez Puértolas, and Zavala (1983), Tusell (1990: 651–62, 707–23, 737–46, 789–95), Ramos Gascón (1991: vol. ii), and Tusell (1998) are particularly useful for their focus on cultural developments.

1.2. SPRINGTIME FOR FRANCO: FROM 1939 TO THE EARLY 1950S

The text that unavoidably marks the beginning of the contemporary era in Spain is General Franco's declaration of total victory on 1 April 1939: 'En el día de hoy, cautivo y desarmado el Ejército Rojo, han alcanzado las tropas nacionales sus últimos objetivos militares. La guerra ha terminado' ('With the capture and disarming of the last of the Red Army, national forces have on this day achieved their final military objectives. The war is over'). What had been planned as a swift *coup d'état* to 'save Spain from anarchy' had led to three years of vicious Civil War and half a million deaths. The generals who had led the insurrection in July 1936 against a democratically elected government now celebrated the triumph of the 'national' cause and set about trying the supporters of the Republic on charges of rebellion, executing tens of thousands of them and imprisoning hundreds of thousands more, determined to exact retribution and eradicate their enemies together with everything they stood for. The exultant victors declared the dawn of a new age: 'Nada choca más que el entusiasmo de los vencedores ante el espectáculo de una España arruinada y hecha trizas por culpa de la contienda fratricida' (Tusell 1990: 575) ('There is nothing more shocking than the enthusiasm of the victors at the sight of Spain ruined and torn apart by fratricidal conflict'). This 'New Spain' paradoxically defined itself largely in terms of tradition: a desire to reverse the social and political developments of the modern age and return the nation to its true historical destiny.

By the end of the war the Spanish economy was severely enfeebled. Recovery was painfully slow, hindered by a policy of autarky which aimed to avoid imports and foreign investment and imposed strict central controls on production, prices, and distribution. The pursuit of a defiantly self-sufficient planned economy reflected the totalitarian instincts and fervent nationalism of the regime, the effects of which were exacerbated by the Allies' ostracism of Spain after the Second World War. Autarky gave rise not only to stagnation but also to inefficiency, increased exploitation of the working class, and widespread corruption, leaving most of the population in extreme hardship while an elite prospered through political favouritism and the black market. The 1940s came to be known as the 'years of hunger': agricultural and industrial production remained below the levels of the early 1930s, harvests were poor, distribution was inefficient and corrupt, and wages were kept low. Progressive social and economic reforms initiated by the Republic were reversed: large landowners were now the main beneficiaries of irrigation and resettlement schemes; trade union rights and minimum wage agreements were abolished; the collectivist experiments of the wartime revolution were overturned; all traces of Catalan and Basque autonomy were eradicated. Inevitably, inadequate nutrition and poor living conditions for the majority of the population were accompanied by widespread disease. Franco had promised

'Ni un hogar sin lumbre, ni un español sin pan' ('Not a single home without light and heat, not a single Spaniard without bread'), and the government did introduce food rationing and set up rudimentary social and health services, but these were inadequately funded, unevenly distributed, and politically conditioned. The 1940s were also the years of harshest political repression and unashamed totalitarianism, as the new regime proceeded to wipe out all vestiges of the Republic and establish complete control over the nation, using draconian measures such as the Ley de Responsabilidades Políticas (Political Responsibilities Act) of February 1939 and the Ley de Represión de la Masonería y del Comunismo (Repression of Freemasonry and Communism Act) of 1941 to criminalize political opposition. While the *vencidos* (vanquished) were punished or forced into inner exile, the *vencedores* (victors) enjoyed the spoils of victory with the blessing of the Catholic Church. The military takeover was sanctified as a holy *Cruzada* (Crusade), a second reconquest of Spain bringing the triumph of Christian civilization over atheism and communism. Until his death Franco was the most ardent exponent of a worldview described in Spain as *maniqueísta* (Manichaean), a black-and-white, moralistic vision of history in terms of an absolute division and constant struggle between good and evil.

1.2.1. *The triumph of anti-culture*

While both sides during the war had, unsurprisingly, made intensive use of culture for propaganda purposes, major differences of approach had become evident. The leaders of the Republic had regarded culture as an emancipating force and had set up literacy campaigns and projects designed to widen access to the arts, a trend intensified by the outbreak of war and the radicalization of politics in the Republican zone.[1] In contrast, the Nationalists tended to be more interested in purging, controlling, and unifying Spanish culture than in promoting diversity, creativity, or popular involvement. The Falangist Ernesto Giménez Caballero boasted that the abandonment of 'el mundo de la cultura' ('the world of culture') and the embrace of a fanatical 'mística de la anticultura' ('mystique of anti-culture') had won them the war (Rodríguez

---

[1] See Graham and Labanyi (1995: 124–66).

4   First Perspectives

Puértolas 1986: 363). Virulent anti-communism, religious orthodoxy, and a narrow, heroic vision of Spain's cultural traditions dominated Nationalist wartime propaganda, creative writings, and visual arts. Almost all the star figures of the creative boom of the 1920s and 1930s had sided with the Republic, reinforcing the conservatives' instinctive hostility to modernism and the avant-garde. Federico García Lorca had been murdered at the beginning of the war and Miguel Hernández died in prison in 1942. The poets, dramatists, and novelists who fled into exile included Rafael Alberti, Max Aub, Francisco Ayala, Alejandro Casona, Rosa Chacel, León Felipe, Jorge Guillén, Juan Ramón Jiménez, Antonio Machado, and Pedro Salinas. Prominent painters, musicians, philosophers, and historians joined the exodus that left post-war Spain drained of cultural and intellectual energy. The victors branded them all as traitors and set about attempting to obliterate their legacy.

Franco's government had already equipped itself with its most effective instrument for controlling cultural expression: the Ley de Prensa (Press Law) of 1938, which remained in force until 1966. The law imposed censorship on all forms of publishing, radio, and film, and was extended to cover theatre and music in 1939 and public lectures in 1940. The system worked principally through advance censorship (*censura previa*): all material had to be submitted for approval before publication. Censors could prohibit publication altogether or demand that offending sections be removed or rewritten. Before a play could be performed, the script had first to be approved, then a censor would attend rehearsals and the first night, checking for improvised additions, gauging audience response, and reporting back to head office. Strict guidelines (*consignas*) were issued daily to newspapers specifying what they should and should not cover, and a special licence was required for any periodical publication. Allocation of scarce supplies of paper was also used as a form of censorship favouring official, Falange, and Church publishers.

From 1938 responsibility for the administration of censorship and propaganda lay with the Delegación de Prensa y Propaganda (Department of Press and Propaganda) under the Minister of the Interior, Ramón Serrano Suñer. In 1941 control passed to the Falange, in the form of its Vicesecretaría de Educación Popular (Office of Popular Education), then in 1946 to the Dirección

General de Prensa, part of the Ministry of Education, and finally to the Ministry of Information and Tourism in 1951. Much of the work was done by freelance readers, including some authors (notably, Camilo José Cela), while religious and moral questions were referred to representatives of the Church. The criteria were largely taken for granted—any 'offence' against the head of state, the political institutions of the regime, the Church, or its teachings on dogma and morality was self-evidently inadmissible—but in practice were applied unpredictably, especially towards the end of the dictatorship.[2] The zealous attention to detail in protecting the public from immoral influences, especially in visual material, often went to ludicrous extremes (retouching comic strips to cover up women's legs, toning down the mildest of slang expressions, removing the most oblique references to extramarital sex).

One of the fundamental principles the regime was determined to defend was the unity of the Spanish nation centred on Madrid, a project seen as cultural and linguistic as much as political. The devolutionary initiatives of the Republic were annulled, while the apparatus of education, propaganda, and censorship was deployed to discredit regionalism and eradicate public use of the Catalan, Basque, and Galician languages. To speak or write in anything other than Castilian—the 'language of empire'—was condemned as unpatriotic, even unchristian, and in the 1940s could earn a beating from jackbooted Falangists. Names of people, streets, towns, and commercial products could be recorded only in their Castilian versions; even inscriptions on gravestones had to be in Castilian; books in Catalan, Basque, and Galician were destroyed, and publishing in these languages (regarded as inferior 'dialects') was made virtually impossible throughout the 1940s. Basque and Galician were more severely affected than Catalan: only thirty books of any kind were published in Basque during the 1940s (half of them religious texts), and only three in Galician between 1939 and 1947. This suppression was gradually relaxed, but in a selective manner: religious and literary writing could be published in Catalan, Basque, or Galician whereas only Castilian was deemed suitable for factual or analytical material

---

[2] A circular of 1940 giving guidelines for censors is reproduced in Abellán (1987: 38–40). See also Abellán (1980*b*: 19, 249–50), and Graham and Labanyi (1995: 169–70, 207–14).

(science, philosophy, sociology), while foreign-language books could be translated into Castilian but not into the other languages. Some banned works in Catalan, Basque, and Galician were approved when translated into Castilian.

1.2.2. The discourses of the regime's 'families'

Although the impact on the population of this project of political and cultural control often gave the impression of a monolithic political structure, the regime in fact consisted of a shifting and competitive coalition of right-wing forces bound together by little more than instinctive anti-communism and the personal prestige of Franco as *Caudillo* (leader, warlord). The most culturally influential 'families' were the Church and the Falange, while the role of the armed forces and the monarchists, if less well defined in ideological terms, was politically and economically significant. Rather than a single coherent ideology or cultural project, several overlapping political and moral discourses were blended together in a common language of crusading *Nacional-catolicismo* (National Catholicism) that, long after the war was over, continued to define the culture of Francoism in political speeches and publications, the press, education, and the arts. The orthodoxy, morality, and anti-materialism stressed by the Church overlapped with the Falangists' notion of 'spiritual' patriotism, with traditional bourgeois ideals of the respectable Christian family, and with a military emphasis on leadership, order, and national unity.

Having converted military command of the rebel forces into supreme power as head of government and state, Franco remained virtually unchallenged at the centre of this shifting coalition of forces, retaining control by playing the various 'families' off against one another. Although clearly a shrewd manipulator of men and ideas, he clung to absurdly simple-minded obsessions about communist–masonic–Jewish conspiracies.[3] He regarded himself as a soldier above all, and the forces under his command as the rock on which the unity, dignity, and stability of the whole country were founded. Since government was seen primarily as a military operation in pursuit of practical goals, military officers carried out a

---

[3] Preston (1993) and Vázquez Montalbán (1992) provide detailed and ultimately damning portraits of the dictator.

remarkably wide range of public functions at all levels—legislative, administrative, economic, judicial, and cultural. The key rhetorical terms were of command (*mando, caudillaje,* or *capitanía*), unity, discipline, and obedience. He distrusted intellectuals (partly as a reaction against the prominence in the Republic of academics, writers, and philosophers) and showed little interest in the arts, an attitude shared by no-nonsense soldiers and obscurantist Catholics alike.

The 'family' of monarchists was more diffuse, including generals, bankers, industrialists, and landowners, all nervous of the revolutionary fervour of the Falange and in favour of more traditional kinds of conservatism. Behind official rhetoric of austere spirituality and totalitarian social justice, the reality was that the Crusade had been fought largely in defence of established capitalist and aristocratic interests. Franco declared the transformation of Spain into a truly classless society, but his smug claim in a speech of 1942 points to the real agenda: 'Nuestra Cruzada es la única lucha en que los ricos que fueron a la guerra salieron más ricos' (Rodríguez Puértolas 1986: 332) ('Our Crusade is the only conflict in which those who went to war rich came out of it even richer'). The political history of the Franco period was to be punctuated by tussles over the question of restoration (sharpened by the liberal Lausanne Manifesto issued in 1945 by the son of the last king, Juan de Borbón, and settled by Franco in 1969 with the declaration of don Juan's son, Juan Carlos, as his successor).

The Falange (Phalanx), a political movement based on the party founded by José Antonio Primo de Rivera in 1933, combined Catholic nationalism with Italian-style fascism to produce the most clearly defined ideological component of the Nationalist alliance and the only one aiming at mass political mobilization. In its origins it was a revolutionary, anti-bourgeois movement that advocated patriotism, discipline, and social justice. Primo's Falange Española had merged with the more radical JONS (Juntas de Ofensiva Nacional Sindicalista: National-Syndicalist Action Groups) in 1934, and had then (after Primo's death) been brought under Franco's control by the Decree of Unification of March 1937, which absorbed the FE de las JONS, along with 'traditionalist' right-wing movements, into the 'Partido Único' (single party) known officially as FET y de las JONS (Falange Española Tradicionalista y de las Juntas de Ofensiva Nacional Sindicalista) or, more broadly, as the Movimiento Nacional (National Movement). The Falange was responsible before, during, and after the war for some of the most brutal persecution of Republican sympathizers and for extremes of violent intolerance. The blue shirts, the raised-arm salute, the yoke-and-arrows emblem, and the anthem 'Cara al sol' ('Facing the sun'), together with stirring rhetoric about Spain's imperial destiny, seemed to dominate public life in the immediate post-war period. The early successes of Germany and Italy in the World War appeared to present an opportunity for the realization of dreams of reviving imperial glories, and the Falange played a key role in shifting Spain's position from neutrality to pro-Axis 'non-belligerency' and recruiting volunteers for the *División Azul* (Blue Division) dispatched to fight alongside German troops on the Russian front in 1941. Although progressively drained of its radicalism, the organization became a crucial part of the machinery of the Francoist state, particularly as an instrument for managing the press and propaganda, local government, social services (especially through its women's organization, the Sección Femenina), and the *sindicatos verticales* (government-controlled trade unions—'vertical' in that they were designed to connect the employee, the employer, and the state rather than creating 'horizontal' solidarity amongst workers).

Up to the late 1940s the Falange was the dominant cultural force of the regime. It ran its own newspapers, magazines, and radio stations, as well as the Escuela de Periodismo (School of Journalism), by which all journalists had to be licensed, and founded a national theatre company (Teatro Nacional de Falange) in 1940. It also exercised control over the universities, the state publishing house (Editora Nacional), and the appointment of editors of privately owned publications. The cultural ambitions of Falangists were not limited to propaganda and control, since the heroic ideals of empire, virility, self-sacrifice, and patriotic Catholicism inspired a great deal of creative energy. Alongside sycophantic tributes to José Antonio and the *Caudillo* and stirring images of joyous young warrior-mystics marching athletically towards the dawning of a glorious new age, there were also thoughtful explorations of faith, suffering, and national division. Some Falangists showed an acute awareness of the loss of talent caused by the war and a determination to prove that the arts could thrive within the ideological constraints of the new Spain. Poets such as Dionisio Ridruejo, Luis Rosales, Luis Felipe Vivanco, and Leopoldo Panero aspired to a recovery of some of the prestige of the pre-war generations and acknowledged the cultural influence of writers in exile—'la España peregrina' ('wandering Spain'). The literary and cultural journals associated with the Falange represent various attempts to reconcile this ambition to achieve cultural credibility with the ideological imperatives of the state (see Chapter 2). *Vértice*, the official monthly magazine of the FET y de las JONS (1937–46), published literary supplements containing articles, poems, stories, and plays by leading Falangists, established figures such as Azorín and Eugenio d'Ors, and a few young writers not directly associated with the regime. The government's 'political and spiritual' weekly *El español* (1942–7, revived in 1953 and 1963), set up by the Falangist Juan Aparicio under a classic Francoist motto—'Una Poética. Una Política. Un Estado' ('One Poetics. One Politics. One State')—published articles, short stories, and novels in instalments, determined to prove that Spanish fiction writing was thriving and superior to foreign works available in translation. *La estafeta literaria* (*The Literary Post*) (1944–6, revived 1956), also the creation of Aparicio, contained literary news and criticism, reviews, surveys, and poetry. *Escorial* (1940–50), the literary monthly founded by Ridruejo with Pedro Laín Entralgo, José María Alfaro, and Luis Rosales, followed a more independent path, publishing work by writers outside the Falangist establishment, including the philosopher Julián Marías and the poets Vicente Aleixandre, Dámaso Alonso, and Blas de Otero. Ridruejo himself, together with other purists, was becoming alienated from the regime, increasingly disillusioned at what they saw as Franco's betrayal of the ideals of José Antonio. The poetry journal *Garcilaso* (1943–6) sought to fuse classicism and aesthetic purity with the patriotic spirit of the regime. A number of other periodicals associated with the Falange flourished briefly in this period: *Fantasía* (*Fantasy*) published creative writing; *Y* was the official magazine of the Sección Femenina; the *Revista de estudios políticos* (*Political Studies Review*) was the journal of the Instituto de Estudios Políticos. The official students' union, SEU (Sindicato Español Universitario), published various periodicals. *Juventud* (*Youth*) and *La hora* (*The Hour*) began as loyal vehicles of youthful Falangist enthusiasm but by 1950 were beginning to harbour some dissident voices. Ironically, it was possible to publish material in Falange-run periodicals (largely exempt from the normal processes of censorship) which could not have appeared elsewhere.

The Falange also exerted an important influence on publications intended for children. The *formación política* (political education) that was a compulsory part of the primary and secondary curriculum for boys and girls had a specifically Falangist syllabus, set out in textbooks such as the various editions of the *Enciclopedia intuitiva, sintética y práctica* by Antonio Álvarez Pérez. The Falange published its own children's books and magazines combining illustrated stories, comic strips, and superficial educational material with heavy-handed political and religious indoctrination. By the mid-1940s, the weekly *Flechas y pelayos* (1938–48) contained little overt propaganda and more comic strips, its lack of popularity in comparison with the magazine *Chicos*, the comic strip (*tebeo*), and various adventure strips now undeniable. Children may have been voting with their pocket money, but in any case, the world was changing and the tide was turning against the Falange.

With the explicit support of the Vatican, the Church had provided crucial moral legitimization for the Nationalist 'Crusade'. While bishops gave fascist salutes at rallies and parades, all aspects of public and private life were redefined in conservative religious terms: the term *Nacional-catolicismo* summed up this unquestionable fusion of religious orthodoxy and patriotism. Catholicism constituted the essence of a unified Spanish identity, the natural moral foundation for family life, education, science, culture, and public affairs: 'No se puede ser español y no ser católico, porque si no se es católico, no se puede ser español' (Manuel García Morente in Rodríguez Puértolas 1987: 994) ('It is not possible to be Spanish and not be Catholic, since if one is not Catholic one is not Spanish'). In the absence of political parties, Church organizations functioned as youth movements, workers' associations, and pressure groups, the most influential of which, the ACNP (Asociación Católica Nacional de Propagandistas: National Association of Catholic Propagandists) and Opus Dei, pursued an explicit strategy of influencing public policy and grooming their followers for senior positions in business and government. Although the direct political role of the Church was limited before 1945, specific ecclesiastical privileges were embedded in the state from an early stage: control of education, tax exemptions, the obligatory appointment of clerics to official bodies. In return, the Church confirmed the support it had given Franco during the war and imposed on the population an intolerant, authoritarian form of Christianity. The official philosophical basis of the Church's teachings was Neoscholasticism, which in theory rejected modern rationalist thought in favour of a return to traditional sources such as St Augustine and St Thomas Aquinas. Religious dogma not only justified the Church's own ideological hegemony and stifled independent thinking, but also legitimized the authoritarianism of the regime and the aggravation of social inequality. The traditional ideal of the family as defender of social stability and instiller of Christian values was sanctified, and its specifically patriarchal nature was reinforced by education at home and in schools (and extended beyond school by the Sección Femenina) explicitly directed at preparing girls to be submissive, dutiful wives and mothers (see Chapter 4).

Inevitably, Catholicism pervaded and constrained cultural and intellectual activity of all kinds, especially through the Church organization Acción Católica. The religious press was extensive, including Acción Católica's official gazette, *Ecclesia*; the daily *Ya* (*Now*); *¡Tú!* (*You!*), a weekly newspaper published by the Catholic workers' association Obreros de Acción Católica; *¡Zas!* (*Zap!*) and *Trampolín* (*Trampoline*), children's magazines published by Acción Católica. The Church was given extensive control over primary and secondary education, while the university system, having been purged of all subversive influences at the end of the war, was defined as having an explicitly religious function, in which it was to be guided by the Consejo Superior de Investigaciones Científicas (Higher Council for Scientific Research) with a remit to combine the teachings of the Catholic tradition with the demands of modernity. The CSIC soon came to be dominated by Opus Dei, which, in addition to exercising influence over universities and education, established its own higher education institutions for the formation of professional elites: the University of Navarra (1952) and its business school in Barcelona, the Instituto de Estudios Superiores de la Empresa (1958). *Arbor*, a magazine founded by Opus members in 1943, became the official journal of the CSIC in 1945 and a useful weapon in the Catholic campaign to wrest power from the Falange.

The Church played its part in the construction of cosmetic constitutionalism, increasingly distancing itself from totalitarianism and favouring monarchism, but insisting on the maintenance of orthodoxy in religious and moral matters. The ACNP's Alberto Martín Artajo, as Foreign Minister, led the negotiations that produced the Concordat with the Vatican of 1953. Although in practical terms this agreement did little more than consolidate existing arrangements (the status of Catholicism as the single state religion, Franco's power to appoint bishops, state funding for the Church, ecclesiastical control of marital law, legal recognition of religious orders), it had considerable importance in terms of achieving diplomatic respectability and formalizing a relationship between Church and dictatorship that hitherto had been largely taken for granted.

1.2.3. Alternative voices in the 1940s

The Republic continued for a while to have an existence in several forms. An increasingly frustrated government-in-exile succeeded to some extent in winning support from the Allied powers, but hopes of military intervention against Franco after the defeat of Germany were dashed. Armed guerrilla resistance within Spain after 1945 by former Republican fighters, known as the *maquis* as many of them had been active in the French Resistance, continued into the 1950s but failed to spark off the mass revolt hoped for. More lasting was the influence of artists and intellectuals in exile, continuing evidence of the existence of the 'other Spain'. Although most of their work was excluded from Spain until the 1960s, an infrastructure of congresses, periodicals (including *España peregrina*, founded in Mexico in 1940), and publishing houses helped to maintain their cultural prestige. Periodicals in Spain such as *Ínsula* (founded in 1946) played an important role in keeping up contact with exiled writers.

Within Spain, the mass of population (still more than 40 per cent agrarian until the 1960s) was engaged in a daily struggle for survival, largely indifferent to the propaganda and to the shifts of political and cultural influence within the regime, starved of genuine news but increasingly well supplied with films, sentimental narratives, and comics. However, a few creative texts that gave voice to real experience in powerful ways were beginning to emerge in the 1940s. These landmarks of *ruptura* (rupture, breaking-out) by Cela, Carmen Laforet, Antonio Buero Vallejo, and others will be discussed at length in subsequent chapters.

1.3. MAKING THE DICTATORSHIP WORK: CHANGE IN THE 1950S

None of the shifts of power of the late 1940s and early 1950s amounted to real democratization—the leading Catholic and monarchist influences were not necessarily any more liberal than the Falangist establishment. Nonetheless, signs of *apertura* (opening-up) in economic and cultural spheres became increasingly evident during the 1950s. More conciliatory, liberal voices began to be heard in the universities, in Catholic publications and workers' organizations, and in the Church itself. José Ortega y Gasset, who had returned from exile in 1948, was distrusted by the regime but had a profound influence on essayists and philosophers such as Xavier Zubiri, Pedro Laín Entralgo, José Luis López Aranguren, and Julián Marías,[4] and even on Joaquín Ruiz Giménez, who as Minister of Education from 1951 gave some encouragement to intellectual liberalization. However, the progress towards *apertura* was far from continuous, and pressure from hard-line factions (orchestrated by Opus Dei) led to the dismissal of Ruiz Giménez in 1956, setting a pattern of moderate opening and right-wing backlash that was to be repeated several times.

By the middle of the 1950s, the effort to overcome Spain's diplomatic isolation had achieved its main objectives. In addition to the Vatican Concordat, the government signed an agreement with the USA in 1953 which brought substantial loans in exchange for the provision of facilities for military bases, paved the way for Spain's admission to the United Nations in 1955, and began to open up the Spanish economy to US products and investment. Liberal hopes that the Americans would also demand political changes were short-lived: Franco's virulent anti-communism was now a useful asset. What was urgently required, however, in order to respond to these new circumstances (and to strong economic growth in the rest of Europe) was economic liberalization and modernization. Although Franco and the old guard were reluctant to abandon the spirit of autarky, a government reshuffle in 1957 brought to power a new generation of technocrats associated with Opus Dei, whose

---

[4] For a study of these and later essayists, together with extracts from their writings, see Gracia (1996).

Stabilization Plan of 1959 began to put in place the structures that would allow rapid economic development in the 1960s.

In the short term, economic 'stabilization' resulted in recession, increased unemployment, and widespread hardship, sharpening social tensions. Apart from the Barcelona tram boycott of 1951 and the strikes that followed it, popular discontent had so far been contained, but by the late 1950s unrest among students and workers was becoming an increasingly significant fact of political life. The crackdown of 1956 was provoked largely by student demonstrations, which broadened from a specific campaign against the SEU into a major political protest. Clandestine trade unions were also increasingly active, particularly Comisiones Obreras (Workers' Commissions, by 1960 dominated by the Communist Party), which grew up in opposition to the official *sindicatos*. Opposition in various forms was finally becoming visible and audible.

1.3.1. Expressions of dissent

There was still no sign of a significant relaxation of restrictions on publishing and other forms of expression (indeed, the censors were busier than ever), but by the mid-1950s cultural production was generally becoming more and more independent of the spheres of influence of the 'families' of the regime. A Catalan cultural identity was re-emerging, and Barcelona was also an important centre of activity for writing and publishing in Castilian. Writers and academics, including former Falangists, were discovering existentialism and Marxism, seeking ideas and inspiration abroad, and entering into impassioned argument about the relationship between writing and society (see Jordan 1990, 1995). 'Realism'—although by no means the only defining feature of literary production at this time— was a central preoccupation and focus for debate, as an aesthetic issue that was also, unavoidably, a political one. The most characteristic products of this climate (discussed in Chapter 7) were novels and short stories by writers such as Ignacio Aldecoa, Josefina Rodríguez, Jesús Fernández Santos, Rafael Sánchez Ferlosio, poetry by Gabriel Celaya and Blas de Otero, and plays by Alfonso Sastre.

At the beginning of the 1960s, Franco and his regime were politically secure and confident of achieving economic prosperity without relinquishing control. Yet they had failed to eliminate the 'other Spains' and no longer dictated all the terms of cultural interaction.

1.4. CRACKS AND FISSURES: 1962–1975

As well as the obvious feature of all written works of imagination and synthesis, that their truths and realities are mediated not immediate, two factors in particular complicate our task as readers of locating Spanish writing of this next period in the relevant contexts. One is the continuing, if changing, role of ideological control and censorship, the privileging of certain ideas and styles, and the pressure on alternative expression to silence or disguise itself; the other, the existence of increasingly dominant, established voices of individuals and groups of writers in exile, mainly in Europe and the Americas, in dialogue with their more silenced partners who are at first in inner exiles of varying kinds and then, as the 1960s progress, increasingly exposed to the possibilities of freer expression within Spain.

The period is one of a complex and zigzagging process of *apertura* arising partly out of the fact that in power politicians had been replaced largely by professionals ('technocrats') who were in particular associated by the end of the regime with Admiral Carrero Blanco, Franco's right hand in government from September 1967 until becoming President in 1973, and one of a small number of politicians whose aim was to allow Spain to open itself out to and align itself with Europe, culturally as well as economically. With hindsight, in the knowledge of the date of the dictator's death, historians have been able to read into the 1960s a sense of an ending which by the early 1970s was finding explicit expression in Spain, once Franco had nominated Juan Carlos de Borbón y Borbón as his successor (in 1969, after long procrastination) and suffered the first of a series of life-threatening illnesses culminating in his death on 20 November 1975.

In 1962, the year of Franco's seventieth birthday (4 December), pressures on the old regime were bearing down variously. A large-scale strike in the mining country of Asturias gave focus and impetus to a growing wave of organized working-class resistance, and allegations of torture of strike leaders led to protests in the capital by leading intellectuals and students. At a meeting in Munich to consider Spain's official request for entry into the European Economic Community the moderate left was able to mobilize effective opposition and to gain greater visibility. The lay members of

Hermandades Obreras de Acción Católica (HOAC) (Workers' Brotherhoods of Catholic Action) and Juventudes Obreras Católicas (JOC) (Young Catholic Workers)—grass-roots working-class movements concerned with the interface of Christian teachings and labour conditions, setting up alternative union structures—were two increasingly visible signs from the mid-1950s into the 1960s of the precariousness of the old discourses of religious and national unity, as were the views of some priests themselves. A revival of Catalan and Basque nationalism was supported by younger members of the clergy who rejected the ideology of National Catholicism. Eventually the Spanish Church hierarchy sought to distance itself from the regime in response to changes in Spanish society and events outside Spain such as the reforms of Pope John XXIII and the Second Vatican Council (1962–5) which promoted a more liberal outlook defending political pluralism and human rights. Thus, in 1973 the Spanish bishops voted for the separation of Church and state.

As part of a larger change of government, in 1962 pragmatic liberalizer Manuel Fraga Ibarne was appointed Minister of Information and effectively chief agent of censorship—the laws on which he quickly set to work changing. This appointment had an important effect on the traffic of books and thought. Though of cost-restricted availability, Marxist literature was cautiously allowed in bookshops, and, as Carr and Fusi imply (1981: 127), by 1969, not only might you have studied Marx, Gramsci, or Marcuse at university, but you could choose between three editions of Che Guevara's Bolivian diaries. Equally, though, liberal-minded publishers still ran a serious risk of being closed down. The Ministry became increasingly tolerant with weeklies and monthlies: Fraga allowed the establishment of *Cuadernos para el diálogo* in 1963 (a progressive Christian Democrat publication which steadily became, for the late 1960s, the main voice of centre-left opposition), the culturally open *Revista de Occidente*, and—storing up trouble for the future—the *Gaceta universitaria*, the voice of an increasingly dissident and massively growing sector of lecturers and students, inscribed in an ongoing history of increasingly resonant protests and strikes (from the first in 1956 to crises in 1965, 1969, and—now with the whole sector out in solid protest—in 1974).

Fraga's 1966 Ley de Prensa (Press and Publications Law)—which removed the obligation to deposit proofs with the censor *prior* to publication—was outwardly liberal (for example, the press was no longer designated as a public service) but in fact strictly policed; in the novelist Miguel Delibes's words 'antes te obligaban a escribir lo que no sentías, ahora se conforman con prohibirte que escribas lo que sientes, algo hemos ganado' (in Sánchez Aranda and Barrera 1992: 411) ('Before they used to make you write what you didn't believe; now they are content to forbid you to write what you believe. At least that's something'). Issues of newspapers and magazines could be withdrawn from circulation and fines imposed for infractions (still the same vague touchstones: undermining the principles of the regime; offending against the Church and Catholic dogma; affronting decency). This was to affect numerous publications, including the *Gaceta universitaria* (eventually forced into closure through bankruptcy in 1972), the satirical magazine *La codorniz*, and the newspaper *Madrid* (forced to close in 1971, with some of its team going to the new *Time Magazine*-style *Cambio 16*). On the other hand there were many examples of rapid liberalization and the introduction of new debates. The post-1966 era saw a change in the magazine *Triunfo*, to take a prominent case, from being a light, leisure-oriented publication from 1946 to 1962 to a more news-oriented one and, in the period leading up to the end of the regime, an increasingly powerful voice raised in support of new freedoms. Essayist Eduardo Haro Tecglen's chronicles of May 1968 in Paris are a key moment, as Manuel Vázquez Montalbán's 'Crónica sentimental de España', from 1969 on, is another.

These years were ones of vast and extremely rapid social change (the destabilizing social effects of which were avidly and luridly chronicled in popular newspapers such as *El caso* and *Por qué*), and, except at the turn of the decade, of gradual liberalization. During the 1960s and 1970s a number of legal reforms were passed to improve the situation of married and working women, marking a shift in attitudes as Spanish society became increasingly urbanized and industrial. The number of women in higher education also increased significantly over the course of the 1970s, as did the publication of feminist essays and book-length studies. Women were active across the spectrum of oppositional groups including neighbourhood and housewives' associations, trade unions and clandestine women's groups, often linked to the illegal political parties, and Catholic action groups.

Industry, backed by strong foreign investments (partly attracted by cheap labour), saw spectacular growth during the period with the highest annual growth rate in Europe in 1960–75 (matched only by Japan), and productivity surpassing that of Germany while doubling that of the UK (to the cost of an over-exploited workforce and the gain of the under-taxed). By the start of the 1970s Spain was in the top dozen industrial nations, although per capita income was still 25 per cent less than the European average in 1975. Tourism, rising from an already substantial 6 million visitors in 1960 to 30 million in 1975 (and 42 million in 1982: more than one tourist per indigenous Spaniard), meant a boost to reserves, a further impetus for a booming construction industry, and the establishing of service industries as a major player in Spain. It also meant a further set of cultural contacts with the world 'beyond the Pyrenees', albeit more symbolic than real: Spain—or its coasts and monuments—was newly open to the world, had a market image. Demographically, Spain was continuing to be rapidly transformed. On top of the 2 million driven out of rural areas by poverty in the 1950s, through the 1960s the smaller provincial towns and cities were severely affected by the concentration of almost half the population in just eight provinces. The growth of economic activity in Madrid, Valencia, Zaragoza, Catalonia, and the Basque Country was matched by a growth in barely controlled development of trading and industrial estates and of housing at the peripheries of the cities, in particular Barcelona. The philosopher Julián Marías was able famously to qualify Spain as no longer *subdesarrollado* (underdeveloped) but *mal desarrollado* (poorly developed). Movement towards a more liberal society beyond the merely economic was visible, but unevenly developed: in 1965 the Student Union, SEU, which its members had divorced completely from the official union structures, was suppressed and lecturers and professors arrested and suspended (most famously Enrique Tierno Galván, later to be mayor of Madrid under socialism); in 1967 the unofficial, alternative trade union movement Comisiones Obreras (CCOO) was outlawed; and in 1970 a sequence of incidents across Spain—the most notable and publicized a trial of ETA militants in Burgos—provoked widespread demonstrations of solidarity against the government and the effective end of the so-called Years of Peace. The assassination in December 1973 by ETA of the man who had charge of the measures against such unrest, Carrero

Blanco—when angry despair at the news of the coup against Allende in Chile was fresh in the minds of the left—led to what was, retrospectively at least, a symbolic and premonitory funeral cortège and burial. Essayists and columnists noted and analysed the twists and turns, either by insistently highlighting them, or by setting them apart (notably in a resurgence of an old obsession with *costumbrismo*, the evocative chronicling of lost local customs, in conservative newspapers such as *ABC*). Novels set in Spain, however, when dissident in quality (though the majority consumed were not), had largely shifted their interests from social realism, always of limited readership, to formal experimentation and self-reflexivity, in many cases similarly limiting but of sufficiently wide-reaching transformational effect to justify the application of the term *nueva novela española* (New Spanish Novel) to a phenomenon as much inflected by the challenge of exciting new writing from Latin America as by social change and the transit out of immediacy of the harsh years of hunger and the consolidation of the regime's ideology. Novelists and short-story writers within Spain and with no visible quarrel with the regime did continue to turn to retelling the Civil War and mulling over the nature of (middle-class or picturesquely peasant) social relations in the twenty-five and more years of 'Peace' or, working in another mode, tended to treat the domestic, erotic, marital, and bourgeois themes which seem still to sell novels across Europe. The first half of the period is notable, however, for a radical recuperation of this otherwise tired version of the genre in the form of psychological realism. Writing by women combines lyrical subjectivity and social critique in novels which focus on psychological analysis and emotional probing of characters through narrative devices such as introspection and retrospective recall, multiple perspectives, and stream of consciousness. The effects of history were, arguably, far more sharply chronicled and their emotional patterns more clearly delineated in these ways than by many of the established male writers. Though tendencies can, as above, be ascribed in very broad terms within the plurality of narrative approaches, many literary histories (and syllabuses) focus on the contributions of individual writers. Indeed, this period, with its financial empowerment of the middle classes (the main buyers of books) and its quest among intellectuals and the politically or patriotically committed for prophets, hate figures, and heroes, marks the start of a cult of the writer (mainly male, and prose-producing) as personality.

The responses of poetry within such a changing Spain may provisionally be summarized by reference, in descending order of direct contact with historical realities, to: the slow conversion of *poesía social* (Social Poetry: a sometimes oblique form of political commitment) into *poesía civil* (Civil Poetry: less clearly politically aligned, though not simply humanist) and the persistence of strong, oppositional voices of the 1950s; the growth of what would later become known as *poesía de la experiencia* (Poetry of Experience: colloquial, anecdotal, and philosophical); the Barcelona School of writers; the poetry of the so-called *novísimos* (translatable as the New New Poets) which drew selectively on contemporary popular culture (especially films, rock music, and strip cartoons) and consolidated, sometimes in traditionalist and sometimes in parodic mode, notions of the language of poetry as difficult, 'clever', cultured, and self-referential. Poets writing in exile are conventionally represented as carrying forward the innovative 'spirit' of that earlier group of writers (although in reality by the 1960s all had radically changed their style).

1.5. CHANGES: 1975–1996

En estos días están sonando las campanas fúnebres de un mundo legendario que termina [...] Hay que [...] proclamar [...] que este país es viable, es capaz de autogobernarse y hasta de ser feliz.

(As these days unfold, the funeral bells are tolling for a legendary world coming to its end. [...] We must [...] proclaim [...] that this country is viable, capable of governing itself and even of finding happiness.)

These were the words of the editorial of the (confiscated) November 1975 special issue of *Cambio 16* on the death of Franco after a long and much chronicled multiple syndrome of terminal illnesses. As the institutions of Francoism, and the new king as head of state, carefully negotiated their way towards what was planned as an evolutionary leaving behind of the old system there was a less quiet mood among intellectuals and political commentators of the right and the left. The next five years saw a significant increase in the activity of essayists and columnists in the sphere of open political, social, and cultural comment,[5] much of it competitive, often combative, and turned toward a male-led version of history even in the most liberal publications of which the newspaper *El país* (established in 1976 and by 1980 overtaking in circulation figures both *ABC* and *La vanguardia*) is the most famous example; and the attempted coup fronted by Colonel Antonio Tejero's raid on the parliament in February 1981 provided something of a thematic climax. In a special issue on the event, the magazine *Interviú* (at that stage still an intriguing mix of unenlightened pornographic titillation and a forum for serious antiestablishment comment albeit mostly by men) was one (to take an example among many) which devoted a special issue to immediate comment on the event: Manuel Vázquez Montalbán (famous for his ironic idea that 'Life was better against Franco', lamenting the lack of a coherent response to the Transition) declares that if the king had not intervened as he did (contacting key military figures and asserting his authority) 'las vedetes de la democracia estarían en los paredones o en los campos de concentración, mientras los peatones de la democracia caerían como moscas [. . .] Y puedo contarlo. E *Interviú* puede publicarlo' (Vázquez Montalbán 1981) ('the stars of the democratic show would be up against the wall or in concentration camps, while the extras would be dropping like flies on the streets [. . .] And I can say this. And *Interviú* can publish it').

Unemployment was escalating (from 3.2 per cent in 1974 to 12 per cent in 1980), the oil price crisis of the early 1970s had dented the armour of steady boom, and inflation began to spiral; however, Spain's relatively strong economic situation facilitated the profound and complex process of reform as much as the huge social changes of the past fifteen years and the long matured expectation of change. The first years of the Transition were, of course, not free of unrest. There was a wave of protests and strikes in 1976. Increasing pressure from terrorism included, as well as intensification of ETA's activities, right-wing hit squads targeting liberal magazines and, notably, in 1977 a law firm with PCE connections, causing seven deaths. That same year marked the legalization of the

---

[5] For a middle-of-the-political-road example, see the special number on 'La cultura española durante el franquismo' in the liberal Catholic-controlled Reseña (13/100, Dec. 1976).

PCE and the real beginning of the formation of the political parties (including, crucially, those representing nationalist interests in the Basque Country, Catalonia, and Galicia—in order of affiliation more or less from left to right) who would fight the democratic elections of 1979.

The drawing up of the new constitution, approved in a referendum in December 1978, was a complicated tussle with the language (and realities) of nation, state, nationalities, and communities, individuals, citizens, rights, beliefs, and the Church (all references to which had in first drafts been omitted). The new contract it explicated led over the next years to enabling laws on divorce (in 1981) and abortion (in 1985), educational reform, and a stepped process of devolution to the regions and autonomy for Catalonia, the Basque Country, Galicia, and other important geopolitical and cultural units with a greater or lesser degree of overlap with historical boundaries and names. After the 1982 elections, when the socialist PSOE under Felipe González won an exceptionally convincing mandate to govern, these processes of change were in the hands of the left, albeit, as the years moved on, an increasingly centrist-tending left.

In some ways political change and transition had been anticipated by the shifts in literary writing at the end of the 1960s already briefly described, and proscribed voices—becoming increasingly available through the 1960s—emerged stronger but totally familiar, reinstalled now in a context of justification of much of what they had spoken out for. The soon loosely tagged Generations of 1970 (or 1968) are noted for experimentalism across all genres, as well as, in narrative at least, for their always knowing and frequently morally honest compromises with an acceleration in the commercialization of writing as product. By the 1980s the fields of reference of imaginative writing, without having to respond so much to punctual historical and politically produced personal trauma, extend widely; out, indeed, beyond the thematic areas we have chosen for the current study, but with a particular emphasis on these. On the one hand there is a concern to radically rewrite and on the other urgently reclaim the values, and sometimes the trends, ideas, and stories, of the preceding forty-odd years. A New Novel and a New Realism can confidently be said to have become installed at this time, moving on into further dominance into the 1990s. But equally there are returns, in some ways paradoxical ones, to the avant-gardisms and libertarianisms not only of the 1960s but of the early years of the century: the much cited *movida*s (leisure-, image-, and music-led youth culture booms) of Madrid, Barcelona, Corunna, Valencia, Bilbao (and a long tail of others) attest vividly, and radically to this. Some new writing responds directly to social change, to personal freedoms, but also to civic problems: to the effects of unemployment rising into the 20 per cents and hitting the young disproportionately; the spread of AIDS linked in more solid ways than in other European countries to the use and commerce of drugs; visible racism and the emergence of ultra-right groups (*cabezas rapadas*, an updating of the skinhead); a return of old inequalities of wealth; homelessness; and, under the conservative Partido Popular, from 1994, a cut back on welfare and benefits. Novelists continuing to write about the closed-in domestic and emotional issues of the well-off middle class find the usual market, but this is much enhanced by impressive publicity campaigns and a radical change (in the major cities at least) to the spaces and circumstances in which books are displayed and bought. Poetry picks up on the new lessons of the culturally voracious, eclectic style of some of the 1968 poets but also moves back towards purism, and out towards social documentary and, in particular, commentary on identities national, sexual, and regional (supported, until a drawing in of horns in the early 1990s, by generous localized subventions and a politics of positively separatist affirmation). In essays, nurtured by a liberalized daily, weekly, and monthly press (whose boom we shall be charting in later chapters), the writings of left-wing sociologist Jesús Ibáñez, philosopher Fernando Savater, and polymath chronicler of daily life Francisco Umbral all began in the late 1970s to form, for differing constituencies, a substantial sense of the progressive intellectual's role in the new histories unfolding. Spain had, by the 1990s, put itself back on the intellectual map as a significant set of commentating and philosophizing cultures. It should be borne in mind, however, that reading newspapers was still, in 1985 (according to a survey by the Ministry of Culture),[6] a regular habit for less

---

[6] Ministerio de Cultura, Secretaría General Técnica, 'Encuesta de comportamiento cultural de los españoles', Oct. 1985. Gómez García (1980) is of considerable interest on the post-constitution cultural picture away from the cities and the centre.

than half the population (40 per cent, indeed, had read nothing at all in the three months prior to the survey date) and circulation figures for the quality dailies never exceed 1 million in the period 1980–93. Nonetheless, in 1985, hearteningly, the same percentage (5 per cent) of respondents were reading 'ensayo' (essays, opinions, factual accounts) as were reading science fiction, and among these essayists would figure the names now routinely included in daily columns and the revealingly named, revered, and reviled 'firmas' ('names'; literally, signatures or autographs) of the glossy weeklies.

The policies of the PSOE built up regional and national cultural infrastructures and led to international recognition of Spanish culture which was not just restricted in its causes to the notoriety of big names such as Camilo José Cela (winner of the 1989 Nobel Prize, and in some ways a strange bedfellow for the previous Spanish winner, the subtle, liberal-leftist poet Vicente Aleixandre). As Chapter 10 will briefly show, by the 1990s Spain, in its writing as well as its statehood, had become multicultural and multilingual, conscious of suppressed and untapped voices within its fluid boundaries, but looking outwards and projecting itself as a culture on the other side of change.

Further Reading

Abellán (1987); Blanco Aguinaga, Rodríguez Puértolas, and Zavala (1983); Carr and Fusi (1981); Graham and Labanyi (1995); Hooper (1995); Julià (1999); Preston (1986, 1993); Shubert (1990); Sieburth (1994); Terry and Rafel (1983: 206–13); Tusell (1998).

2
Rewriting History

2.1 ETERNAL SPAIN: THE MYTHOLOGY OF EMPIRE

The victors of the Civil War quickly set in motion a reactionary project of appropriating and immobilizing Spain's history in the service of the regime's central ideological concerns: the maintenance of national unity, the promotion of the Catholic faith as the essential determinant of national identity, and the legitimization of authoritarian government as the necessary means of defending these ideals. Certain periods of history were celebrated as divinely ordained stages in a heroic imperial destiny, and selected heroes of the past (el Cid, Columbus, the Catholic Monarchs, the conquistadors) were used as the focus for ideals of *Patria* (Fatherland), *Raza* (Race), and *Hispanidad* (Hispanic universalism), often directly linked with the personality cult of the *Caudillo* or with José Antonio Primo de Rivera.[1]

The first phase of this vision is the coming together of the medieval Christian kingdoms in the common struggle to reclaim Iberia from Islam and form a single nation, united by a single faith. A shifting, contradictory pattern of power struggles between warlords, of mixing and coexistence of diverse cultures and religions, is reduced to a simple ideal of *Reconquista* (Reconquest). The mythology of this *Cruzada* (Crusade) binds permanently together the elements of military conquest, religious unification, and formation of the state, culminating in the reign of the Catholic Monarchs, who capture the last Muslim stronghold in 1492, bring together the kingdoms of Castile and Aragon, and expel the Jews from their united Christian realm. The survival of Islamic and

---

[1] The principal sources of the right-wing ideas discussed in this chapter are Marcelino Menéndez Pelayo, especially his *Historia de los heterodoxos españoles* (1880), Ramiro de Maeztu, especially his *Defensa de la Hispanidad* (1934), and José Antonio himself.

26 Rewriting History

Judaic influences, the diversity of forms of local and regional autonomy, and the fact that effective centralized government was not achieved until the eighteenth century were ironed out of this Christian and Castile-centred narrative.

The next stage was the expansion of the national destiny into a universal one. By providential coincidence, 1492 also marks the beginning of empire: the nation forged and sanctified by the Reconquest is chosen by God to carry the true faith into the New World. The subsequent decay of a vast and glorious empire was seen as having been brought about largely by foreign treachery and pernicious liberal ideas, eroding the authority of the Church and fomenting social turmoil, the ultimate humiliation being the loss of the last colonies (Cuba and the Philippines) in 1898. The Second Republic established in 1931 had further threatened the very foundations of Church, state, family, and traditional values, in response to which the military rebellion of 1936 had set in motion a new Crusade that saved Spain from anarchy and heresy. Now the Spanish people, reunited and fervently Catholic, had rediscovered their historic destiny and true identity. History had been brought full circle, the apotheosis had been reached, no other way was conceivable. The nation that had turned in upon itself during the centuries of decline was now ready to reclaim its leading role on the stage of world history, at a moment when the rise of fascism in Germany and Italy looked set to reproduce Franco's victory over communism and liberalism on a global scale. For a short time, Falangist rhetoric nourished heady fantasies of a real resurgence of empire. Santiago Montero Díaz, in his *Idea del imperio* (1943: *The Idea of Empire*), considering the possibilities for Spain at this juncture, affirms that 'nuestra Patria sigue conteniendo en sus entrañas sangre y potencia de Imperio' ('we can declare that the blood and potency of Empire still courses through the veins of our Fatherland') and that 'we' well know that 'todo Imperio significa ante todo la realización de un orden ético superior' ('above all any idea of Empire means the establishment of a higher ethical order') which can be achieved only through conquest and victory (in Rodríguez Puértolas 1987: 1073–4).

The various discourses of the 'families' of the regime were thus brought together in a more or less homogeneous mythology of 'la España eterna' ('eternal Spain'). The past was fused with the present, the promise of renewal was rooted in imperial history, and

Catholicism was insistently placed at the heart of national history and identity: thus Manuel García Morente, in his *Ser y vida del caballero cristiano* (*The Life and Experience of a Christian Gentleman*) (1945), insists that because in the constitution of Spain, uniquely among nations, there is historically no difference (nor will there ever be) between the moral, the religious, and the national, 'Ser cristiano y ser español es una y la misma cosa' (Rodríguez Puértolas 1987: 993-4) ('To be Christian and to be Spanish are one and the same thing'). When the fascist fervour of the early 1940s gave way to the more moderate tone of the late 1940s and 1950s, official propaganda still celebrated the idea of Spain as the last bastion ('la reserva espiritual') of Christian civilization.

2.2. EDUCATIONAL TEXTS: INDOCTRINATING THE YOUNG

The education system and publications aimed at the young played an important role in the 1940s and 1950s in consolidating the nationalist-Catholic historical orthodoxy. Drawing on educational policy formulated by Andrés Manjón, founder of the Escuelas de Ave María (Ave Maria Schools) at the turn of the century, the core of the school curriculum was made up of religion and Spanish history, fused together into a grotesquely oversimplified lesson in national identity, patriotism, and obedience, taught through dictation, copying-out of texts, and endless repetition. Exponents of the regime's educational policies were unapologetic about the ideological instrumentalization of the teaching of history. An influential professor of history reminded teachers that their main job was to inculcate a patriotic spirit by deliberately emphasizing 'los hechos que muestran los valores de la raza, silenciando otros que o no la ennoblecen o pueden ser interpretados torcidamente' ('events that demonstrate the virtues of our race, silencing those that do not show it in a noble light or can be interpreted in a distorted way'), the point being to make pupils into Spaniards who *feel* their history ('que sientan la historia'), not just know it off by heart (Cámara Villar 1984: 17).

The textbooks originally prepared for the propagation of this monolithic vision continued to be used in schools, with only minor modifications, into the 1960s. They trace the eternal patriotic and religious ideals embodied in the regime and in the person of the *Caudillo* right back to pre-Christian roots, insisting that Celts, Carthaginians, Phoenicians, Greeks, and Romans were all magically civilized and spiritualized by their contact with the Iberian essence. So were the Gothic and Islamic invaders: 'Aquellos musulmanes eran españoles casi todos. [. . .] Toda aquella civilización maravillosa es "española" ' (F.T.D. 1940: 302) ('Those Muslims were almost all Spaniards. [. . .] That whole marvellous civilization is "Spanish" '); and Spanish too, in this interpretation, are their books, scholars, artists, and poets. Jews, on the other hand, remain a threat to unity, a dangerous, alien race rightly expelled in 1492. The heroic exploits of the Reconquest and the discovery of America naturally feature prominently, together with impassioned refutations of the 'leyenda negra' ('Black Legend') put about by the enemies of Spain. Columbus's mission, as he is deemed to have told Queen Isabel, was to discover new lands and 'enseñar a todas las gentes a ser buenos y a rezar' (Serrano de Haro 1953: 60) ('teach all the people in them to be good and to pray').

The political and moral lessons for the present are spelt out insistently and unequivocally. A standard history book of the late 1950s exhorts primary school pupils to imitate the heroes and martyrs of the past; cultivate the 'virtudes de la Raza hispana' ('virtues of the Hispanic Race'); work hard and obey the authorities; repudiate the 'funestas doctrinas' ('destructive doctrines') of liberalism, freemasonry, and separatism; and 'abrazar con entera decisión los ideales patrióticos y religiosos de nuestra España imperial' ('embrace wholeheartedly the patriotic and religious ideals of our imperial Spain') (Edelvives 1958: 108). The Álvarez encyclopedia—probably the most widely used and best remembered textbook of the 1950s and 1960s[2]—presents Spanish history in two different ways: more or less objectively, as an academic subject, and, subsequently, in a dogmatic and partisan way, as part of Falangist *formación política* (political education). The overall message is familiar: when Spain has neglected her global mission to propagate and defend the Christian faith, her greatness has been diminished; now the nation is reunited and back on course, and

---

[2] The Álvarez encyclopedia seems to have acquired an ironic status as a nostalgic icon, and is now available in a facsimile edition (Madrid: EDAF, 1997).

everyone must contribute to the fulfilment of its destiny by 'cumpliendo fielmente las consignas del Gobierno y cultivando las virtudes morales y religiosas que hicieron famosos a nuestros antepasados en los tiempos imperiales') (Álvarez Pérez 1964: 607) ('faithfully complying with the orders of the government and cultivating the moral and religious virtues that made our ancestors famous in imperial times').

2.2.1. Children's magazines and comic books

Children's magazines and comic books are another influential, formative group of writings of the 1940s into the 1950s. The Falange's children's magazine, *Flechas y pelayos*, combines patriotic propaganda and religious doctrine with comic strips and stories celebrating 'heroes of the fatherland' such as el Cid, the conquistadors, and José Antonio. The same ideas recur again and again: a united nation favoured by God, a superior race with an imperial destiny, the Crusades of the past repeated in the victory of 1939, the heroic leaders of the past reincarnated in Franco. Letters and drawings from well-drilled young readers vie with one another to show how well they have assimilated the rhetoric and become writers and artists for the regime. But by 1946, the explicit propaganda has all but disappeared from *Flechas y pelayos*. The patriotism is blander, and history is gradually becoming merely a setting for adventure stories rather than a means of overt indoctrination. It was not just that times—and official rhetoric—were changing: there were much more attractive accounts of historical heroism on the market, especially the *cuadernos de aventuras* (adventure comic books). Despite the often poor quality of the draughtsmanship and of the paper on which they were printed, these stories of cowboys, medieval knights, pirates, explorers, world war, and science fiction enjoyed a boom during the 1940s and 1950s. The most popular were series with historical settings, the undisputed leader of which was *El Guerrero del Antifaz* (*The Masked Warrior*, drawn by Manuel Gago and published by Editorial Valenciana between 1946 and 1966, with reissues continuing into the 1980s).

El Guerrero del Antifaz is the story of a medieval Christian nobleman brought up as a Muslim who seeks to avenge the killing of his mother and prove his true identity (the Muslim ruler Alí Kan had kidnapped his mother, brought up her child as his own son, and made him a Muslim warrior, then murdered her just as she was revealing the truth to her son). He repudiates his Muslim identity, dons a mask, and embarks upon a ferocious personal crusade against Alí Kan. In the course of more than 600 violent, action-packed episodes, a crudely Manichaean vision of the Reconquest is played out again and again. The hero is noble, austere, and invincible, driven by righteous hatred of the Moors, who are by definition treacherous and depraved. The hero represents not just an eternal Christian essence of Spain, but more precisely the struggle to throw off an imposed 'foreign' identity, overthrow a tyrannical usurper, and reclaim a true Christian identity. Other *cuadernos de aventuras* with historical settings—such as *El Cachorro* (first issued 1951: *The Cub*)—also tend to have revenge as their motivating force. Essentially, they offer a defence of the concept of the just war, and therefore an echo of the regime's justification of its own use of extreme violence against its enemies and the sacrifices having to be made by its supporters (Vázquez de Parga 1980: 102). On the other hand, these avenging heroes are too individualistic, their motives too obsessively personal, to match perfectly either the fascist ideals of comradeship, discipline, and selfless service or the Catholic emphasis on family and community.

An interesting contrast to *El Guerrero del Antifaz* is provided by *El Capitán Trueno* (*Captain Thunder*), a medieval adventure series that began publication in 1956. It became almost as popular as its predecessor, using a similar formula, but with significant differences of tone and content. The Crusade is now in the Holy Land, and Capitán Trueno is driven less by the pursuit of revenge and ethnic cleansing than by a love of adventure for its own sake. Good and evil are no longer so clearly defined, the hero is more human and playful than the stern, obsessive Guerrero del Antifaz, and there is much less violence. While such changes may have been prompted to some extent by the growing influence of British and US comic books, they clearly suggest a less oppressive social climate. History is used less as a vehicle for propaganda than for escapism; the brutality that seemed unexceptional to readers who had only recently emerged from a Civil War is no longer appropriate. By 1963, when the regime was emphasizing peace and prosperity, even the official censors were becoming squeamish, and some issues of *El Guerrero del Antifaz* had to be retouched to tone down the depiction of violence.

2.3. POETRY OF THE 1940S: VICTORY, 'ROOTEDNESS', UNCERTAINTY

The heroic rhetoric of the post-war cartoons celebrating the 'heroes of the fatherland' is also the vehicle for the exalted sentiments of Falangist war poetry lionizing Franco, José Antonio, and the Falangist leader Arrese, frequently in the language of the medieval epic. There is, thus, writing which not only seeks to elevate the present by rewriting the past but which attempts selectively to mimic or adapt languages of that past. Dionisio Ridruejo's *Poesía en armas* (1940: *Poetry in Arms*) shows, also, a typically combative strain in direct response to past violence and present challenge as well as a counterblast to Republican war poetry of commitment and struggle. Thus in poetry in the first half of the 1940s one sees a persistent muscularity and a programmatic abhorrence of delicacy and decadence. Two poems involving rivers—a 'Romance al río' ('Ballad to a River') and an 'Oda a Burgos' ('Ode to Burgos')—by José María Alfaro, appearing in the poetry pages of the weekly *El español* (1942), see one river as 'hierro en fiebre de conquista' ('iron rushing in feverish conquest') and another, the Duero, again as iron, this time anchoring the villages on its banks. Both poems have images of fire, movement, and heroism, inscribing energy and steady purpose on the water. A later poem 'Castilla', by Lope Mateo (co-editor in chief of *Sí*, the Falangist daily *Arriba*'s literary supplement), sees Castile, in a distortion of a key idea in the thinking of the writers of the Generation of 1898, as the strong-armed embodiment of the salvation of Spain, and here the river is one of (Falangist) blue shirts and (Carlist) red berets as Castile rises up in defence of Spain against the left:

> Entonces, fiera, te erguiste
> y por tus robustas venas
> tornó como hace mil años
> a latir la sangre nueva.
> (in Rodríguez Puértolas
> 1987: 449)

('So, proud and wild, you arose | and through your robust veins | there flowed again | new blood as it had a thousand years ago.')

Such treatments of natural topography contrast tellingly with Antonio Machado's famous poems on Castile and the upper reaches of the Duero in his *Campos de Castilla* (1912 and 1917) in their quiet, philosophically and metaphorically more densely textured inscriptions of new meanings onto the historical geography of Spain. As the violent immediacy of the outcomes of the war receded, loud triumphalism, moment-specific propaganda, and automatic rhetoric became less common in literary writing although the exaltation of past glories and present strengths persisted in both tone and theme. However, given the political investments in central Spain as a source of spiritual strength as well as a site of abstract patriotic aspirations—carried over in varying degrees of sophistication from Unamuno's *En torno al casticismo* (1895: *On Spanishness*), Ángel Ganivet's *Idearium español* (1897: *Ideas of Spain*), the essays of Menéndez Pelayo and Ramiro de Maeztu, early Azorín, and Ortega y Gasset's *España invertebrada* (1920: *Invertebrate Spain*) as well as from Machado—the leisured post-war reader taking refuge in poems appearing in quality newspapers and magazines or in state-backed and prize-promoted collections would find with little surprise hundreds and hundreds of poetic texts refining down the essence of 'Spain', empire, Castile, God, and the past.

2.3.1. Poetry periodicals of the 1940s

In the early post-war years José Antonio Primo de Rivera's understanding of the Falange as 'un movimiento poético' ('a poetic movement') found resonance in many manifestos and speeches, editorials and poems; as Rodríguez Puértolas (1986: 49–50) summarizes this topos of European fascism, 'el jefe fascista es un artista él mismo, y el movimiento por él dirigido una obra de arte [. . .] defensor y organizador de la verdadera cultura' ('the fascist leader is himself an artist, and the movement he heads a work of art [. . .] the defender and organizer of the one true culture'). There is much evidence of this romantic notion in the luxuriously produced *Vértice*, the house magazine of the Falange. In February 1941 it announced 'efusivamente' ('effusively') the publication of its first complete poetry section, full (as the magazine boasted) of 'autoridad lírica' ('lyrical authority') and of poetry (by Juan Aparicio, Gerardo Diego, Jorge Guillén, Manuel Machado, and José María Pemán) which 'penetra en el alma humana' (*Vértice* 1941) ('penetrates deep into the human soul'). Although *Vértice* was clearly designed for an upper-middle-class and pseudo- or truly aristocratic readership and, as Fanny Rubio (1976: 46) points out, was '[llena] de nostalgias burguesas, de evocaciones de [...] los felices años finiseculares [...] y de bellas elegías culturales' ('full of bourgeois nostalgia, evocations of [...] the happy years of the turn of the century [...] and of fine high cultural elegies'), in the postwar phase of the magazine the voice of 'lyrical authority' in the service of politics frequently intervenes in verse and prose in far from languorous tones, reaching out instead for dignity, austerity, and authority. The fortress archive at Simancas, in a poem by Lope Mateo, in typical manner encapsulates under considerable sentimental pressure a past of war and mystic endeavour which looks back not to the turn of the century but into the preceding five years and beyond them to the Golden Age of conquest:

> Hoguera de soledades
> en la meseta encendida.
> Así, de cara a la vida,
> petrificada en historia,
> lanzas—Blasón y Memoria—,
> torres de luz y de gritos:
> ¡tempestad de manuscritos
> en un poniente de gloria!   (Mateo 1941)

(Beacon of solitude | ablaze on the meseta. | Thus, confronting life, | yet fixed in history of stone, | you cast—heraldic, memorial—, | towers of light and of the cries of men: | a tempest of manuscripts | in a sunset of glory!)

A fascination with uprightness, heavenward aspiration, stone structures, memorials, and words of glory can easily be traced through exalted lyrical writings in the 1940s and indeed on into the next decade. Behind it lay Ridruejo's mostly earlier *Sonetos a la piedra* (1934–42: *Sonnets to Stone*), and the discourses of virility and purity of the new regime. Refined versions of the style include Ridruejo's 'A un pino solo' ('To a Lone Pine Tree'), which appeared in the issue of *Vértice* following that of Mateo's poem. Here history is all but excluded in favour of the eternal, and yet spirituality is inevitably bound up with strife and tension. The poem employs the image of a rooted tree, offering a clear sign of such a poem's place in what came to be known as a sub-tradition of *poesía arraigada* ('rooted' poetry)—poetry written by those who felt that the Nationalist victory had restored to them a voice, a tradition, a set of images. Key to the development of such a writing, and less partisan than *Vértice*, is the poetry magazine *Garcilaso* (1943–6). As well as wanting to recuperate the values of empire and of the poetic renaissance whose initiation is conventionally attributed to the eponymous sixteenth-century soldier-poet, *Garcilaso* attempted to maintain a sense of poetry's supposed disinterested, pure, and human qualities. This meant in part bypassing the immediate past by publishing well-known poets of the Generation of 1927 (though not, of course, the left-wing Alberti, or Lorca), including Gerardo Diego, whose earlier 'Al ciprés de Silos' ('To the Cypress at Silos') had looked back to Antonio Machado in topography and forward to Ridruejo in its application of the sonnet form.

Another important poetry magazine of the Establishment, *Escorial* (1940–50), with Ridruejo as one of its founders, laid its general emphases on classical style. It is usually accepted that its title was a direct statement of an aspiration to recuperate the expansionist and spiritual glories of the seventeenth century, but a 1970s version offered by the then ex-Falangist Gonzalo Torrente Ballester (Benet et al. 1976) suggests that the name was coincidental (the apartments rented for the purposes of producing the magazine being decorated with illustrations of the famous monastery) and 'no apuntaba para nada a las glorias pretéritas [. . .] sino a una obra maestra de la arquitectura [. . .] un modelo de estilo' (62; 64) ('in no way was meant to draw attention to past glories [. . .] but rather to an architectural masterpiece [. . .] a model of style'). This attention to 'style' made *Escorial*, indeed, a propitious site for the development of some carefully modulated and highly refined expressions of what can only be called dissent. In 1945, characteristically, *Escorial* was open to poems by Carlos Bousoño, whose earlier melancholy, religious poems were already beginning to transmute into intense, existentialist interrogations of faith; by José María Valverde, whose *Hombre de Dios* (1945: *Man of God*) rehearses some of the crises of faith which are the substance of the left-wing Blas de Otero's* *Ángel fieramente humano* (1950: *A Fiercely Human Angel*); and by Eugenio de Nora whose anonymously published *Pueblo cautivo* (1946: *A Captive People*) wears its affiliations clearly on its title-page.

2.3.2. Paradoxes of faith

Although it is now seldom represented in anthologies or on syllabuses, traditional poetry on Catholic themes had as much of a boom in the 1940s and 1950s as did that which under the generational labels of 1936 and 1950 has attracted more attention in later years. Luis Rosales's 'Misericordia', from *Segundo abril* (a collection written between 1938 and 1940, in Pamplona and Burgos: *A Second April*), although remaining unpublished until 1972, offers an arresting example of how the best of this discourse of austerity can participate both in traditional Catholic belief and a more primitive, pantheistic vision which sees God—directly exhorted in the manner of the Psalms—as a landscape 'en sereno equilibrio' ('in balanced serenity'), and as 'mansedumbre sin voz, hierba de siempre, sosiego de mis ojos' (Rosales 1972: 31) ('mild and voiceless presence, the ever-growing grass, solace for my eyes'). The plea is that God should suppress the poet's smile of intense aesthetic pleasure at the prospect of this and give him instead 'esa sobria y precisa alegría que no turba ni ofende' ('that sober, precise happiness that neither troubles nor offends') (31).

Religious poetry in this period often leads in mildly unorthodox directions, in particular to diverge from the official tones of heroism and virility. In the many poems to and about the Virgin there is (of course) little room for robust neo-imperialism and it is easy to detect a tendency to an exaggeratedly feminine representation of the scenarios narrated, even (or especially) by male writers. *Vértice*'s Christmas and New Year Special in 1941 reprinted (along with immensely lavish full-colour reproductions of scenes from van de Weyden) two 'Romances a la inmaculada' ('Ballads to Our Lady of the Immaculate Conception') which had won Adriano del Valle the Sánchez Bedoya Prize at the end of 1938, leading to their publication in *Falange española* the following year. Here Mary Mother of God is conventionally represented as delicacy, purity, and loveliness but Joseph is enveloped in a refined sensuality far from his rude masculine calling: in his workshop 'el serrín es polvo de oro | y el engrudo es hidromiel' (Valle 1941: 19) ('the glue is sugared water, | the sawdust, gold-dust'). Valle, who had worked alongside Ridruejo in the war in the Press and Propaganda Delegation, is a key figure in that vast and (to present tastes) somewhat monotonous tradition of cross-writing by which popular, folkloric conceptions of the saints and the Holy Family colourfully oust the barer biblical truths. Winner of many establishment prizes and an important minor player in official cultural politics, Valle makes good the bonds between Marianism and official state discourse and yet also disrupts the classicizing and normalizing project. In *Arpa fiel* (1941: *A Faithful Harp*), the lighter verses to Mary in popular metres quite properly, in internal political terms, sit side by side with poems (mostly more formal sonnets) dedicated to Spain and Italy but also with further verses 'A la mujer española' ('To Spanish Women') and 'A la poesía' ('To Poetry') suggesting, by juxtaposition, a heterodox erotic and aesthetic perspective on religious devotion. In his occasional prose writings on religious festivals in Seville there is a strong recapitulation of *fin de siècle* decadence mixed in with the Andalusian *costumbrismo* (an often exoticized writing on rural and regional life and landscapes). 'Un encuadre cinematográfico de Sevilla' ('A Cinematographic Framing of Seville') brings a spectacular excess of light, colour, and sentiment to the overshadowed days of 1944 in its description of the progress through the streets of Seville of a Virgin on her float; and the poetic essay 'Stella matutina' of 1953 is indecently concerned with the heady aromas, pistils, and coronas of the flowers of spring which go against nature in order to be out in time for the processional commemorations of the Passion (Valle 1992: 194–5). This sensual language was to reappear towards the end of the 1940s in the poetry of some of the writers in the Córdoba magazine *Cántico* to similarly tacit, transgressive effect.

2.4. DRAMA: RESTAGING THE PAST

Several plays from 1939 and 1940 express the euphoria of victory through celebrations of Isabel la Católica and the formation of the empire, finding female icons to match the Virgin. Poets Luis Rosales and Luis Felipe Vivanco published *La mejor reina de España* (*Spain's Greatest Queen*), and in a similar vein the Jesuit Ramón Cué published *Y el imperio volvía* (*And the Empire Was Returning*). The 'Victory Year' also saw the première of *La santa hermandad* (*The Holy Brotherhood*, about the Inquisition) by Eduardo Marquina and *La santa virreina* (*The Saintly Vicereine*) by José María Pemán, who was also the author of history books for use in schools. Pemán's play is based on the story of the Countess of Chinchón, wife of a viceroy of Peru in the late seventeenth century, who is supposed to have discovered the medical value of quinine. Pemán's preface to the 1939 edition emphasizes his desire to pay homage to Spain's 'great colonial achievement' as an 'obra por esencia misionera, humana, civilizadora' (Pemán 1939: 7) ('a humanizing, civilizing mission'). Spain not only brings the gospel to heathen peoples but also (in a perverse reworking of Enlightenment thinking) scientific knowledge too. Pemán's confident discourse elides numerous contradictions: obscurantist Catholicism appears to be no obstacle to enlightened scientific discovery; a humanistic mission is expressed in combative terms of conquest and taming of wild forces; indigenous knowledge is dismissed but simultaneously coveted and exploited (in the case of the secret of quinine).

Marquina's drama ends with these exultant words: '¡Paso a España! Los verdugos de ayer hinquen la rodilla a la doble majestad de estas flechas y este yugo ... Caen las sombras incoloras y alza el Imperio español su frente rubia de amores. Después de la noche el sol' (in Andrés-Gallego et al. 1995: 246) ('Make way for Spain! Let the executioners of yesterday fall to their knees before the double majesty of these arrows and this yoke... The dim shadows fall away and the Spanish Empire lifts its fair head with love. After the night, the sun').

As in poetry, the evocation of artistic forms of the past serves ideological purposes of the present, and plays such as *La santa virreina* pay homage in their language, characters, and dramatic structure to the *comedia* of the Golden Age. Avant-garde writers such as Federico García Lorca had sought in the 1920s and 1930s to rediscover and experiment with a diverse classical heritage neglected during the nineteenth century. Now, in the hands of Pemán and other conservative playwrights, such forms represent little more than a deferential nod towards tradition and a rejection of modernism. Both history and literature are seen as unproblematic and fixed, but there are underlying contradictions: avowedly apolitical aestheticism serves a regime founded on puritanical, anti-intellectual instincts; the ambition of defining the essential historical character of the people is pursued by glorifying the traditions of monarchy, aristocracy, and absolute state control.

In 1944, with Falangist hopes of a resurgence of empire on the back of Axis victories not quite extinguished, Isabel la Católica was still a potent icon. Eduardo Juliá Martínez's play *Se ensanchaba Castilla* ... (1944: *Castile in Expansion*) features a visionary Isabel, supported by a steadfast Fernando, bringing peace, unity, and imperial glory to a grateful Spain. The significance of these plays here is not that they are all particularly virulent expressions of imperialism but that they emerged when they did, celebrating the new regime by defining civilization and progress in terms of religion, tradition, order, and that unique sense of national destiny centred on Castile. The unity and order they idealize are necessarily achieved by means of military victory, and yet it is interesting that their heroes are women. Queen Isabel and the *santa virreina* represent empire with a feminine touch; the implacable masculine spirit of the Crusade is softened by the gentleness of the Virgin Mary; not conquest but the triumph of love is the theme. On her deathbed, Juliá Martínez's Isabel entrusts the empire to her husband with these words:

> Y cuidad que el corazón
> siembre el amor en el suelo,
> que a nuestro Imperio dió el cielo
> por el genio de Colón.
> Amor nos fizo triunfar.
> (Juliá Martínez 1944: 68)

(And see to it that the heart | sows love in the soil | that heaven gave to our Empire | thanks to the genius of Columbus. | Our triumphs were wrought by love.)

2.5. PROSE WRITING IN THE 1940S

There are three particularly famous, canonical literary texts of this period—Camilo José Cela's *La familia de Pascual Duarte* (1942: *The Family of Pascual Duarte*) and *La colmena* (published in 1951, but completed in 1945: *The Hive*), and Carmen Laforet's *Nada* (1945: *Nothingness*).[3] Gonzalo Torrente Ballester and Miguel Delibes were also establishing their careers. To all these we shall be returning in later chapters to discuss specific issues. In imaginative non-fiction, Cela brought out his evocative *Viaje a la Alcarria* (1948: *Journey to Alcarria*)—as much a meditation on writing as a representation of a part of 'la España profunda' ('deepest Spain': a term signifying remote areas, but also conservative values and

---

[3] However, the clear best-seller of the post-war period, significantly, is *Camino* (*The Way*), originally published as *Consideraciones espirituales* (1934: *Spiritual Thoughts*), by the founder of the Opus Dei, José María Escrivá de Balaguer. As of March 1996 there have been some 298 editions, and almost 4 million copies in forty-one languages sold (Pope 1999: 138).

wisdom). The state-owned Editora Nacional published some key texts in the history of Spanish ideas and the essay, all of which were to be, in different ways, the focus of debates in years to come: among them, philosopher Xavier Zubiri's *Naturaleza, historia, Dios* (1942: *Nature, History, God*) and a series of works by essayist Pedro Laín Entralgo on culture and Spanishness. Prolific middlebrow novelist Juan Antonio de Zunzunegui saw his boom years (writing mostly on provincial life around Bilbao and middle-class neighbourhoods of Madrid), and Ignacio Agustí—a major Catalan novelist working in Castilian—with his second big success, *El viudo Rius* (1945: *Rius, the Widower*), inaugurated a largely Barcelona-based saga in a series ending in 1972 with *Guerra civil* (*Civil War*). Carmen de Icaza consolidated a career as a stylistically impressive and interestingly ambiguous reactionary writer of nonetheless sharply unconventional novels for women; and the well-wrought romantic fantasies of Concha Linares Becerra and Rafael Pérez y Pérez provided distraction and alternative histories and distant pasts aplenty. But the more immediate and painful history of the Civil War itself was, of course, a pressing theme.

2.5.1. Heroism and red terror: Falangist accounts of the war

Within Spain, accounts of the war could at first only be written by the victors. Two kinds of narrative predominated: the celebration of patriotic heroism in combat and the denunciation of anarchy, brutality, and depravity in the 'red' zone. *La fiel infantería* (1943: *The Loyal Infantry*), winner of the 1943 José Antonio Primo de Rivera National Prize for Literature, and Rafael García Serrano's contribution to the first of these genres, contains this stunningly insensitive image: 'Recorríamos España en alegre turismo armado. El turismo que precisamente le estaba haciendo falta a España' (57) ('We were joyful armed tourists on a jaunt around Spain. Just the kind of tourism Spain was in need of'). Nationalist soldiers are pictured marching with the weight of history behind them gladly and manfully into war (though also foul-mouthedly and into brothels, which led to the book's withdrawal: Pope 1999: 137). The protagonist feels some anguish at having to 'disparar sobre un hombre que dice madre igual que tú' (87) ('shoot at a man who says mother the same as you'), but convinces himself that it is necessary to kill: 'Con la razón y el arma en los brazos. La muerte es un camarada más de los soldados, y en nuestro campo se mataba de frente' (88) ('With right on our side and our weapons in our hands. Death is just another comrade to a soldier, and on our side we killed face to face').

In Tomás Borrás's *Checas de Madrid: Epopeya de los caídos* (1940: *Chekas in Madrid: Epic of the Fallen*) there is no such soul-searching. The book is a nauseatingly exaggerated catalogue of the alleged *terror rojo* (red terror) of Republican Madrid during the war: the descriptions of genocide, torture, corruption, treachery, ugliness, fanaticism, and depravity are graphic and relentless. All the Manichaean stereotyping and grotesque distortion of wartime propaganda is deployed: the Nationalist cause is pure, decent, pious, and patriotic; the Republican forces, 'esta galería de monstruos que es la España roja' (286) ('this gallery of monsters that is Red Spain'), are evil wreckers, hating spiritual values 'por envidia, como el sapo a la estrella' (286) ('out of envy, as a toad might hate a star').

2.5.2. A longer perspective on the Civil War

When the boom in triumphalist and sometimes rancorous narratives of the struggle for victory faded away, the war and the harsh years of the early 1940s became, gradually at first but, by the 1960s, in a dazzling explosion of creativity, the agenda of the left (see Chapter 8). Narrative texts on these issues written in exile— Arturo Barea's *La llama* (1944: *The Flame*),[4] Manuel Andújar's *Cristal roto* (1945: *Broken Mirror*), Concha Castroviejo's *Los que se fueron* (1957: *Those Who Went Away*) and *Víspera de odio* (1958: *The Eve of Hatred*), Max Aub's prolific output of novels and short stories from the mid-1940s to the mid-1960s, and works by Francisco Ayala and Ramón José Sender*—form a counterpoint, in their clear position-taking, to quieter and supposedly balanced accounts within Spain, of which the most significant example is perhaps José María Gironella's *Los cipreses creen en Dios* (1954: *The Cypresses Believe in God*), the first in a trilogy on the Civil War and one of the best-sellers of the 1950s.

[4] This is the last book of the trilogy *La forja de un rebelde*, originally appearing in English (1941–4): see Barea (1972).

Rewriting History 41

A resurgence of what would once have been Nationalist fervour was going to have to wait for an unexpectedly long time, until after the death of Franco. The direction that the transition to democracy began to take led to reactions from the right, not just in active forms such as the famed coup attempt by Colonel Antonio Tejero of February 1981 but also in fierce literary and journalistic battles and soul-searching, as in Dionisio Ridruejo's *Casi unas memorias* (1976: *Almost Memoirs*). In the field of the novel, favourite names of the Franco years were spurred to new publications by the decline and death of the *Caudillo* and by subsequent events. Fernando Vizcaíno Casas's *La España de la posguerra* (1975: *Spain in the Postwar Years*) and *...Y al tercer año resucitó* (1978: *...And in the Third Year He Rose Again*) are full of retrospection, with the latter satirizing the left and wishfully thinking that the spirit of Franco could live on. Cela's *Oficio de tinieblas 5* (1973: *Tenebrae*) and *Mazurca para dos muertos* (1983: *Mazurka for Two Dead Dancers*) are both concerned to redress the balance of blame and praise. A late resurgence of Falangist opposition to Francoism in the second of these two novels is accompanied (unsurprisingly) by an emphatically rightwing, nostalgic view of a deterministic bond between man and nature, of ineluctable cycles, and the Galician land as source of authenticity but also of sempiternal evil. Equally convinced of the irrelevance of ideas of the social constructedness of reality or of political agency is Fernando Sánchez Dragó's vast *Gárgoris y Habidis: Una historia mágica de España en cuatro volúmenes* (1978: *Gárgoris and Habidis: A Magical History of Spain in Four Volumes*), a heady combination of 'anarchist millenarianism with a compendium of the clichés inherited by Spanish fascism from the 1898 Generation and Ortega' (Labanyi 1989: 218). Its 1995 sequel (Sánchez Dragó 1995) is fulsome in its praise of Cela, half unwittingly reproducing the language of thirty-five years back: 'representa la unidad de España en tiempos tan difíciles para los españoles como los que ahora corren [...] Cela, o el inmenso espectáculo de la libertad [...] Cela, nuestro resumen' (257–8) ('he represents the unity of Spain in difficult times like these for Spaniards [...] Cela, or the great spectacle of freedom [...] Cela, our epitome'). Rafael García Serrano's autobiographical novel *La gran esperanza* (1985: *The Great Hope*) looks back directly to the violence of war and insists on the Nationalists' qualities of 'disciplina', 'vocación militar', 'sosiego y mesura' ('discipline', 'military calling', 'calmness and moderation'), keeping violence in check behind Nationalist lines, 'pero la balanza se desequilibró ferozmente por la enloquecida bestialidad de la zona roja' (García Serrano 1985: 58) ('but the scales were savagely unbalanced by frenzied brutality in the Red zone'.

The reprinting in 1983 of Ernesto Giménez Caballero's *Genio de España* (1932: *Spirit of Spain*)—a foundational text of Falangism—and the compilation in 1984 of a series of essays entitled *Cataluña con Franco* (*Catalonia with Franco*)—the title pointedly avoids the now more usually employed preposition 'under'—serve as reminders of the potency of the language of the old crusades and the longevity of their echoes. *Cataluña con Franco* laments the 'decadence' of Catalonia since the death of Franco, and reviews in detail the cultural, ecclesiastical, and legal measures— for example, the team of lawyers working on the Carta Municipal of Barcelona of May 1960 are compared to hard-working honest peasants digging deep in rich tradition—which in the view of its authors had served so well to unite a Catalonia, 'esta tierra tan española' (Aguirre et al. 1984: 14) ('this so very Spanish land'), already bound together in its fervent adoration of Our Lady of Montserrat (96) (whose Festival is proudly chosen for the publication date of the volume). The claims here, against prevailing liberal opinion, are that Catalan culture, and specifically literary endeavour in the Catalan language, were far from suppressed during the Franco era: the regime supported the traditional Jocs Florals (a festival of traditional verse and song) and the establishment of numerous poetry prizes (including the Rosselló-Poncel Prize, with Salvador Espriu, one of modern Catalonia's most famous literary names, on the jury) (259–87), and the Barcelona-based Nadal, Destino, and Planeta prizes for narrative flourished. In short, in this version of affairs, there was no question of a silencing or desertion of Catalan writing and culture: 'la labor oficial [. . .] estuvo presente' (288) ('official effort and support [. . .] was ever-present').

Lastly, and into the 1990s now, another reissue by a prestigious Falangist attests to the power and fascination of the remembered imagery and actions of the traumatic 1930s. Agustín de Foxá's *Madrid de corte a cheka* (1938: *Madrid, from Royal Court to Prison Camp*), a fictionalized autobiographical account of the transition from the end of monarchy through the Second Republic and into the Civil War, Falangist activism, and the life of the aristocratic and pseudo-aristocratic right under first the Republic then the *terror rojo*, was reprinted by Planeta in 1993, as Spain approached its decision to oust the PSOE from government, and went at once into three runs. Its virulent critiques of the left in power perhaps rang bells, and readers on the mid- to far right may well have been pleased to note how old scapegoats might serve to expiate Spain in weary disenchantment in the 1990s, recognizing in their own time what Foxá identifies as the canker of the early 1930s: 'enfermizos intelectuales de sexualidad mal definida' ('sickly intellectuals of ill-defined sexuality'), reading about sex, contraception, Marxism, and trips to Russia (Foxá 1993: 78; 108–9) (though for Russia, in the 1990s, read Cuba).

Further reading

Blanco Aguinaga, Rodríguez Puértolas, and Zavala (1983); Rodríguez Puértolas (1986, 1987); Sopeña Monsalve (1994).

3
Reclaiming History

3.1. ESSAYS IN NEW HISTORY

By the 1950s, although Falangist fundamentalism had given way to a more pragmatic but still authoritarian political climate, the heroic vision of history remained essentially intact in official versions. In the meantime, however, it was beginning to be questioned in a variety of ways by essayists, historians, and creative writers. Exiled philosophers such as Fernando de los Ríos, Américo Castro, Claudio Sánchez Albornoz, José Gaos, Eduardo Nicol, and María Zambrano had already been reflecting from an instructive distance on questions of historical development and national identity. They evoke alternative traditions: not the glories of conquest but the voice of conscience of Bartolomé de las Casas; Spanish Humanism in place of Tridentine Counter-Reformation; the eighteenth century as a time of constructive enlightenment rather than heresy and renunciation of Spanishness. Although many of these accounts seek essentialist definitions of Spain which may in some respects sound similar to the official notion of *Hispanidad*, they do at least see the whole project as problematic, and present the lessons of history as open to philosophical debate rather than as monolithic dogma.

In Spain, the historian Jaume Vicens Vives had been developing an incisive critique of the dominant mode of unprofessional, ideology-driven dabbling in history ('ideologismo historizante') throughout the 1940s, although he was denied a university chair until 1947. His rigorous, modern methodology, based on solid economic and sociological evidence collected at a local level, began to have a significant impact after his founding of the journal *Estudios de historia moderna* in 1951, an impact that was ultimately political as much as academic, since its focus on Catalan history posed a serious challenge to the regime's dogmatic centralism. A few other historians were also quietly engaged in undermining aspects of the official orthodoxy: Manuel Giménez

Fernández sought to demystify notions of the Catholic unity of the sixteenth century; Ramón Carande's work on Carlos V showed the terrible cost of empire rather than exalting it; and Julio Caro Baroja continued to study the marginal cultures of the Spanish past, including, famously, the Basques (Carr and Fusi 1981: 111). The eighteenth century, which had been condemned by Marcelino Menéndez Pelayo (republished by Editora Nacional in the 1940s) as a century of betrayal of the national tradition and had been neglected in the post-war period by historians anxious to study centuries with a greater affinity to the 'national spirit', was by the end of the 1950s receiving more attention from historians, encouraged by the technocrats brought into government after the abandonment of autarky and the end of international isolation. The Enlightenment was politically useful in that it represented a period of reforms designed to promote economic and administrative progress without the need to change the fundamental structures of an authoritarian system, and, as we shall be seeing below, was also to prove richly suggestive for some imaginative writers.

3.2. POETRY: BECOMING COMMITTED

While the two principal literary genres in which there is extended, contestatory engagement with issues and protagonists from recent and distant Spanish history are theatre and narrative, epochal changes were being created in poetry through the 1940s and 1950s as it fought to write itself into history (as 'social poetry') or to construct itself as an ideal space, above—or beyond—mere events (as 'pure' poetry, *poesía pura*). Of particular interest are the ways in which the ideals of the literary power bases around the magazines of the early to mid-1940s are countered and converted. In 1944, the year of the publication of Dámaso Alonso's *Hijos de la ira* (*Children of Rage*), whose anguished topicality and free form was a double rebellion against the sanctioned poetry already discussed, the magazine *Espadaña* was founded in León. It was to be a focus for a new poetry, distancing itself from 'official' poetry, but also from the 'pure', metaphysical poetry and the interest in transcendent meanings in vogue just before the war (Rubio 1976: 268–9). There is a straightforward commitment to answering the two questions put in issue number 24: '¿Merece la pena escribir?, y, en todo caso, ¿para quién?'(269) ('Is it worth writing? And in any case, for whom?'). This focus came about despite the discrepancies of views amongst its co-editors which came to furious conclusion (and the end of the magazine) in 1950—'Va sonando la hora en que los poetas opten entre los sucios harapos académicos y la autenticidad revolucionaria' ('The hour is now striking when poets must choose between donning the dirty rags of academic values and embracing revolutionary authenticity'), wrote Miguel Labordeta (269). *Espadaña*, though, stood on the whole for anticlassicism and anti-formalism; it was anti-*Garcilasista*, if nonetheless open to poets like Carlos Bousoño.

That key double question—why? and for whom?—was to resound for many years, years in which new realisms were being forged in the other literary genres. The answer given by Gabriel Celaya in Francisco Ribes's *Antología consultada* of 1952—having joined the Communist Party and become a focus for militant *antifranquista* political and cultural activism—was 'Hablemos de lo que cada día nos ocupa' ('Let's talk about what concerns us every day'); poetry is 'un instrumento para transformar el mundo' (in Riera 1988: 429) ('an instrument with which to change the world'). This is the line followed to considerable poetic effect in the *Cantos íberos* (1955: *Iberian Chants*), *De claro en claro* (1956: *Clearer and Clearer*), and *Poesía urgente* (1960: *Poetry of Urgency*): his famous set of formulations about poetry in 'La poesía es un arma cargada de futuro' (1955: 'Poetry is a Weapon Armed with the Future') is, in retrospect, a defining formulation of *poesía social* (with, here, strong overtones of the recently published *Odas elementales* of the Chilean Pablo Neruda whom Celaya so much admired).

It is this kind of writing, as well as the debates in *Espadaña* (amongst other magazines), and around the *Antología consultada*, which in the 1950s built up a core sub-genre of poetic realism gradually joined by important voices which had, in earlier years, reacted quite differently to the facts of war and its aftermath. Thus, one of *Espadaña*'s two co-founders, Victoriano Crémer, shifts from the oblique, veiled dissenting voice of *Caminos de mi sangre* (1947: *Paths of my Blood*) towards clear historical revisionism in *La espada y la pared* (1949: *The Devil and the Deep Blue Sea*); the other co-founder Eugenio de Nora's earlier (and anonymously published) *Pueblo cautivo* has denunciations, passages of testimony, and references to the facts of war, exile, and death; and Blas de Otero moves from dissident religious writing where the poet is akin to an Old Testament prophet imploring a cruel and distant God on behalf of a suffering but unspecific people in a ruined, allegorical landscape, in *Ángel fieramente humano* (1950: *A Fiercely Human Angel*), to directly politicized writing in *Pido la paz y la palabra* (1955: *I Ask for Peace and Time to Speak*), and *Que trata de España* (1964: *On Spain*). Suddenly, again, a new protagonist in poetry is the *pueblo*; as in Antonio Machado, before the Civil War, poetry is not merely transcendent but 'palabra en el tiempo' ('the word intersecting time'), and Spain a site whose *intrahistoria* it is the urgent, special task of poets to articulate.[1]

3.3. DRAMA: HISTORY IN MOTION

The première in 1958 of Antonio Buero Vallejo's* *Un soñador para un pueblo* (*A Dreamer for the People*) was an influential sign of the growth of interest amongst dramatists in opening up Spanish history to reinterpretation and critique. Many history plays written during the dictatorship performed a particularly important function in challenging the Francoists' hijacking of ideas of national identity by presenting history as a dynamic, open process. Previously idealized elements are problematized or satirized, while neglected or despised elements are brought into the foreground. Links with the present are sometimes explicitly signalled by means of anachronisms or framing devices, or suggested by analogy. One advantage of using a historical setting in a time of strict political control is that it may afford a disguise under which expressions of dissent can be smuggled past the censors, but the kind of historical theatre under consideration here has broader aims, exploring tensions between temporal distance and aesthetic distancing, between historical time and stage time, between recorded fact and

[1] *Intrahistoria*: a term coined by Miguel de Unamuno to refer to the relative lack of change in the everyday lives of the mass of the population (still predominantly agricultural in the early years of the century) under the surface of historical events. Feminist historians have reclaimed the term 'intrahistoria' to refer to the study of the history of everyday life in which the personal and the social intersect (as in Martin Gaite's *El cuarto de atrás*).

dramatic fiction, and ways in which attitudes and ideologies in the present rewrite the past. After 1975, when the urgency of reclaiming history from right-wing manipulation has diminished, there still remains the enormous task of opening up and problematizing history: investigating its continuing relevance to the present, using it to explore issues of individual and collective identity, class and gender relations, myth and memory, the rituals and victims of power.

3.3.1 Reassessing the protagonists

Un soñador para un pueblo, based on the anti-reform riots of 1766 known as the Esquilache rebellion, made a subtle but significant contribution to emerging debates about the eighteenth century and current processes of reform. Buero's positive presentation of Esquilache and Carlos III as enlightened modernizers, struggling against a conservative aristocracy and the inability of the common people to recognize their true interests, could be read as a 'reactionary' defence of both eighteenth-century absolutism and the emerging new face of Francoism. However, the most significant implication of the play is that real change requires both the dismantling of established power structures and the genuine involvement of the people. Esquilache realizes belatedly that his aim of improving the material conditions of the masses before they are given any real responsibility has underestimated both the obstructive force of the established order and the potential capacity of the people for taking responsibility on their own terms. Left-wing unease at the apparent representation of the people as loutish riff-raff in contrast with an undeservedly favourable view of their rulers was ironically shared by right-wing critics, who accused Buero of betraying the precious Spanish national spirit for the defence of which the rioters of 1766 should be celebrated (García Escudero 1959, 1960). However, Buero's play challenges such notions of national identity by asserting that patriotism need not manifest itself as nationalistic xenophobia and makes the *pueblo* (in the form of the maidservant Fernandita) the ultimate judge of moral value. Furthermore, Esquilache's self-sacrifice—he advises the king to concede the rebels' demands to avoid the bloodshed that a military solution would bring—implicitly questions the legitimacy of Franco's government: he decides that his aims, however rational, cannot

Reclaiming History 49

justify the suffering of a Civil War. He admits that he is tempted by the intoxicating lure of military power, yet he resists the temptation and wins a small but significant moral victory. Buero's treatment of the historical material emerges as a complex, self-conscious process of selection, reshaping, and reinterpretation. The defiant declaration made by Esquilache to the Duke of Villasanta—'la Historia se mueve' (Buero Vallejo 1994: 86–7) ('History moves on')—becomes his consolation in defeat and reaches out to a present-day audience.

Buero has applied this thoughtful, dialectical approach to other periods and historical figures. Each play develops a key conflict between forces of change and immobility around an artist or intellectual whose importance lies not so much in being the prime mover of events as in being an unusually perceptive observer of them. Like Esquilache, Velázquez in *Las meninas* (1960: *The Maids of Honour*), Goya in *El sueño de la razón* (1960: *The Sleep of Reason*), and Larra in *La detonación* (1977: *The Shot*) develop a special understanding of the impact of historical processes on the lives of the people around them. The personal crisis of each protagonist is intricately linked, through powerful theatrical images, with the public crisis of the historical moment and the privileged perspective of each of them is complemented by a relationship with a representative of the powerless masses. History is shown to be driven largely by crude forces of self-interest and abuse of power, but certain individuals exemplify the difficult lesson that real human progress can only be made through individual and collective empowerment.

Since the 1960s, the critical exploration of Spanish history has been a major concern of a number of younger playwrights. The strategy of thoughtful re-evaluation of well-known personalities and episodes so successfully developed by Buero has also been pursued by Ana Diosdado, whose *Los comuneros* (1974: *The Communards*) dramatizes the rebellion of the Communities of Castile in 1517 against Carlos I (the Emperor Charles V). The revolt of the *comuneros* can be seen as local, popular resistance to centralized authoritarian government, or as an expression of chauvinism and the defence of established interests against foreign interference. Diosdado's treatment, while generally supporting the justice of the *comunero* cause, is careful to take into account both sets of connotations. Juan de Padilla, the leader of the rebels, is an idealist tortured by doubts about whether the devastation of war can be justified, about the purity of his own motives and the nature of justice. King Carlos emerges as neither tyrant nor hero, a self-doubting prisoner of the political forces over which he nominally presides. By means of a complex structure of flashbacks, dream sequences, and simultaneous actions, Carlos appears both as the youth of 1517 and as an old man, and is made to be both a protagonist and a spectator of the story, as well as a commentator on the events and an arranger of the dramatic re-enactment. For a moment he clutches at an illusion of understanding and repentance, imagining that he can change the story, but his older self knows that the story is already history. The real audience, though, is given the opportunity to see that things could have been different—and therefore can be different in the future.

When Carlos's mother Juana de Castilla (known as Juana la Loca) makes a brief appearance, the *comuneros* attempt to persuade her to back their rebellion but find that she has withdrawn into a private world of fantasy and nostalgia. Although she is as sad and mad here as popularly supposed, she has a humanizing effect on both Padilla and the young king. This intriguing figure is the protagonist of *Juana creó la noche* (1960: *Juana Created the Night*) by José Martín Elizondo and *Juana del amor hermoso* (1982: *Juana: A Love Too Beautiful*) by Manuel Martínez Mediero. Both plays present Juana as a tragic victim of the power games controlled by the men around her. Conventionally written off as unfit to reign, an embarrassing parenthesis between the devout resoluteness of her mother Isabel and the imperial grandeur of her son, Juana emerges in these versions as humane and far-sighted, driven into solitude and hallucination because she is potentially dangerous and because she puts love above politics.

The young Juana who appears in *Juego de reinas* (*A Pair of Queens*, written in 1990 and staged as *Razón de estado* in 1991) by Concha Romero is a weaker character. Sentimental and happy to submit herself unquestioningly to her husband's authority, she disappoints her mother Isabel, who is presented as an intelligent, independent-minded woman who questions established gender roles and urges Juana to stand up for her own ideas. Romero's *Las bodas de una princesa* (1988: *Marriage of a Princess*) traces the development of Isabel's independent spirit up to the time of her marriage to Fernando. The queen traditionally revered above all for her piety is built up by Romero into a strong-willed woman who challenges patriarchal assumptions and finds her own balance between her personal independence, her responsibilities as queen, and her emotional needs.

3.3.2. History and the people

An affectionately quirky and down-to-earth image of Isabel emerges from *Isabelita tiene ángel* (1976: *Isabelita Touched by an Angel*, revised in 1992) by José María Rodríguez Méndez. This is a very private Isabel, a devout, no-nonsense woman pushed against her will into a decisive role in history. The thread she is spinning during her encounters with the slightly shabby angel who flaps in through her window becomes a poetic motif standing for her historical role as the force of love and faith which unites the hearts and kingdoms of Spain—in some respects, this play echoes the kind of idealization we have seen in Chapter 2 (and no excuse is made for her anti-Semitism). However, she constantly deflates the angel's insistence on her historical importance, and their whole relationship has an odd tone of whimsicality that undermines any ideological seriousness (culminating in the angel hauling her up with the thread into heaven to the warbling of a celestial choir).

Rodríguez Méndez is an unashamed traditionalist and self-proclaimed defender of the Spanish language. He maintains that the true (popular) spirit of Spanish culture has always opposed the structures of power, and his own work constitutes an effort to combat Spain's institutionalized lack of a theatre culture by reclaiming the classical legacy and the whole notion of Spanishness from the Establishment, which tends to manipulate and falsify culture through dictatorial controls or (after 1975) through commercialization and public subsidy.[2]

A project of reaffirming the popular, dissident roots of the Golden Age legacy is continued in dramatic homages to St John of the Cross, St Teresa of Ávila, and Cervantes. Rodríguez Méndez brings out the rebelliousness of the two saints, presenting their principled campaign for ecclesiastical reform and their writings as the product not only of spiritual purity but also of social concerns. *Teresa de Ávila* (1981), a 'dramatic oratorio' composed largely of

---

[2] These theories are set out in several essays published in the 1960s and 1970s, particularly Rodríguez Méndez (1971, 1974).

selections from the saint's own writings, emphasizes her visionary awkwardness and refusal to conform. In *El pájaro solitario* (1974: *The Solitary Bird*, revised for publication in 1993), Juan de la Cruz escapes naked and delirious from imprisonment in Segovia and is rescued from the authorities with the help of whores and ruffians in the streets. Ordinary people respond instinctively to the mystical purity of Juan's poetry, which, although obviously different from the baroque slang dazzlingly recreated in the street scenes, seems to be mysteriously connected to it. At the end he declares his faith in the *pueblo* to the nuns who have taken him in: 'Es el pueblo el que ha de salvarnos, hijas mías' (Rodríguez Méndez 1993*a*: 79) ('It is the people who will save us, sisters'). Rodríguez Méndez's prologue to his homage to Cervantes and the Spanish language, *Literatura española* (1978: *Spanish Literature*), reaffirms the centrality of Santa Teresa and San Juan, Fray Luis de León and Cervantes to 'la literatura española del pueblo, la literatura española para el pueblo' (Rodríguez Méndez 1989: 18) ('Spanish literature, a literature of the people, literature for the people'). In this play, an aged Cervantes sits at his window chatting to the people who go by in the street: other writers (an arrogant Lope de Vega and a surprisingly down-to-earth Luis de Góngora) and fictional characters from his own work. Once again, Rodríguez Méndez insists on the writer's affinity with the common people and their language and on their affection for him, suggesting a kind of creative symbiosis in which great artists are inspired by the people, who in turn incorporate elements of art into their culture.

Rodríguez Méndez is also the most prominent exponent of another mode of historical theatre that explores *intrahistoria* much more than *Historia*, calling attention to marginalized or suppressed interests and voices and often foregrounding women's experience. History is seen from the point of view of its victims rather than its protagonists—ordinary citizens who are represented as having little control over events but nevertheless fight for collective ownership of their history and their cultural identities. Rodríguez Méndez focuses on working-class communities in the late nineteenth and early twentieth centuries, celebrating but also showing the decay of the popular spirit he calls *machismo español*. The concept is elaborated in his *Ensayo sobre el machismo español* (1971: *Essay on Spanish Machismo*), which traces the evolution of national identity through a selection of popular literary and theatrical archetypes ranging from the seventeenth century to the 1930s, each simultaneously representing an expression of arrogant individuality, the ethos of a particular community, and a version of Spanishness. *Machismo*, in this sense, is a dissident force of realism with the capacity to 'destruir esos grandes mitos, esas grandes hipocresías, sobre las que se ha asentado frecuentemente lo que se conoce por el nombre de Civilización' (Rodríguez Méndez 1971: 166) ('destroy those great myths, those grand hypocrisies, on which what goes by the name of Civilization has often been founded'). The *Ensayo* shows how, after the Civil War, *machismo* finally disintegrates and popular creativity is replaced by football, television, and consumerism. Rodríguez Méndez's plays recreate the languages and cultural practices of ways of life in which such creativity is still alive but under threat, and construct versions of national identity based upon acts of creative resistance to authority.

Bodas que fueron famosas del Pingajo y la Fandanga (1965: *The Famous Day When Pingajo and Fandanga Got Wed*, first staged in 1978) is set in Madrid in 1898. Pingajo (a conscript recently returned from the defeat of Spanish forces in Cuba) and the other marginalized but flamboyant characters illustrate very clearly the notion of cultural identity as performance. The men play games and revel in language, celebrating the spirit of their community, but the popular spirit embodied in *machismo* is a complex mixture of defiance and abjection. The representation of these people and their culture is far from idealized: there is ugliness, ignorance, and brutality, their rebellions are ultimately futile, and Pingajo's death at the end of the play is grotesque, a moment of intense tragicomedy. The men may make fun of patriotic ideals, yet their own language and behaviour are in certain ways still influenced by those same ideals. The most telling examples of this ideological ambiguity are in the final scene, in which the women express well-directed anger at the ruthlessness with which the state is ridding itself of Pingajo while other remarks suggest a pathetic inability to escape ideological conditioning. They have brought a scrap of material in the colours of the national flag in which to wrap his body, 'como se hace con los gloriosos' (Rodríguez Méndez 1979: 117) ('like they do with war heroes'). The women reappropriate the nationalist symbolism of the flag and make it their own. Although they are in some ways the victims of conventional *machista* behaviour, including physical abuse, they too are participants in the performance of cultural identity. Moreover, they make the only coherent statements of resistance to oppression, offering an image of strength and solidarity in contrast to the black comedy of Pingajo's last moments. Ultimately, the men's arrogant display of *machismo* is revealed as shallow and fragile; they are crushed by the state, leaving the less ostentatious but more durable women to represent the underlying spirit of their community.

For *Historia de unos cuantos* (1972: *Anyone's History*, first staged in 1975), Rodríguez Méndez takes characters directly from popular cultural forms (nineteenth-century *zarzuelas*), gives them substance by locating them in a realistic historical and political context, and develops them over the years between 1898 and the 1940s. These people, more firmly rooted in a Madrid working-class community than the delinquents of *Bodas*, develop a political consciousness, but the possibility apparently offered by the Republic of gaining some control over their history gives way to bitter disillusionment even before the devastation of the Civil War. All the male characters are killed save Julián, who is revealed to be a self-serving political opportunist and traitor to the Socialist Party, leaving the indomitable figure of Mari-Pepa as the only surviving embodiment of *machismo español*, stubbornly clinging to the remains of her sense of identity and place: 'Yo aquí, en mi barrio, en mi casa. En lo mío, en lo que me queda, en lo que nos queda' (Rodríguez Méndez 1982: 202) ('I'm staying here, in my neighbourhood, in my home. With what I know, with what I've got left, what we've got left').

José Martín Recuerda has also produced a series of history plays in which the voices of the oppressed and the marginalized make themselves heard forcefully. As in Rodríguez Méndez, colloquial language and traditional forms of popular culture are central to the evocation of this spirit of resistance. Martín Recuerda's texts build their primary dramatic conflicts around well-known historical figures, using groups of relatively unindividualized characters to represent the common people, but the *pueblo* is still the primary focus: the significance of the famous protagonists is defined principally in terms of their relationship with the sufferings and heroism of the ordinary people around them.

Mariana Pineda, the liberal dissident executed by Fernando VII's government in 1831, is the powerful figure at the centre of *Las arrecogías del beaterio de Santa María Egipciaca* (1970: *Inmates of the Convent of Saint Mary of Egypt*, first staged in 1977). This 'Fiesta española' transforms her from the sentimental Romantic heroine created by Lorca in 1927 into a much tougher, more independent rebel against tyranny and hypocrisy and her fellow inmates (a mixture of political prisoners and 'fallen women') turn their imprisonment into a rebellion which is sexual as well as political, expressed in impassioned words but also through their bodies, as they gesticulate, dance, tear their clothes, stamp their feet, and hammer on the doors of their cells.

None of these plays by Rodríguez Méndez and Martín Recuerda offers a positive image of the political mobilization of the poor or a coherent story of organized labour. Alfonso Sastre's* *El camarada oscuro* (1972: *The Unknown Comrade*) is one of the few attempts during the dictatorship to dramatize an explicitly left-wing view of history. It is an episodic chronicle following the humble life and harsh experience (including warfare, imprisonment, and torture at the hands of Franco's police) of the orphan Ruperto, an inconspicuous and politically naive member of the Communist Party. Fluid staging is required, incorporating an array of classic techniques of political theatre: recordings, songs, projections, newsreels, leaflets distributed amongst the audience. The complexity of the intended effect on an audience is increased by a Pirandellian ending, in which the author himself is present at Ruperto's death and is arrested at the funeral by policemen who proceed to practise their riot control procedures on members of the audience, as the curtain falls 'como señal de que esta obra dramática ha terminado mientras la vida y la muerte continúan' (Sastre 1990: 148) ('as a sign that this performance has ended whilst life and death go on').

Como reses (1987: *Like Cattle*), by Luis García Matilla and Jerónimo López Mozo, also uses an episodic structure, multiple spaces, songs, and recordings to trace the growth and destruction of working-class political consciousness (between 1909 and 1939). The municipal abattoir in which most of the action is set acts as the focus for individual relationships, collective solidarity and conflict, the impact of economic and political forces on the lives of ordinary people, and their possibility of influencing history. The movement of national history is played out in miniature through the key issues of workplace politics which intersect with questions of gender and sexuality (the status of the female workers and one character's struggle to win his comrades' acceptance of his homosexuality). The crude, bloody physicality of the hacking-up of carcasses on stage creates an effective stage image of honest hard labour, but also disturbingly suggests the brutal sacrifice of the people in wars and oppression.

Alongside the serious reappraisals of famous figures and the dramatizations of popular 'history from below', a third mode of historical theatre has been significant, particularly in the late 1960s and 1970s. This type aims at *desmitificación*—the debunking of officially sanctioned myths through satire and parody (often influenced by the aggressively expressionist *esperpentos* written by Valle-Inclán in the 1920s), using exaggeration, non-naturalistic staging, and black comedy to bring out forcefully the political processes behind the personalities and events. Works by Alberto Miralles, Carlos Muñiz, and Domingo Miras are representative of this mode.

While many of the plays discussed above have either focused on prominent women or given considerable importance to the collective role of women in social history, there have also been some attempts to dramatize an explicitly gendered or feminist history. *Las mujeres caminan con el fuego del siglo* (1982: *Women March in Step with the Fire of History*) by Lidia Falcón* is set in Barcelona on 14 April 1981, the fiftieth anniversary of the declaration of the Republic. Two indomitable women as old as the century narrate, sing about and re-enact significant moments from their lives for the benefit of 17-year-old Esther, streetwise and cynical but ignorant of history and in despair about an unwanted pregnancy. Montserrat is from a wealthy family, for which Patro worked as a maid, and this social difference constantly cuts across their shared experience of powerless womanhood and progressive politics. Patro regards the feminist convictions that Montserrat developed during the heady days of the Republic as bourgeois theorizing irrelevant to the everyday grind of working women, and her great-granddaughter Esther also dismisses all that as 'un rollo de señoritas' (Falcón 1994: 55) ('boring stuff that posh women go on about'). At the end, however, it is Montserrat who proposes a practical solution to Esther's immediate problem: a family planning service run by a feminist group which may be able to arrange an abortion in England.³ As they set off, Montserrat remarks: 'Me parece que antes de morirme todavía haré feministas a estas dos' (58) ('I might just make feminists of these two before I die').

3.4. REPRESENTING ORDINARY HISTORIES: RAMÓN JOSÉ SENDER AND IGNACIO ALDECOA

A major figure whose writing shifts focus radically in the twenty-five-year period following the Nationalist victory, and yet stays fixed on the meanings for the individual inserted in specific histories, is Ramón José Sender. Although *Carolus Rex* (1963), a critical portrait of the early reign of Carlos II, places him in line with the history plays just discussed, before the war Sender had written novels rooted in the working-class movements of the early part of the century, particularly anarchism. *Mister Witt en el canton* (1936) had offered a romanticized image of its anarchist characters, emphasizing their courage, solidarity, and virtue (with a particular lyrical emphasis on violent male heroism), and *Contraataque* (1937: *Counter-attack*) had a clear heroic vision: these contrast with the later, more complex, and bitter account of the war and its protagonists' motivations in *Los cinco libros de Ariadna* (1957: *The Five Books of Ariadne*). In the novels of the 1950s and onwards, protagonists display states of mind which could equally be read as madness or visionary insight, contributing to the blurring of perspective away from the stark confrontations established in the earlier works and departing from the more polarized visions of both right and left. Irony and humour compound the unsettling nature of narratives like *Bizancio* (1956: *Byzantium*) while the futuristic *Ariadna* (1955: *Ariadne*) is constructed around abrupt shifts in time, place, and narrative perspective as the writing attempts to simulate the chaos and confusion which Sender now attributed to the Civil War.

Crónica del alba (in three volumes, each of three separate novels, 1942–66)⁴ is a complex, layered narration. Framed as the

---

³ Abortion was not legalized in Spain until 1985. In 1986 Falcón published a play on the theme set in the early 1980s, *¡Parid, parid, malditas!* (*Breed, Breed, you Bitches!*).
⁴ For English translations of the first three books see Sender (1957).

memoirs of a Republican soldier, feverishly jotted down in a prison camp during the final days of the Civil War, the text has elicited autobiographical readings because the fictional author bears Sender's middle name and maternal surname. Yet such readings are difficult to sustain: the device of the memoirs allows the individual witness to develop into a collective voice through a proliferation of texts within the text, through the two narrative voices—of a young Pepe Garcés narrating his life as it unfolds and the voice of the older Pepe (and his reconstructed status as saint, poet, and hero)— and the existence of a further implied narrator in the construction of scenes in such a way as to elicit adult responses of various kinds from readers to which the boy narrator is oblivious. The fictional author dies on 18 November 1939, after entrusting his notebooks to his friend, a saintly figure who shares even his meagre rations in the camp. The text—headed by an epigraph on the custom of nomadic peoples of gathering up their memories prior to going to war—opens with a protest against his imprisonment and a declaration of faith in the power of writing as memory and witness:

Por primera vez en mi vida, los hombres me limitan el espacio. No pueden mis pies ir a donde irían ni mis manos hacer lo que querrían. Sin embargo hay una manera de salir de todo esto. Pero no basta con soñar. Hay que escribir. Si escribo mis recuerdos tengo la impresión de que pongo algo material y mecánico en el recuerdo y en el sueño. (Sender 1984: 17)

(For the first time in my life other men restrict my space. My feet cannot go where they wish nor my hands do what they want. However, there is a way out. But it is not enough to dream. I must write. If I write down my memories I have the impression that I am putting something material and mechanical into memory and dream.)

Sender—himself in a sense one of the nomads (being in exile)— sets a fictionalized memoir against the discourse of the regime, offering a problematizing counter-history and suggesting the limitations of any one memory or history by creating multiple layers of stories and histories which are at variance with the Francoist regime's vision of rural Spain and Spanish history. A shepherd whom the hero befriends on a childhood holiday offers a pantheistic and holistic account of life which is favourably contrasted with Pepe's father's fervent glorification (and rather shaky knowledge) of the Roman Empire, and with the scientific indifference of the doctor who drily questions the sacred status of skeleton remains discovered by Pepe; the local priest engages with Pepe's enquiring,

Reclaiming History 59

restless spirit whereas his father manifests rigid incomprehension by nailing up the window which provides access to one of his son's favourite liminar areas, the roof (where he studies on the threshold between unfettered natural instincts and the various forms of social control that operate within the household). The castle that was once the boy's holiday playground allows both a demythification of a supposed glorious medieval military history, and, when it becomes the scenario of a bloody siege during the Civil War and is finally occupied by representatives of both Republican and Nationalist forces, a development of alternative visions. Besieged by troops from both sides, it facilitates the substitution of the sanitized and orthodox Catholic vision of heroic Francoism by an earthy, semi-pagan, multicultural, and oppositional version of events, textually reinforced by songs incorporated in the text, the tales told by the shepherd, and a frequent recourse to humour (amid the tragedy).

Ultimately, *Crónica*'s evocation of an innocent anarchism, a rural boy's childhood fascination with manly pursuits involving weaponry, hunting, and a heroic military history, gives way to the horrific realities of war. A war, moreover, now seen as a multiple betrayal of the people by all those who claim to represent it, as is symbolized in the denouement of book III by a woman widowed in the conflict giving birth to a child in the castle yet no longer believing in anyone or anything.

Sender's preoccupation with history viewed from a rural perspective continued in *Réquiem por un campesino español* (1960: *Requiem for a Spanish Peasant*)[5] which is notable not only for its critique of the collusion of the Catholic Church in the oppression of the Spanish peasantry, but, structurally, for the narration of the life and death by execution of Paco el del Molino through a triple perspective: the repentant parish priest; the critical commentary of his acolyte; and popular history in the form of the *romance* (popular ballad) which the villagers have created around Paco, who, following legislation by the new Republican government, had led them to claim their land rights. While much of the narration is omniscient, the repetition of 'Mosén Millán recordaba . . .' ('Mosén Millán remembered . . .') foregrounds the subjective

---

[5] Originally published as *Mosén Millán* (1953). For an English translation see Sender (1960).

nature of the account. The official prohibition of alternative histories—the acolyte is warned by a powerful local grandee, don Gumersindo, that if he continues to sing the *romance* the mayor will put him in gaol—is dramatized by having the more detailed account of Paco's life and death narrated as the inner monologue of the priest, in parallel to the fragments of the ballad. As Ovejero (1982: 217) points out, the reader thus becomes a witness and jury in the inner drama of the priest's account. Where the priest is Paco's failed spiritual father, his godmother Jerónima, midwife and healer, and taunter of the priest in vivid songs and phrases he cannot decipher, represents an alternative spiritual mother. With her skills in childbirth and traditional medicine, her gossip network and storytelling power, Jerónima is a female counterpart to figures like the shepherd in *Crónica del alba*, using her matriarchal power to support Paco where the priest tries, but fails, to check him. The massacre of men and women at the time of the uprising by the *señoritos* (landowners) marks the destruction of both progressive peasant politics and popular rural wisdom. Nonetheless, the refusal of the remaining villagers to attend the requiem mass, and the intrusion of Paco's horse into the church, suggest continued, if oblique, resistance to the official order: the priest hopes the mass will bring peace to Paco's soul and social peace to the village, but it serves only to confront him with his role in Paco's death and his consequent social isolation.

While the first book of *Crónica del alba* is set in pre-war Aragón and *Réquiem por un campesino español* situates us in a less specific rural setting but equally distant time-frame, Ignacio Aldecoa's *El fulgor y la sangre* (1954: *Blood and Radiance*) begins in the Castilian meseta in the early 1950s, the Francoist heartland, and looks back to key moments of the recent past—the declaration of the Republic in 1931, the revolution of October 1934, and the outbreak of the Civil War in 1936—through the memories of the main characters, in particular the women. From their different backgrounds and places of origin they have all ended up in the isolated barracks of the Civil Guard in an anonymous village, eternal outsiders who long for change and recall a more dynamic past. Situated in the ruins of one of Castile's many medieval castles, known generically as 'el castillo' in the novel, the barracks offer a symbolic corrective to the regime's military triumphalism and rural idealism. Through this location Aldecoa is able to depict the

Reclaiming History 61

medieval past as in ruins and the historical processes it represents as brought to a halt by Franco's project of immobilization. While the children—all boys—of the castle's occupants play enthusiastic war games, like the *flechas* (Falangist cadets) of the comics they devour to offset their boredom, their mock battle scenes are paralleled by brutal memories of real wars recent and distant, recalled both in individual testimonies and through collective histories (one character, María, actively engages with and inscribes herself into local history through hearing the mayor's accounts, and herself experiences the outbreak of the war; another, Felisa, remembers her father and gives us a complex picture of rural working-class Spaniards, caught up in events not through specific ideological or political affiliations but in their attempts to alleviate their grinding poverty).

The women's stories provide a panorama of different experiences of gender as well as class and rural or urban situations which cut across several generations. Sonsoles's much-loved grandmother offers her a grim, stoical image of marriage against the idealized version of the Church, while still advocating it as the natural course for a woman. Living in a working-class area of Madrid, Carmen's mother has rigid ideas about which professions are suitable for a 'decent' woman and believes that women should give up working outside the home when they marry, yet her daughters manage to negotiate greater freedom and pleasure than she intends, while, in a small rural town, Felisa asserts her right to marry the man of her choice despite the objections of her older brother—on political grounds—and her father's attempt to invoke paternal authority to prevent the match.

The apparent plurality of these experiences is undercut at several points (Zatlin 1984), opening up the novel and its sexual politics to several readings. The immobilized regime of the castle is a timeless existential *ennui*, or a critique of the immobility imposed on ordinary Spaniards by Francoism; in another direction, the structuring of the text brings to the surface what is repressed in Franco's Spain and allows forbidden connections to be reforged. The flashbacks remind us that there have been different social orders in Spain, that urban and rural workers and peasants have struggled for better conditions, and that some women have experienced other ways of life. This is not a romanticized vision, given the harshness of many of the characters' past conditions, nor is the characters' desire limited to a nostalgic return to the past. Above all they desire change.

3.5. DECONSTRUCTING HISTORY

The official triumphalist historiography of the regime, discussed in section 2.1, set out to suppress alternative accounts which did not conform to the unitary orthodoxy of 'One Spain, one race, one religion' (Herzberger 1991: 251) through a monologic discourse which claimed the authority of Truth. However, transgressive works published in the 1960s and 1970s by authors such as Juan Benet, Juan Goytisolo, Luis Goytisolo, Carmen Martín Gaite, Luis Martín-Santos, Elena Quiroga, and Gonzalo Torrente Ballester not only attempt to express what is repressed in Franco's Spain, as in Aldecoa, but furthermore foreground the contingent nature of history and testimony through narrative techniques which make explicit the constructedness of experience through its mediation in language.

In Juan Goytisolo's* trilogy *Señas de identidad* (1966: *Marks of Identity*), *Reivindicación del Conde don Julián* (1970: *Count Julian Redeemed*), *Juan sin tierra* (1975: *Juan the Landless*),[6] and Juan Benet's 'Región' novels—including *Volverás a Región* (1967: *You'll Return to Región*), *Una meditación* (1970: *A Meditation*), and *Un viaje de invierno* (1971: *A Winter's Journey*)—the illusion of referentiality is displaced as history is embraced as fiction (Herzberger 1991: 254). Goytisolo's counter-mythifications of Francoist ideology through corrosive parody and subversion have been accused of perpetuating the mythical vision which they set out to subvert (Labanyi 1989: 196). However, the focalization through a narrating and remembering self serves to emphasize the discursive nature of all myths thereby opening them out to dissent and dynamic transformation. The use of multiple, shifting perspectives and fragmented composition in Luis Goytisolo's 'Antagonía' tetralogy initiated by the ground-breaking *Recuento* (published in Mexico, 1972: *Looking Back*) also serves to accentuate anxieties around the reliability of memory. Both Benet and Martín Gaite, in their fiction and essays, focus on the importance of ambiguity in narration.

---

[6] The first two novels were published in Mexico and the latter initially banned by the censors.

3.5.1. Carmen Martín Gaite: *El cuarto de atrás*

Ambiguity is one of the key features of Martín Gaite's* 'novel of memory' *El cuarto de atrás* (1978: *The Back Room*).[7] Whilst the references to historical, political, and cultural figures lend the text an air of veracity, reality and fiction cannot be clearly distinguished in a text which defies generic definitions to blend together sociological document, autobiographical memoir, romantic fiction, and the fantastic. Franco's funeral in 1975 provided the impetus for Martín Gaite to consider writing her memoirs. However, bored by the plethora of memoirs which came out at the time, she let the project drop:

> Se me enfrió, me lo enfriaron las memorias ajenas. Desde la muerte de Franco habrá notado cómo proliferan los libros de memoria, ya es una peste, en el fondo, eso es lo que me ha venido desanimando, pensar que, si a mí me aburren las memorias de los demás, por qué no le van a aburrir a los demás las mías. (Martín Gaite 1992a: 128)

(It went cold, other people's memories made it cool off. Since the death of Franco you will have noticed how memoirs have proliferated, it's a plague, that's what has really put me off, to think that, if I get bored reading other people's memoirs, what's to say mine won't bore other people.)

She also had the project of writing a fantastic novel, inspired by her reading of Tzetvan Todorov's *Introduction à la littérature fantastique*. Approximately midway through *El cuarto de atrás* the narrator has the idea of combining these two projects into a composite text which suspends distinctions between the fantastic and the real. Through the course of a stormy night, the narrator C., who is closely identified with the author herself, converses with a stranger dressed in black. As they talk a stack of pages grows beneath his hat. At the close of the novel the narrator falls asleep and is later awoken by her daughter. The stranger has gone but before leaving he has ordered the pages and placed them where Todorov's book had previously been. They are marked 'El cuarto de atrás' and begin with the same phrase as the novel. The reader is left unsure as to whether what has been recounted is a dream experience, is drug-induced hallucination, or actually happened.

This self-referential text which relates its own genesis can be

---

[7] For an English translation see Martín Gaite (1983).

classified as a work of historiographic metafiction in which history is articulated as a dynamic process rather than a static product. A variety of discursive practices are incorporated in order to question the authority of official discourses. The narrator notes the contradictory versions prevalent in both literature and historical accounts according to the perspective of the person doing the narrating:

[T]ampoco la historia es esa que se escribe poniendo en orden las fechas y se nos presenta inamovible, cada persona que nos ha visto o hablado alguna vez guarda una pieza del rompecabezas que nunca podremos contemplar entero. (Martín Gaite 1992a: 167)

(Nor is history that which is written in order of dates and presented as something unchangeable, every person who has ever seen or spoken to us keeps a piece of the puzzle that we can never contemplate in its entirety.)

As in Juan Goytisolo's trilogy, history is evoked from an interior, personal perspective through an act of subjective remembering in a first person autobiographical narrative. The use of the first person highlights the mediation of history and, through the interplay between past and present, confronts the reader with a multiplicity of perspectives and the demonstration that the narrator of an autobiographical text is to some extent unreliable in that the narration is not only influenced by present perceptions and articulation through language, but also by the wish to present oneself in a certain manner. Memories are not only positioned in history, they produce it or reinvent it.

El cuarto de atrás is a contestatory account of the narrator's childhood and youth during the Civil War and post-war period. However, this is not only a narrative of personal identity but a work which gives insights into Spanish society and culture at that time. In particular it focuses on the process of growing up as a woman faced with restrictive norms of behaviour. The novel performs a cathartic function in that it includes accounts of the Civil War and political references previously suppressed by censorship. Not all of the memories invoked are pleasurable; some, such as the imprisonment of her friend's parents and execution of her uncle, are extremely painful events. By confronting them the narrator's anxiety about them would seem to decrease.

The integration of the personal and the social has been identified as a feature of women's writing in Spain in the late 1970s and early

1980s in a process in which the boundaries between fiction, history, biography, and autobiography were dissolved (Davies 1991: 215).[8] Indeed, it is easy to confuse the narrator C. with the author Carmen Martín Gaite as the memories invoked by the former can clearly be recognized as the biographical details of the latter. However, by not naming the narrator Martín Gaite distances herself from her despite the obvious identification between them. Thus the self at the centre of this text is shown to be a subjective, fictive structure which engages in a continual act of self-invention. *El cuarto de atrás* combines a commitment to testimonial, historical narrative with aesthetically self-conscious, experimental writing which represents experience whilst interrogating the very premises of a representative fiction. Experience is shown to be mediated through discursive practice and the heterogeneity of the discourses invoked, transformed, and reinscribed in the novel serve to call into question authoritative, hegemonic discourse with its claim to the metanarratives of history and truth.

3.5.2. Exotic and shady histories

The engagement with historical discourse has perhaps intensified during the post-Franco period as attempts have been made to recover previously suppressed versions of history. Novels such as Benet's *Saúl ante Samuel* (1980: *Saul before Samuel*) and Jesús Fernández Santos's *Los jinetes del alba* (1984: *Riders of the Dawn*) re-examine the psychological aftermath of the Civil War. This need to reinvent the past has led to the growth of a heritage industry with the refurbishing of museums and increased focus on local history (Labanyi 1995*b*: 402). However, many literary texts problematize this project of recuperation, whilst in the late 1980s and 1990s writers have engaged in increasingly exotic textual play (Labanyi 1999: 152). Antonio Gala's enormous commercial success *El manuscrito carmesí* (1990: *The Crimson Manuscript*) and Terenci Moix's *Nuestra virgen de los mártires: Novela de romanos* (1983: *Our Lady of Martyrs: A Roman Novel*), *No digas que fue un sueño: Marco Antonio y Cleopatra* (1986: *Don't Say it Was All*

---

[8] The integration of the personal and the social is also a feature of the writing of Julio Llamazares in the 1980s and 1990s, in which history is expressed through landscapes which are repositories of both personal and collective memory.

a Dream: Mark Antony and Cleopatra), *El sueño de Alejandría* (1989: *The Dream of Alexandria*), and *Venus Bonaparte* (1994) make use of the inclusion of multiple cultural references and different registers, with an emphasis on the historical exotic. The blend of intrigue with cultural references to the worlds of art and literature in the self-conscious historical thrillers of Arturo Pérez Reverte have led to comparisons with Umberto Eco (Moral 1999: 124).

However, not all pastiche of popular cultural forms serves to exoticize history: the *novela negra* (detective fiction) form has been used to engage in the ironic critique of socio-historical reality. Whilst writers such as Andreu Martín and Juan Madrid focus on the contemporary social crisis which followed the Transition, others have used the genre to interrogate the past. Joaquín Leguina's *Tu nombre envenena mis sueños* (1992: *Your Name Poisons my Dreams*) is an account of the murder of three Falangist businessmen in 1942. The story is fragmented into the accounts of the two investigating policemen, Paco Valduque and Ángel Barciela, and Julia Buendía who had family connections to the victims. Although the crime is resolved to the satisfaction of Paco and Ángel's superiors who wish to avoid scandal and political upset, the case remains full of inconsistencies which are only filled in by the later confession in letter form to Ángel by Julia in 1953. Both Ángel and Julia ironize the notion of truth, 'La verdad no existe en términos absolutos, todo el mundo la adapta a su leal saber, entender y sentir, a sus intereses de cada momento' (Leguina 1996: 119) ('Truth does not exist in absolute terms, everyone adapts it to their personal knowledge, understanding, and feelings, to their interests at that time').

Contradictory versions of the truth are most evident in the radio broadcasts by Radio Nacional de España and the BBC which Ángel listens to. The objectivity of the Spanish media—and supposed neutrality of the Spanish state—is humorously called into question when Ángel recounts a joke about the ironically named newspaper *Informaciones* directed by Víctor de la Serna, 'Hitler da una rueda de prensa en Berlín y le preguntan cómo va la guerra. Él contesta: "Muy bien, va muy bien, aunque no tan bien como dice el *Informaciones*" ' (128) ('Hitler gives a press conference in Berlin and they ask him how the war's going. He answers: "Very well, very well, but not as well as they say in *Informaciones*" ').

The rewriting of history according to the political mandate of whoever is in power is the focus of an extended discussion between the main characters Ángel and Julia when they visit El Escorial. Ángel parodies Nationalist rhetoric in his description of the monastery palace as the eighth wonder of the world. He gives the motivation behind the construction of the palace as the fear of death experienced by all those in power and then draws an analogy with the Valley of the Fallen being built by Franco nearby. Julia contests the account of Felipe II as a bitter despot obsessed by power, arguing that both sides—the Nationalists in their adoption of imperialist rhetoric and the opposition in its adherence to the *leyenda negra*—have adapted history to their own design. Elswhere the novel humorously debunks such heroic myths by reducing patriotism to stoically surviving the years of hunger which followed the Civil War.

The ironic, highly intertextual style of many *novela negra* texts is also a key feature of 'historical' novels written by women in the 1980s such as *Cántiga de agüero* (1982: *Canticle of Omens*) and *Los perros de Hecate* (1985: *Hecate's Hounds*) by Carmen Gómez Ojea, and *El rapto del Santo Grial* (1984: *The Kidnapping of the Holy Grail*) by Paloma Díaz-Mas. These playfully parodic and irreverent texts meld together mythical and historical references to interrogate patriarchal discursive conventions through metafictive narrative technique and deconstruct hierarchical power relations encoded in gendered discourses such as those discussed with relation to the family in the following chapter.

Further reading

Abellán (1978); Davies (1991); Herzberger (1995); Labanyi (1999); Romeu Alfaro (1994).

4
Keeping it in the Family

4.1. CONSTRUCTING THE MODEL

A crucial component of the Francoist vision of an ordered, unified, and uniquely spiritual nation was the idealization of the family. For Catholics and conservatives, the traditional model of dominant, breadwinning father, submissive, nurturing mother, and numerous obedient children was the 'natural' foundation of Spanish society which had been threatened by the Republic and almost destroyed by a war that was blamed on the 'Reds'. Millions of families had suffered loss by death and exile or had been torn apart by ideological differences. For hundreds of thousands of families the post-war years were overshadowed by absence, imprisonment, and persecution. For the victors, though, the family had now been restored to its rightful place in public and private life, connecting, as Helen Graham has observed, 'vertically with the state rather than horizontally within society' and thus reinforcing 'the unity and power of the state', in particular by 'promoting [society's] "privatization" or "atomization" based on the "haven" of the private household at whose centre was the "mother" '(Graham 1995: 184, 186–7).

The state, the Church, the Falange, and the education system emphasized three dimensions of the ideal Catholic family: sexual morality, with sexuality restrictively understood as procreation, women's identities defined by motherhood, and deviant behaviour policed and proscribed; spirituality, with the family as both its own congregation and a means of imparting doctrine (Graham 1995: 187); and authority, with the father as leader—validated by the hierarchical structure of the Church and by the Holy Family itself—providing for, protecting, guiding, and disciplining his wife and children. These principles were enacted in specific legal and economic measures, most of which remained in force throughout the dictatorship. Divorce, contraception, and abortion were prohibited, civil marriage was abolished, and all printed and visual representations of sexuality and material regarded as an incitement to immorality were censored. Married women's total legal and economic dependence on their husbands was enforced, married women were discouraged from working outside the home, and there were financial incentives for large families.[1]

The message for women and the younger generation was, unsurprisingly, also relayed in the popular press. ¡Hola! magazine (in amusing contrast to its later interest in glamorous affairs and erotic excitements) took a coy look at courtship in the spring of 1948, urging the bride-to-be to enjoy the day but also to ask, 'en oración reposada [. . .] que Él te conceda la mayor gracia que puede anhelar una mujer digna: ser madre' (Guzmán 1948: 11) ('in quiet prayer [. . .] that He grant you the greatest gift that a worthy woman can desire: to be a mother').

The coercive effect of such values and the policies that enforced them fell disproportionately on women: the peasant working alongside her menfolk in the fields and bearing the whole weight of running the household; the urban working-class woman obliged by poverty to take a menial job in which she could be exploited without any legal protection (while also fulfilling her responsibilities in the home); the middle-class woman discouraged from gaining qualifications or seeking a career, with no control over her family's money or property; all denied control over their own fertility and threatened with social extinction if they failed to find and keep a husband or gave in to temptation before marriage. And all were expected to model themselves on the impossible ideal of the Virgin, maternal but chaste, resilient but submissive, the centre of the family yet existing only to serve the other members of it.

Religious organizations at all levels played their part in the pro-family strategy. The Catholic workers' organizations, for example, would protest against unscrupulous employers and campaign for better working conditions, but were reluctant to defend the specific rights of women at work. ¡Tú! (You!), the newspaper of the HOAC, is clearly directed primarily at male workers. Its regular women's section in 1946 is entitled 'Tu hogar: Para la mujer obrera' ('Your Home: For the Working Woman'), offering advice on childcare, home decor, and the importance of keeping the house

---

[1] For further detail on family policy see Gallego Méndez (1983); Graham (1995: 184–6); Nash (1991); and Scanlon (1986).

and yourself spotless so that your husband can be proud of you if he happens to bring a friend home after work. By 1950, the section bears the less specific title '¡Tú! y ellas' and seems to have a slightly wider focus. Women's employment is recognized, even cautiously celebrated, but always with the assumption that only certain kinds of work are appropriate (teaching is the only occupation to be wholeheartedly approved of) and that a woman's true place is in the home. In a patronizing piece from 1950 entitled '¡Oh, la mujer!'('Oh, Woman!') the paper expresses its admiration for women's adaptability and readiness to take on 'all kinds of jobs' including 'men's work', but warns: 'No ha de olvidar que es mujer y que cuanto lleve a cabo ha de hacerlo teniendo en cuenta su condición y su misión especial. Su deber primordial está en ser hija, esposa y madre' (¡Tú! 1950) ('[A woman] should not forget that she is a woman and that in everything she does she should bear in mind her nature and her special mission. Her prime duty is to be a daughter, a wife, and a mother').

4.1.1. Falange and family

Just as a relatively liberal voice such as ¡Tú!'s finds itself tied up in contradictions as it seeks to protect women from the detrimental effects of labour, so the Falange's Sección Femenina played a paradoxical role as 'the transmission belt for state directives to women', using middle-class women to police other women, thereby blurring 'the rigid division between public and private' (Graham 1995: 187). While the Falange promoted the Catholic family, at the same time it contained the potential to destabilize that ideal, providing a possible opportunity for a form of 'horizontal' association, even a kind of alternative family. Its rhetoric emphasizes virtues of manly comradeship and patriotic self-sacrifice together with the asceticism of the monk or mystic. The Sección Femenina offered an active social and educational role to unmarried women which to some extent removed them from their parents' control and diverted them from the primary approved activity of preparing themselves for marriage. Pilar Primo de Rivera herself (sister of José Antonio and leader of the SF) never married and her public political profile was extraordinarily high for someone who preached the sanctity of women's domesticity. The young Falangist was treated as a child of the *Patria*, being moulded physically and mentally to serve the

Father/Motherland under the guidance of older 'brothers' and 'sisters' in the Movement, spending time away from home at parades, camps, and training sessions. Mari-Pepa, the cute but slightly naughty little cadet used by *Flechas y pelayos* to appeal to its female readership, even absconds from convent school in one episode in order to see a Falange parade (no. 51, 26 November 1939). She is severely scolded by the Mother Superior, but her patriotic fervour clearly does her credit. The Sección Femenina's own children's magazine, *Bazar* (founded in 1947), projects a genteel, domestic image far removed from the militant cuteness of Mari-Pepa in Falangist uniform in the *Flechas y pelayos* of the early 1940s. The cover of every issue of *Bazar* features a picture of Guillermina, a dainty, blonde, blue-eyed, well-dressed, obviously middle-class little girl, engaged in everyday, family-based activities of play, worship, learning, and domesticity. Girls are invariably timid, boys tend to be boisterous, and the humour must have seemed feeble even to the average 10-year-old in 1947.

In practice the Falange could hardly be said to have posed a serious threat to the family. Its own rhetoric of 'verticality' and hierarchy clearly put obedience before comradeship, and the role of women within it was always unequivocally defined in terms of nurturing, domesticity, and preparation for marriage and motherhood. Both the Sección Femenina and the Church set out to discredit feminism and notions such as equality between the sexes in texts such as *Dos sendas de mujeres* (1948: *Two Paths for Women*) by Carmen Buj and *La mujer en la vida* (1953: *Women's Role in Life*) by Padre Delgado Capeáns (discussed in detail in Scanlon 1986: 329–38).

With respect to the moral dimension of the family, the discourse of the Falange is entirely in line with that of the Church. Strict control of sexuality (especially women's) is seen as an essential part of the Spanish tradition; the Republic, socialism, atheism, and liberalism of all kinds are associated with immorality and decadence. The defence of the moral strength and purity of the family is therefore not just a spiritual issue but a patriotic one. An article in the Falangist newspaper *¿Qué pasa? (What's Going On?)* in 1941 (Illán 1941) warns of the inner enemies (inappropriate, ungodly passions) and the apparently ubiquitous external threats, the moral infections and 'incitements to licentiousness' that undermine family values through commerce, the media, 'falsa ciencia o ciencia inoportuna, modas de vanguardia exhibicionista, artimañas femeninas para disputarse los supervivientes de las guerras, la miseria, que lo hace olvidar todo' ('false science or inappropriate science, exhibitionist avant-garde fashions, the wiles women use to compete for the survivors of wars, and poverty, which makes people forget themselves'). Worst of all is 'la justificación ideológica del mal. Esa plaga pestilente de literatos e intelectuales, elegantes asesinos del alma nacional' ('the ideological justification of evil. That foul plague of writers and intellectuals, elegant assassins of the spirit of the nation'); but the new Spain, 'que mira la familia como a la niña de sus ojos y quintaesencia de su viabilidad' ('which regards the family as the apple of its eye and the key to its success'), is alert to such threats.

4.1.2. Leader of the family, father of the nation

The vocabulary of family values constantly overlaps with the language used to refer to the regime's aspirations for Spain: unity, order, decency, spirituality, tradition, and, above all, firm leadership. Thus the Álvarez encyclopedia's summary for schoolchildren of the ideal role of the father (in the 'formación político-social' section for boys of a 1964 edition) clearly echoes Francoist arguments for benevolent but strict *caudillaje*:

> Toda agrupación, para conseguir sus fines, necesita un jefe. El jefe de la familia es el padre. Como tal, trabaja y manda. Trabaja para dar ejemplo y para procurar el bienestar de los demás miembros; manda, para que bajo su amorosa autoridad cada cual cumpla su misión: la madre administrando el hogar y los hijos preparándose para una vida moral y materialmente digna. (Álvarez Pérez 1964: 592)
>
> (Any group of people, in order to achieve its ends, needs a head. The father is the head of the family. His role as head is to work and to command. He works so as to give a good example and to ensure the well-being of the other members of the family; he commands so that, under his loving authority, all members of the family may fulfil their mission: the mother looking after the home and the children preparing themselves for a morally and materially decent life.)

The personality cult that was constructed around Franco combined a strictly military notion of command with an image of the *Caudillo* exercising 'loving authority' as the father of the nation and, from the 1950s on, 'the benevolent and beloved patriarch of the Spaniards' (Preston 1993: 784). This image was sustained by a self-perpetuating discourse which is half pompous and half sentimental, particularly in the popular press. It was common for Spain to be interpellated here (as in church and in political speeches) as an extended family with the *Caudillo* at its heart, but also, of course, with the Pope and God as higher father figures. In the Holy Year of 1950, *¡Hola!* magazine (*¡Hola!* 1950a) makes a double appeal to its readers, saying how it is 'at the humble service of Pope Pius XII' and, later in the spring, reporting on the marriage of Carmen Franco Polo, Franco's daughter, to the Marqués de Villaverde as a hugely welcome event in the social life of Spain and offering 'felicitaciones a nuestro invicto Caudillo y a su egregia esposa' ('congratulations to our unvanquished Caudillo and to his illustrious lady wife').

Franco was anxious to present himself as a family man (and magazines like *¡Hola!* vividly colluded with this) yet the family life of the Francos has been full of ironies and inconsistencies. Franco was bitterly disappointed by the dissolute behaviour and liberal views of his own father, who abandoned the family in 1907, and of his maverick brother Ramón—demons which his novel/filmscript *Raza* (1942: *Pedigree*) (written under the pseudonym Jaime de Andrade) attempted to exorcize. He only fathered one child (Carmen); and his claims to austerity of lifestyle were mocked by his wife's and immediate family's accumulation of wealth and social climbing, as well as the sexual and financial indiscretions of several of his much photographed grandchildren. For a leader who prided himself on impartiality and detachment, he was surprisingly dependent on members of his family, as is revealed years later in the playfully parodic account in Manuel Vázquez Montalbán's *Autobiografía del general Franco* (1992: *Autobiography of General Franco*).

4.2. DECONSTRUCTING THE MODEL

Critiques of traditional models of the family have been constant features of Western cultures throughout the twentieth century. In Spain, though, the overt political manipulation of the family by the Franco regime and the insistence with which it was mythologized have given an especially sharp edge to literary texts that question, undermine, or oppose the Catholic-conservative ideal.

4.2.1. Camilo José Cela:* patricide and matricide

From the perspective of the 'family values' of the 1940s and their enforcement through censorship, it seems extraordinary that Camilo José Cela's *La familia de Pascual Duarte* (1942: *The Family of Pascual Duarte*),[2] a novel dealing with rape, matricide (and other murders), premarital sex and pregnancy, abortion, prostitution, and adultery, should have been published in 1942 and survived a full year before a second edition was temporarily prohibited in 1943 and a police raid (which failed to net a single copy) signalled a hardening of attitudes towards this remarkable text. Martínez Cachero (1997: 107) reports the claim that Cela was protected by powerful supporters in the Delegación Nacional de Prensa against sustained pressure from various sectors, of which a review in *Ecclesia* is representative. Rating it as dangerous for the general public, it goes on, 'Obra literaria notable; no se debe leer, más que por inmoral, que lo es bastante, por repulsivamente realista. Su nota es la brutal crudeza con que se expresa todo [. . .] sus personajes [. . .] superan el horror y la repugnancia (*Ecclesia* 1944) ('A notable literary work; it should not be read, not just because it is immoral, reason enough, but because of its repulsive realism. This is evident in the brutal crudeness with which everything is expressed [. . .] the characters [. . .] surpass horror and repugnance'). *Tremendismo*—a darkly pessimistic mode of realism based on deliberately crude representations of violence and crime, focusing on the morally and physically repellent, and using forceful, direct language—was the least pejorative of the labels attached to a series of texts produced in the 1940s, this one included, which were considered dangerously violent, morally dubious, and politically suspect by critics affiliated to the new regime who saw it also as the infiltration by stealth of the defeated (communist) enemy into the pure literature of a new generation, earning it tags like *miserabilismo* (miserabilism) and *excrementicialismo* (excrementalism) (Martínez Cachero 1997: 114).

This novel represents a shocking alternative to the official image of family and village life and, more subtly, the family of the nation, for although it is set in the 1920s and 1930s it is open to contemporary interpretation by its readers in the 1940s and 1950s. In that

[2] For an English translation see Cela (1965).

respect, our initial point of departure might most usefully be not so much the horror of matricide which so disturbed the reviewer in *Ecclesia* but 'metaphorical parricide' (Schaeffer 1988). The assassination of don Jesús González de la Riva, Conde de Torremejía, by Pascual during the period of 'revolution' is after all the ostensible reason for Pascual's death sentence whereas the murder of his mother goes unpunished by society. Ultimately, the former was more directly threatening to the social order even if the latter elicited more anguish from the literary critics of the Catholic Church.

Constructed ostensibly as a document of confession and atonement written as Pascual awaits his execution, dedicated to the dead Count and entrusted to the Count's friend and lawyer, the text also comprises the comments of the 'transcriptor' and letters elicited by him from Pascual's confessor. Contradictions between these various accounts, important gaps and silences in the text—including Pascual's failure to recount his version of the assassination of the Count—all contribute to what the majority of critics have characterized as the complex ambiguity of this novel which challenges the polarized world-view of the regime as much as its idealized image of family life.

Where Pascual's father swings between drunken, violent rages and helpless tenderness towards his baby daughter, Pascual is more self-consciously torn between the pressures of the patriarchal honour code (whose 'moral' code ironically led him to pressurize his first wife to abort the baby conceived while he was in prison) and his spontaneous tenderness and affection as father and husband. The novel represents, in fact, a lack of positive authority in all the spheres promoted by the new regime: biological, political, and religious father figures are all abusive and inadequate while neither biological mother nor motherland nurtures or provides for her sons and daughters. This is a text which offers a coded call for Spanish society to address its past—in Pascual's frequent references to the importance of memory—and to move on from it, in a reconfiguration of the traumatized family of the nation with its bruised and battered children.

4.2.2. *Families of the underclass*

In the narratives and plays of the social realism of the 1950s and early 1960s, it is the brutalizing circumstances of poverty, emigration, and social injustice that make the family ideal impossible to put into practice. Paternal prestige is damaged by the inability to bring home an adequate wage; the myth of the contented *ángel del hogar* (guardian angel of the hearth) is demolished by the realities of domestic violence, squalor, and the need for women to take on low-paid menial work at the same time as bearing the full weight of housework and childcare; and children grow up selfish and cynical. The real effects of the social and economic policies of the regime (and, in a more general way, of industrial development without adequate welfare provision) are shown to work against its promotion of the traditional family model. The nostalgic evocation of supportive village communities built around extended families is contradicted by rootlessness and urban deprivation, and mocked by the crude improvization of the shanty towns in which people struggle to keep families together and create some sense of community.

In *La camisa* (1962: *The Shirt*), a grittily realistic play by Lauro Olmo, a fundamentally decent, loving family is under pressure from long-term unemployment, disappointed hopes, and extreme poverty. The husband Juan's proud but doomed insistence on attempting to fulfil his duty as a patriarchal breadwinner is linked to a paradoxical sense of patriotism—an ironic echo of the rhetoric of Numantian resistance used by the government in the post-war period to persuade the Spanish people that their suffering was worthwhile: 'Han nació aquí, Lola. Su hambre es de aquí. Y es aquí donde tienen que luchar pa saciarla' (Olmo 1968: 74) ('They were born here, Lola. Their hunger comes from here. And here is where they have to struggle to satisfy it').

The second-hand shirt that Lola buys for her husband in the hope that it will help him to get a job as a bricklayer becomes a bitterly ironic symbol of the social role he is prevented from performing. The image of the respectable *padre de familia* crumbles, the shirt is torn in two by a despairing Juan, and it is Lola who faces up to reality and decides that she must go abroad to work. The women in general are pragmatic, understanding, and resourceful, much more willing than the men are to help one another out. They collaborate in sustaining the discourse of *machismo*, but only up to a point, since it is they who see most clearly that it is in crisis. In contrast, an uglier face of *machismo* is exposed in a sub-plot involving Ricardo and María. This couple is presented initially as the comic stereotype of the good-for-nothing drunkard and the nagging wife who belts him from time to time with a frying-pan, and the other men make jokes at their expense accordingly. However, things turn nasty when Ricardo beats María up badly, causing her to miscarry: as Lola heads for the station at the end, María cries out in despair: '¡Sácame de aquí, Lola!' (108) ('Take me away from here, Lola!').

In *Tiempo de silencio** (1962: *Time of Silence*)[3] by Luis Martín-Santos, similarly stark contradictions between the family ideal and the brutal realities of urban deprivation are explored. The novel picks up again on the 1950s themes of internal migration and conditions for slum-dwellers: a young medical researcher, Pedro, participates in the illegal abortion of Florita, a relative of his assistant Amador. Florita's family live in the slums in the south of Madrid where, like the rats bred for Pedro's experiments, they are confined in miserable conditions with Florita and her younger sister sharing their parents' bed. Her father, Muecas, engages in incestuous relationships with both daughters, maintaining his position of authority through domestic violence in a grotesque distortion of the regime's values, 'Porque el Muecas se sentía, sin saber lo que significaba esta palabra, patriarca bíblico al que todas aquellas mujeres pertenecían' (1989: 66) ('For Muecas felt himself to be, without knowing the meaning of that word, the biblical patriarch to whom all those women belonged').

4.3. FAMILY DRAMAS

The bourgeois household has traditionally been the favourite setting and subject of serious drama and comedy. While much of the mainstream theatre of the decades since 1939 has continued this tradition in an unproblematic way, dissident playwrights have focused productively on the family as a site of conflict, oppression, or frustration.

4.3.1 *Rafael Alberti: the collapse of the bourgeois family*

Rafael Alberti's 'Drama of a Spanish family', *De un momento a otro* (*Any Moment Now*), was originally conceived during the war

[3] For an English translation see Martín Santos (1964).

for a production by María Teresa León's Guerrillas del Teatro which did not take place, but the text was not completed until 1940 or 1941, when the author and his wife were in exile. Its hero, Gabriel, goes through a painful process of rejecting his middle-class family in order to redefine himself in terms of a commitment to the working class and to the anti-fascist cause at the outbreak of the Civil War. He comes into conflict with his brother Ignacio, first within the family home, then in the street fighting following the military uprising of July 1936, in which he is killed.

The family is represented here less as an authoritarian institution than as an essentially bourgeois one, a key component of an exploitative system that uses religion to maintain the passivity of the masses and assuage the consciences of the privileged. Most of the characters simply take the sanctity of the family for granted, clinging to a status quo that is literally disintegrating around them (the house itself begins to crack and crumble in a thunderstorm). Gabriel finds that he must abandon the strong emotional bonds with his mother and sister for the new 'family' and fraternity of labour in the wine warehouse, harbour, fields, and factories: 'Si una vieja familia se hunde, agoniza, otra nueva, distinta, aparece en la tierra. A ella me dirijo' (Alberti 1992: 220) ('If an old family collapses and begins to die, a new, different one appears on earth. That's the one I'm joining').

Although the political message that *De un momento a otro* would have conveyed to a wartime Republican audience in 1938 was a simple call for unity amongst the squabbling factions of the Republic against the common foe, the play is also a thoughtful and moving exploration of the relationship between the middle-class intellectual and the people at a moment of class conflict and revolutionary change, and constitutes a metatheatrical investigation of the ideological implications of different modes of theatre. At the beginning, Alberti uses the conventions of nineteenth-century bourgeois 'realist' drama; he later shifts into a grotesque expressionist mode reminiscent of Valle-Inclán's *esperpentos* of the 1920s to expose the decay of the old social and theatrical order; finally, an epic, lyrical mode predominates, signifying solidarity and the collectivist ideal.

The second of these modes is essayed again in *El adefesio* (1943, first staged by Margarita Xirgu in Buenos Aires in 1944: the title means a grotesque, outlandish figure) which presents a disturbing, distorted image of a household set 'en cualquier año de estos últimos setenta, y en uno de esos pueblos fanáticos caídos entre las serranías del sur de España' (Alberti 1992: 237) ('in any of the last seventy years or so, in one of those fanatical villages lost amongst the mountains of southern Spain'), and by implication a whole society thrown back virtually into the dark ages. Alberti's vision of a young woman's vitality crushed by a tyrannical matriarch is darker and wilder, and shows the arbitrariness of paternal power more explicitly, than García Lorca's famed *La casa de Bernarda Alba* (1936: *The House of Bernarda Alba*), also premièred by Xirgu in Buenos Aires a year later and a clear thematic model for Alberti. The character Gorgo, like Bernarda, has inherited the position of head of the family and enforces her physical control with a stick, tormenting and imprisoning her niece Altea, an unwilling participant in strange ceremonies parodying family traditions, and ultimately driving her to suicide. One of the other characters spells it out: 'Gorgo manda. Ella es la autoridad. El varón. El hombre' (279) ('Gorgo is in charge. She is authority. The male. The man'). Gorgo finally becomes a tragic figure as she realizes the emptiness and destructiveness of the patriarchal role (for which, grotesquely, she wears a false beard), seeing herself at the end as a monster, an *adefesio*.

4.3.2. Hints of infidelity in mainstream comedy

Inside Spain, such disturbing representations of sexuality and the family stood no chance whatsoever of finding their way onto a stage: the text of *El adefesio* became well known but plans for a production in Spain were blocked until 1976. The links between the family and authoritarianism would be taken up later by radical playwrights such as Arrabal and Ruibal. In the meantime, marriage, infidelity, and relations between parents and children continued to form the main focus of much of the drama that was acceptable to censors and audiences from the 1940s to the 1960s.

Jacinto Benavente had specialized in such fare since the 1890s, and with his popularity re-established in the 1940s (after recanting his Republican sympathies), he continued to exercise considerable influence on younger dramatists. Francisco Ruiz Ramón (1989: 297–319) uses the term *teatro público* to characterize a successful brand of theatre written for a well-defined middle-class public of conservative tastes by authors such as José María Pemán, Juan

Ignacio Luca de Tena, Joaquín Calvo Sotelo, Edgar Neville, José López Rubio, and Alfonso Paso (see also Oliva 1989: 103–32). These prolific dramatists tried their hand at a variety of genres (detective mysteries, history plays, dramas dealing with issues of morality or social conscience), but their most characteristic products are witty situation comedies and domestic dramas in comfortable middle-class or aristocratic settings in which characters tend to fantasize about perfect romances, illicit affairs, and suspected infidelities. Against the background of the fanatical promotion by state and Church of traditional patriarchal ideals, even the blandest, most predictable representations of family relationships could have a mildly disruptive effect. Theatre itself is often used as a metaphor for either the repetitive routines of married life or the liberating power of role-play. Although irresponsibility is ultimately disapproved of and the safe, conservative status quo is usually restored, these elegant diversions insistently adopt an ironic attitude towards conventional respectability, and hint at a secret desire in the officially penitent society of the 1940s and 1950s—and that of the 1960s, guiltily titillated by changing mores—for escape from the tedium of the approved family model. López Rubio's *Celos del aire* (1950: *Jealous of Thin Air*), Neville's *Alta fidelidad* (1957: *High Fidelity*), Paso's *Cosas de papá y mamá* (1960: *What's up with Mummy and Daddy*) and *Historia de un adulterio* (1969: *A Case of Adultery*) are characteristic examples.

The comedies of Enrique Jardiel Poncela and Miguel Mihura also revolve obsessively around the theme of bourgeois marriage, but make of it something at once more frivolous and more challenging, deftly dismantling the familiar logic and the supposed naturalness of social norms. Their plays are full of eccentric situations that become increasingly bizarre yet are taken as normal by the people involved in them while the ordinary routines of polite social behaviour are made to seem odd or intolerable to the protagonists, who long to escape into fantasy and find a pure, idealized form of love free from arbitrary, bourgeois constraints. This whimsical form of absurdism is discussed further in Chapter 7.

4.3.3. Fernando Arrabal: absurdity and cruelty

While the mildly disconcerting comedies of Mihura and Jardiel were viable within Spain, the more radical and disturbing absurdism of

Fernando Arrabal was acceptable neither to audiences nor to the censors. When the Madrid première of *El triciclo* (1958: *The Tricycle*) was received with derisive hostility, Arrabal had already begun to establish himself in France, where his work soon acquired a worldwide reputation. His first play, *Pic-Nic* (written in various versions, in Spanish and French, between 1952 and 1961), simultaneously exposes the absurd futility of war and the emptiness of bourgeois family customs by throwing the two incongruously together, and in *Los dos verdugos* (1956: *The Two Torturers*, first published in French in 1958 as *Les Deux Bourreaux*) it is a father who becomes the victim of the alarming perversion of moral codes characteristic of Arrabal's work. A wife, Francisca, has denounced her husband to two silent, anonymous torturers for some unspecified crime and obtains sadistic satisfaction from hearing him scream, inspecting his wounds, and rubbing salt and vinegar into them. One of her sons, Mauricio, is horrified and condemns her; the other, Benito, defends her and attacks his brother for his lack of respect. Francisca's motives are never clarified, but the situation is certainly not as simple as an oppressed family getting its own back on an authoritarian father. Francisca represents the traditional ideal of motherhood—passive, selfless, long-suffering—taken to a twisted extreme. She laments Mauricio's ingratitude and disloyalty but forgives him and manipulatively begs Benito—'¡Qué martirio! ¡Qué calvario!' (Arrabal 1979: 257) ('What martyrdom! What a Calvary!')—not to be angry with him since 'la familia es una cosa sagrada' (255) ('family is something sacred'). The family values that obliterate a woman's identity independent of her roles as wife and mother have been stretched to the point of ghastly absurdity. The self-denial and self-effacement of the perfect mother have turned into a kind of tyranny demanding the complicity and loyalty of the two sons: 'Sólo pido que no seáis desagradecidos y que sepáis apreciar el sacrificio de una madre como la que habéis tenido la suerte de tener' (259) ('All I ask from you two is a little gratitude and appreciation of the sacrifices a mother such as the one you've been lucky enough to have has to make').

4.3.4. José Ruibal:* scenes of violence

The avant-garde playwrights of the New Theatre* of the late 1960s and 1970s often also present the old values of authority and morality as grotesquely archaic, and parents as totally alien to their children. The nameless mother in José Ruibal's short play *Los ojos* (1969: *The Eyes*) is trapped in and twisted by the ideal of the mother totally devoted to her children. Ruibal dramatizes her loss of independent identity in a shocking way. She incessantly cleans, tidies, and fusses over her son, tolerant of his growing, masculine interest in such things as firearms, cigarettes, pornography, and a large knife which is a prominent prop in the piece. She mimes her lines to a record that she has put on the record-player, as if she were trying to learn by heart the mechanical clichés of the doting but disapproving mother and diligent housewife: eat your breakfast, you'll be late for school, don't pick your nose, oh my goodness what a mess your room is in, I'll tell your father when he gets home . . . (Ruibal 1984: 186–90). Authority, naturally, lies with the father (who does not appear on stage); and though the mother sees everything, she does not tell. Desperate to construct a meaningful role for herself, she colludes in the formation of the classically desensitized and morally unbiddable male child: suddenly, inexplicably, the boy grabs the knife and stabs her brutally in the eyes. As she pathetically wonders if it was something she said, he repeats some of her own learned phrases with cruel irony: 'Ten cuidado, mamá. Arrópate bien, mamá. Come tu bocadillo, mamá. Tus ojos ya no lo verán todo . . .' (191) ('Careful now, mummy. Wrap up warm, mummy. Eat your sandwich, mummy. Now your eyes won't see everything . . .').

El padre (1968: *The Father*), another short *café-teatro* piece by Ruibal, presents another view of the same kind of violent perversion of values and relationships. Here family morality is on the one hand exploited by parents as an instrument of manipulation, and on the other it traps them in self-destructive stereotypes. In *Los mutantes* (1968: *The Mutants*), Ruibal's target is consumerism, which generates a striking stage metaphor: a man and a woman live in an apparently neolithic condition, squashed under a huge stone, but the small space they inhabit is filled with miniature versions of modern domestic appliances. They are literally oppressed by technology and material possessions as well as by the petrified immobility of the overall environment (suggesting, perhaps, continued political fossilization in Spain despite the changes of the 1960s), but while the man thrives and uses the technology and objects around them, his pregnant wife is suffocated by them. This new, technology-intensive model of family life is still an oppressively patriarchal institution mirroring a superficially modernized but politically authoritarian society. In all three plays, Ruibal's main preoccupation is with the ideological impact of language. The unthinking clichés of family relationships and institutions are exaggerated and turned into startling visual metaphors in order to defamiliarize them and blow them apart.

4.3.5. Antonio Buero Vallejo: guilty secrets*

Others writing for the theatre within Spain offer less aggressive critiques in which the family may be reinstated to some extent as a source of emotional support or of moral values more humane than the conservative ideal, but is nevertheless subject to pressure, contradiction, or conflict. Plays by Antonio Buero Vallejo with a contemporary setting tend to focus on families in enclosed domestic settings, often involving a tragic crisis in which one member of a family kills or causes the death of another. The family is used both as a microcosm of contemporary Spain (with the Civil War and its consequences unavoidably in the background) and as a setting for tragic meditations on hope and justice. Characters in these plays seek stability, moral authority, and emotional reassurance from spouses, parents, or children, but the family (and by extension the nation) is shown as deeply troubled by guilt, lies, and secret betrayals.

La doble historia del doctor Valmy (1964: *The Double Case History of Dr Valmy*, first performed in Spain in 1976) is the only one of Buero's plays to have remained prohibited until the end of the dictatorship. Despite a pointedly fictitious setting, the subject of the torture of political prisoners by the police was clearly too dangerous to be aired in public. The beginning of the play offers a conventional, comfortable image of family life, but Mary Barnes's married bliss depends upon not enquiring into the real nature of her husband Daniel's work in the Political Section of the police force, a sinister team whose boss, Paulus, is referred to by his men as 'papaíto' (Daddy). The modern, technologically advanced, free-market society in which they live is poisoned by the barbarism at the core of the state, and the symptoms of this poisoning manifest themselves in ways that directly attack the foundations of family relationships. After being made to crush the testicles of a prisoner,

Daniel has himself become impotent. Dr Valmy's diagnosis is moral as well as clinical: 'Pues es muy sencillo: usted ha elegido arrepentirse mediante la enfermedad, precisamente por no estar arrepentido. [...] Para curarse, tendría que admitir que ha cometido algo injustificable y espantoso' (Buero 1976: 65-8) ('It's very simple: you've chosen a kind of repentance through illness, precisely because you haven't repented. [...] To get better, you would have to recognize that you've done something terrible and unjustifiable'). Daniel's colleagues are also bodily troubled by their consciences: the implication is that the whole society is sick and, moreover, hooked (as is Daniel pharmaceutically) on metaphorical analgesics such as reassuring myths about society as a harmonious family, a fairy tale told by the grandmother, and a banal television advertisement promising worldwide happiness from Finus analgesic tablets. Such micro-narratives are tellingly contrasted with two versions of truth: a factual history of torture sent to Mary by a former pupil and revelations elicited by Dr Valmy in the course of his treatment of Daniel and Mary (the doctor's report is the narrative frame for the whole play, with the events recounted to him re-enacted in the imaginary spaces on either side of his office). Daniel finds that he is trapped in a cycle of violence which ensures that if he refuses to be a torturer he will be made into a victim: the Section is an authoritarian family that brutalizes its sons and will not let them go.

In the meantime, Mary's eyes are opened to the reality of what her husband is involved in, and her horror is projected onto the family. She has a recurring nightmare in which Daniel cuts her fingers off with a large pair of scissors and threatens to castrate the baby with the same scissors. She is terrified that little Danielito will, like his father, be dragged into the patriarchy of violence that tortures its wives and children and turns its sons into torturers. At the climax of the play she clutches the baby, shouting, '¡No te acerques! ¡Es mío, mío!' (126) ('Stay away! He's mine, only mine!'), and shoots her husband with his own pistol, becoming effectively his judge and redeemer. As the men from the Section cross from their side of the split stage and take Mary prisoner, the repressive status quo seems restored. However, the final implication is that theatre, in which stories are not just told but enacted before an audience, can act as a form of cathartic social therapy, and this metatheatrical dimension is completed by the presence of the elegant couple in evening dress who introduce and comment sceptically on the main action, addressing the audience directly (with the house lights up on two key occcasions) to warn them not to believe what they hear. But we learn that they are also Dr Valmy's patients and are thus plunged into the abyss of narrative unreliability, forced to wonder whether Valmy's final diagnosis applies to us, whether the untold first case history is in some sense the audience's own.

In each of Buero's plays, a carefully constructed dramatic image embodies in a unique way the same tragic preoccupations: guilt, justice, self-knowledge, human rights, the possibility of reconciliation. After 1975, the connections between the political legacy of the dictatorship and the betrayals that corrupt the family can be made more explicitly. The protagonist of *Jueces en la noche* (1979: *Judges in the Night*), Juan Luis Palacios, is a politician who has evolved from militant Falangism in his student days to a ministerial post and prosperity under Franco, then to a seat in the newly restored parliament as a member of a moderate party, now planning his next shift towards the left. Both his liberal public image and his apparently perfect marriage turn out to be false, founded on lies and guilty secrets. A complex dramatic structure ties together his reactionary political past, his shady double-dealing in the present, his complicity with an assassination by right-wing terrorists, his superficial Catholicism, and his wife's discovery of the fact that, in order to win her twenty years earlier, he had fabricated the story that Fermín, her idealist left-wing boyfriend at the time, had betrayed her by giving her name to police under interrogation. She resents not only Juan Luis's dishonesty but, more profoundly, his destruction of her capacity to believe in the idealism represented by Fermín.

In the 1980s and 1990s, Buero's plays continue to expose egotism, corruption, and complicity with violence in successive generations of *vencedores* through their guilty secrets and their betrayals of loved ones.

Although the guilty fathers and husbands of recent plays such as *Las trampas del azar* (1994: *The Twists and Turns of Chance*) are clearly identified with the Franco regime, they are subjected to a judgement more moral than political, punished by their consciences for their refusal to accept responsibility for what they have done and to change themselves. Their roles as father and husband, rather than being represented as inherently oppressive, are shown to be corrupted by their own betrayals and by the injustices in which they have been involved. The wives, mothers, and daughters are not merely victims, but important agents of a necessary confrontation with truth.

4.4. WOMEN WRITING THE FAMILY

Critiques of the regime's model of female development as marriage followed by motherhood can be found in a number of novels by women writers which offer alternative life-narratives or *Bildungsromans* which tend to focus on an alienated adolescent growing up in a dysfunctional family.

4.4.1. *Alternative models of female development*

Where *La familia de Pascual Duarte* enacts matricide as an existential necessity for its male protagonist, Carmen Laforet's *Nada* (1945: *Nothingness*) subtly substitutes the mother–daughter bond and female friendship for the various relationships with men that were supposed to characterize a good Falangist woman and bring her contentment: paternal authority followed by submission to her husband and the production of the prized male heir. Elizabeth Ordóñez (1991: 51) has traced the 'double-voicing' of *Nada*, the ways in which it appears to conform to the rules while creating a parallel narrative which undercuts them radically, a strategy which enabled its publication, its garnering of the Nadal Prize, and its dissemination amongst a public which included future women writers such as Carme Riera and Carmen Martín Gaite, for whom the novel offered an alternative to the dominant discourse of femininity.

Yet the trajectory of *Nada*'s protagonist, Andrea, has traditionally been read as the movement from a dysfunctional family lacking proper patriarchal authority and moral guidance into the arms of the ideal Francoist family. Andrea's two uncles represent pariah figures in the regime's terms: Juan, unable to provide properly for his family, and Román, a black marketeer and seducer of young girls, who is at times represented in terms that echo the language of the Nationalist crusade, as a dark, demonic force (his room is furnished with various non-Christian artefacts) that must be destroyed for the sake of those around him. His suicide—anathema for a Catholic—conveniently removes him and Andrea leaves an apparently subdued Juan for the 'salvation' of Ena's father, the exemplary Catalan businessman who meets the basic requirements of the ideal husband and father. Andrea seems then to 'choose' a substitute father or authority figure whose uncomplicated fulfilment of bourgeois conformity surprisingly wins over an adolescent who herself agonizes and deliberates incessantly (and in doing so represents a threat to patriarchal prohibitions, frequently reiterated in narratives of the period, on women apparently 'thinking so much').

At the end of the novel Andrea leaves behind the dark household in Barcelona—with its repressed memories of the Civil War—for a new life in Madrid, the symbolic seat of the regime, with her new 'father' organizing every detail of her supposedly 'chaotic' life. Yet this hardly explains the excitement and sense of transgression with which some women read *Nada* in the 1940s or the reaction of the spokesman for the Instituto Nacional del Libro Español (INLE: National Book Institute) who in 1945 suggested that Laforet was part of an 'Asiatic' menace threatening Western, Christian civilization and values (Ordóñez 1991: 35, 44). Despite the surface conformity of *Nada*, it seems that even some representatives of the regime's cultural discourse intuited a more troubling narrative beneath the apparent resolution of opposing forces of good and evil.

Ana María Matute's *Primera memoria* (1960: *First Memories*),[4] which won the Nadal Prize in 1959, also focuses on a dysfunctional family through the eyes of a young girl, Matia, in the transition to adolescence. The novel is situated in the apparently peaceful haven of the Balearic Islands (probably Mallorca) during the Civil War. Matia—whose mother is dead and whose father is a Republican soldier—has been sent to live with her grandmother, doña Práxedes. Unlike the somewhat pathetic 'abuelita' of *Nada* who cannot hold her family together, doña Práxedes—evoking Lorca's Bernarda Alba—ruthlessly upholds her position as a powerful matriarch within the oppressive island regime. Her status is assured by her wealth and the right-wing credentials of her

---

[4] For an English translation see Matute (1963).

deceased husband. Despite the spatial distance from the Civil War, the fratricidal national conflict is reproduced on the island in the juvenile conflicts between the gangs of the sons of professionals, led by Matia's cousin Borja, and the sons of local tradesmen, led by Guiem. The boys are following adult social conventions in their apparently sharply divided loyalties organized in terms of social class. León and Carlos follow Borja because their father has instructed them to, and he in turn is acting out of fear of doña Práxedes who has assumed the position of patriarchal power on the island with the complicity of the local clergyman, Mosén Mayol. The further conflict between Borja and the idealized figure of Manuel (representing those exploited by the social order) is suggestive of the Cain and Abel motif that is central to Matute's work, as both boys are possibly the illegitimate sons of the nonconformist landowner Jorge de Son Major. The subversive identification of Manuel with Christ breaks the symbiosis between the Church and reactionary forces enshrined in National Catholicism, as is emphasized by the biblical epigraph to the story: 'A ti el Señor no te ha enviado, y, sin embargo, tomando Su nombre has hecho que este pueblo confiase en la mentira. Jeremías. 28, 15' (Matute 1988: 7) ('The Lord hath not sent thee; but thou makest this people to trust in a lie').

Matia ultimately acquiesces in this hypocrisy as, although she is aware of social injustice and initially sides with Manuel, she betrays him by failing to come to his defence when he is unjustly accused by Borja, in a confession to Mayol which is made public, of forcing him to steal money from doña Práxedes. This passive betrayal by Matia can be seen to symbolize the failure by the 'silent majority' (Pérez 1991: 107) to protest against the brutal repression carried out against those deemed subversive by the Franco regime. The adult Matia, as narrator, recognizes the cowardice and treachery of this childish act. All the characters would seem to be trapped by fear, hatred, jealousy, and guilt. Matia makes several references to her isolation and vulnerability. Like Andrea, she is an alienated, marginal figure.

Another text of the late 1950s, Carmen Martín Gaite's* 1957 Nadal prizewinning novel *Entre visillos* (1958: *Through the Shutters*),[5] questions the official version of family life and female

---

[5] For an English translation see Martín Gaite (1990).

development from multiple perspectives: dissident female insiders; a foreign, male, outsider; and the voices of a range of women whose very diversity challenges the idea of a single norm for all, from an economically independent woman, through those enjoying or contemplating new possibilities opening up for women and men in the big cities, to portraits of women whose conformity to the expectations of family and society has brought them only dissatisfaction and frustration. The character Natalia's mother dies in childbirth, a potent reminder of the price many women paid at that time for the large families demanded by the regime or in pursuit of a male heir. On another level, in a large number of novels written by women in this period, including *Nada* and *Primera memoria*, the natural mother is significantly absent, usually dead, perhaps representing models of maternity and more generally of femininity which have been displaced and denigrated and whose absence is supposed to be filled by the Francoist model.

4.4.2. Odd girls out

The figure of the 'chica rara' ('odd girl out'), exemplified by Laforet's Andrea in *Nada*, is discussed in Carmen Martín Gaite's *Desde la ventana* (1987: *From the Window*). These essays on women writers examine a number of post-war novels in which female characters break with the restrictive models of the patriarchal family binding them to a confined domestic space. The protagonists of these novels, which include *Nada*, *Los Abel* (1948: *The Abel Clan*) by Ana María Matute, *Nosotros los Rivero* (1953: *We Riveros*) by Dolores Medio, and *Entre visillos*, are characterized by their desire to escape into the public space of the street and broaden their perspective (Martín Gaite 1992b: 113). Both *Nada* and *Entre visillos* offer education as a counter-discourse to marriage and motherhood in the figures of Andrea and Natalia. Martín Gaite counterposes these texts with the predominant literary model for women at the time, the immensely popular *novela rosa** (romantic novel), written by such prolific authors as Carmen de Icaza and Concha Linares Becerra.

Writers such as Martín Gaite, who contested the happy endings and closure of these texts, were themselves regarded as 'chicas raras', as testified to by press reviews of the time (Martín Gaite 1992b: 121–2). Paradoxically, some proponents of social realism accused these texts of evasiveness due to their perceived obliqueness (Brooksbank Jones 1997: 160) in contrast to male-coded discourses of objectivity. However, these novels focusing on the restrictions imposed on women (particularly provincial women as exemplified in the work of Martín Gaite) did challenge official rhetoric and ideological discourses which attempted to enforce a gendered division between public or political and private or personal spheres of activity.

4.5. MODERNIZATION AND THE FAMILY

Critiques of the family from the second half of the 1960s and the 1970s frequently focus on the impact of modernization and consumerism, not only on working-class but also middle-class family values and women's lives. Greater material well-being may have offered a kind of liberation for women at home, while foreign influences and the expansion of education opened up new horizons for young people, but such developments generated new pressures and did not necessarily alter the patriarchal foundations. Although by this stage well established in intellectual circles and among the university educated, liberal leftist and libertarian attitudes had little immediate, widespread impact within Spain, either in writing or experience. While Manuel Vázquez Montalbán's *Los alegres muchachos de Atzavara* (1987: *The Gay Life of the Boys of Atzavara*), Esther Tusquets's *El mismo mar de todos los veranos* (1978: *The Same Sea as Every Summer*), and Luis Antonio de Villena's *Amor pasión* (1984: *Amour Passion*) and *Chicos* (1989: *Boys*) evoke in retrospect spaces of micro-resistance (on the Catalan coast, in Barcelona, in Madrid, on Ibiza, and in Benidorm) to the dictates of family, marriage, and monogamy, portrayals of domestic realities which emphasize the claustrophobic and the coercive are in the majority.

In a lighter vein, Luis Carandell's popular *Los españoles* (1968) speaks with satirical fondness of the vacuities and low-grade destructiveness of persisting mores. Middle Spain is peopled with fathers and brothers whose one concern for their sisters is that 'las niñas lleguen en perfectas condiciones—como el pescado a la plaza—a la edad en que puedan contraer matrimonio' (Carandell 1968: 26) ('the girls arrive in perfect condition—like fish to market—at the age when they can get married'). In courtship, 'se crea una atmósfera enrarecida y a menudo irrespirable. La libertad sexual que se niega a la mujer antes del matrimonio se permite al hombre que, dadas las condiciones reinantes, tiene que hacer uso de ella a salto de mata y a menudo en condiciones deplorables' (72) ('A rarefied and often suffocating atmosphere builds up. The sexual freedom denied to the woman before marriage is allowed to the man who, given the circumstances, is forced to avail himself of it as and when he can and often in deplorable conditions').[6]

Carandell's series of no-comment reproductions of cuttings from local newspapers, parish magazines, and reports on texts displayed in public spaces, collected as *Celtiberia Show* (1970, with some twenty reprints over the next five years), tell a similar story: while Berkeley and Paris seethe with revolution, in the summer of 1968 the mayor of Santos de Maimona (province of Badajoz) publishes a proclamation whose first article begins 'Se prohíbe toda demostración pública de amor en las calles' (Carandell 1974: 78) ('All public displays of love are banned'); a parish magazine's Ten Commandments for Courting Couples gives as number ten for the *novio* 'no codiciarás las novias ajenas' (68) ('You shall not covet the fiancées of your friends'). It was this kind of world which half of Spain was now learning to laugh at and leave behind.

4.5.1. Families after Franco

Two contrasting publications from 1979 give a good indication of the liveliness of the debate about the future of the family at the time of the transition to democracy: a pastoral statement issued by the Conferencia Episcopal (the governing body of the Church), and a polemical collection of views edited by the feminist writer María José Ragué Arias.

The Church document, *Matrimonio y familia, hoy* (*Marriage and Family Today*), makes a clear call for a profound change in the Church's vision of marriage and family, using a series of terms to do with transformation and renovation: *cambio* (change), *conversión, renovación, actualización* (updating). It announces a definite break with the political role of the Church under the dictatorship,

---

[6] These sexual double standards are discussed at length in Martín Gaite (1994).

rejecting certain forms of authoritarianism and welcoming certain changes in society as having positive effects on the family. The bishops envisage a progressive social role for both the Church and the family in combating the effects of poverty, unemployment, marginalization, social injustice, and even militarism (30–6). They also explicitly renounce the Francoist strategy of using the family to disable other forms of association and warn against turning it into a ghetto cut off from the wider community. Families are urged to show a commitment to a humane, free society through trade unions, political parties, and other associations, 'dentro de un verdadero pluralismo' ('in a true spirit of pluralism') (36). Although the document suggests a genuine enthusiasm for the development of a more enlightened social role for the Church within the emerging culture of rights, personal choice, and *convivencia* (harmonious coexistence), underneath the new democratic language the key elements of doctrine with respect to marriage, sexuality, and the family (especially the condemnation of contraception, abortion, and divorce) remain essentially unchanged.

Ragué Arias introduces *Proceso a la familia española* (1979: *The Spanish Family on Trial*) with a preface designed to denaturalize and historicize the conventional model of the family. Her analysis is based on Marxist feminism, seeing the family essentially as an instrument for the exploitation of women, whose function is to provide men with cheap domestic labour and sexual satisfaction and to reproduce the workforce. Romá Gubern analyses the role of popular culture in the mass media in legitimizing and disseminating the model of the patriarchal family; and novelist Carme Riera describes how the characters she creates in her fiction tend to be alienated from their families: she dreams of fluid family groupings created freely and confidently without dominance or dependence, based 'en el amor y en la libertad sin necesidad de pasar por tamices sociales. Y sobre todo que cada uno de nosotros supiéramos asumir nuestra radical soledad, bella, creadora y sugestiva' (240) ('on love and liberty without needing to be mediated by social institutions. And above all, that each of us could learn how to live with our essential solitude, our beautiful, creative, inspirational solitude'). Meanwhile, philosopher Fernando Savater acknowledges that the family can perform a repressive role as an accomplice of state power, but proposes a subtle defence of it as a provider of emotional support and even as a refuge for individuality.

What is striking about *Proceso a la familia española* is the social effervescence it indicates. In 1979 the Transition is still at an early stage; little has changed, the dead hand of the dictatorship and all its rhetoric can still be felt, but everything is now up for debate, and these people throw themselves into that debate with passion and vision.

4.5.2. *The mother–child bond in women's writing*

Esther Tusquets's loosely linked trilogy of texts published between 1978 and 1980 is ground-breaking for both her self-referential experimentation with form and the transgressive nature of the sexual relationships portrayed: a lesbian affair in *El mismo mar de todos los veranos* (1978: *The Same Sea as Every Summer*), a lesbian–heterosexual love triangle in *El amor es un juego solitario* (1979: *Love is a Solitary Game*), and a marital breakdown in *Varada tras el último naufragio* (1980: *Stranded*).[7] The main protagonists of these novels are alienated, middle-aged women located within the specific social setting of the Catalan upper bourgeoisie, a privileged class portrayed as decadent and complacent. These women are unfulfilled by their roles as wives and mothers. Indeed, a consistent theme in these novels is the failure of mother–child bonding. This is taken to extremes in the conclusion of *El amor es un juego solitario* in which the three protagonists Elia, Ricardo, and Clara engage in three-way sex and sodomy. Set on a Sunday, this sexual encounter breaks numerous taboos including that of incest as Elia has been situated as an eroticized, surrogate mother figure by both her young lovers who articulate a lack of closeness to, and simultaneous longing for, their birth mothers.

Mother–child relationships are likewise central to Rosa Montero's first novel *Crónica del desamor* (1979: *Chronicle of Disenchantment*). It can also be viewed as ground-breaking for its portrayal of sexual relationships from a woman-centred perspective. Furthermore, taboo subjects such as illegal abortion, (un)availability of contraceptives (legalized in 1978), domestic violence, marital rape, and sexual harassment in the workplace are

[7] For English translations of the first two of these see Tusquets (1985, 1990).

tackled in a frank manner. The novel is predominantly focalized through Ana, a single working mother who is exploited by her paternalistic bosses: she works more hours for less pay and without the job security of her male colleagues in order to support her 4-year-old son Curro (slang for 'hard work'). However, motherhood is more than an oppressive social construct and the mother–child bond is, in contrast to Tusquets, on the whole, portrayed in a positive light. The rejection by younger feminist women of their mothers as role models is questioned in the relationship between Ana's friend Elena, a feminist academic, and her mother Antonia. Antonia would seem to be the traditional housewife who has lived her life within patriarchal conventions. However, we learn through Elena's sister Candela that Antonia secretly used contraception and achieved her first orgasm through masturbation after reading one of Elena's books on sexual initiation.

Montserrat Roig also foregrounds the relationship between generations of women in her trilogy, translated into Castilian in 1980, relating the saga of the interconnected Miralpeix and Ventura-Claret families: *Ramona, adiós* (1972, as *Ramona, adéu*: *Ramona, Goodbye*), *El tiempo de las cerezas* (1977, as *El temps de les cireres*: *The Time of the Cherries*), and *La hora violeta* (1980, as *L'hora violeta*: *The Violet Hour*). As in Tusquets's trilogy the characters are located in the Catalan, urban, bourgeois space of Barcelona. Over the course of almost a century, these generations of women struggle against traditional, middle-class family roles. As Catherine Davies notes, despite obvious social and cultural changes affecting women, the protagonists of Roig's novels remain 'caught up in a web of assimilated assumptions involving heterosexual relationships, mothering and homemaking which they consistently resent' (1994: 26). The women are linked through a matrilineal genealogy explicitly set out in a chart at the beginning of *L'hora violeta*. Thus history is focalized through the previously silenced voices of mothers, daughters, and sisters in order to reconstruct the present through interrogation of the past.

4.5.3. *The family into the 1990s*

Dramatic texts written in the 1980s and 1990s continue to subject the family to critical analysis and to explore relationships between men and women and between parents and children. *Bajarse al moro* (1984: *Going down to Morocco*) by José Luis Alonso de Santos traces the reassertion of traditional family values amongst young people apparently defying them. Lidia Falcón's* radical critique of the survival of authoritarian patriarchy will be discussed in Chapter 5 since her plays are essentially about the suppression of women's voices. However, her explicitly feminist approach has been an exception. In the work of other dramatists, the institution of the family in itself is not often the most important factor. The emphasis tends to be on the subjectivity and sexuality of the individual, and one of the most characteristic scenarios has been the chance encounter, away from the familiar parameters of home and family, of two solitary individuals, each in search of pleasure or reassurance or identity. A similar 'intimismo' or focus on the interior self is consistently identified as a feature of the *nueva narrativa** (New Narrative) of the 1980s and 1990s in which self-aware first person narrators, or protagonists, explore issues of identity and subjectivity as traditional markers of identity such as Catholicism and the family lose their cohesive function. The figure of the individual is often located within social or family groupings in the process of breaking down. In a reflection of social changes including the legalization of divorce and rise in number of people living alone in urban centres, a focus on loneliness has become a selling point for novels; for example Juan José Millás's *El desorden de tu nombre* (1988: *The Disorder of your Name*), *La soledad era esto* (1990: *That was Loneliness*), and *Volver a casa* (1990: *Coming Home*) have been repackaged together as a 'Trilogy of Loneliness' (Labanyi 1999: 155). The sense of alienation of the individual is particularly marked in the novels of the youthful Generation X, discussed in Chapter 10, faced with a past they have no nostalgia for and an uncertain future.

Further reading

Davies (1994); Graham (1995); Labanyi (1995*b*).

5
Power and Disempowerment

5.1 GENDERED DISCOURSES OF POWER

The focus on alienated individuals exploring their subjectivity in the writing of the 1980s and 1990s can be traced in the earlier writings of those marginalized by the discourses of the regime. As is evident from the preceding discussion of the construction of the family, women were identified exclusively with the domestic sphere in the family model of National Catholicism. Novels by women highlight the restrictions imposed on them by this paradigm and present a challenge to the discourses of the regime, and the institutions which implemented them, through a variety of strategies which emphasize the use of language, or paradoxically silence, as a tool of empowerment.

5.1.1. Escaping the limits of silence

The intersection between an introspective narrative of self and wider socio-historical issues discussed earlier in relation to *Nada*, *Primera memoria*, and *El cuarto de atrás* provides a useful point of departure for the analysis of post-war narrative written by Spanish women. In texts written during the Franco years, outward conformity is often a mask for inner rebellion by characters such as Matia in *Primera memoria*. Non-utterance or silence becomes an explicit, subversive motif in the stifling atmosphere of post-war Spain. For Kronik an aesthetics of asphyxiation prevails during the immediate post-war period (1981: 201). *Nada* abounds in claustrophobic imagery: doors repeatedly shut behind characters—beginning with Andrea's first, nightmarish entrance into the house at calle de Aribau—enclosing them in dark and dismal rooms. The overall structure of the text is also marked by suffocating repetition and circularity.

The *Bildungsroman* formed by Elena Quiroga's* *Tristura* (1960:

Sadness) and *Escribo tu nombre* (1965: *I Write your Name*), like *Nada*, focuses on the alienation of a solitary individual, the child Tadea, surrounded by a society characterized by social and religious conformity (the Galician upper middle class of the 1920s and 1930s). Silence is emblematic of the repressive atmosphere in which she is brought up and Quiroga's elliptical style elicits reading between the lines for what remains unsaid. Her intimist tone and formal complexity find echoes in the exiled writers Rosa Chacel and Mercè Rodoreda, both associated with vanguardist groups before they left Spain (the Generation of 1927 and Sabadell Group respectively). Both have had particular resonance for younger women writers, in the case of Rodoreda especially Catalan writers such as Ana María Moix who translated some of her works.

Solitude and alienation characterize Rodoreda's two major novels: *La plaça del diamant* (1962: *Diamond Square*) and *Mirall trencat* (1974: *Broken Mirror*), perhaps accentuated by Rodoreda's triple experience of exile: as a Republican, a Catalonian, and a woman. Nonetheless, the focus on everday life in *La plaça del diamant* and the dynastic narrative of *Mirall trencat* provide a bridge to the later testimonial fiction of writers within Spain such as Rosa Montero and Montserrat Roig. *La plaça del diamant* is generally acknowledged to be Rodoreda's masterpiece, receiving both favourable reader response and critical acclaim. But it is often omitted from literary histories published in Spain which exclude novels originally written in Catalan (Pope 1991: 34). Marginalization is a key theme; the protagonist narrator, Natalia, is doubly marginalized as a working-class woman. She suffers the harrowing effects of deprivation in the Civil War to the extent that when she hears that her husband is dead she considers killing her two children and committing suicide. Both before and after the war she also suffers the effects of smothering marriages. Her first husband, Quimet, is tender yet domineering; he renames her Colometa (Little Pigeon). This symbol of love and peace comes to signify entrapment as Quimet turns their flat into a dovecote in a money-raising scheme which reduces Natalia to the status of servant to the doves, hemmed in by their interminable cooing and stench. Unable to communicate with Quimet, she silently rebels by destroying their eggs and slowly killing them off. Although her second husband, shopkeeper Antoni, provides much needed financial stability she remains emotionally isolated. Nonetheless, the novel ends with the possibility of hope for the future. Natalia breaks her silence with a liberating primal scream through which she comes to terms with her destructive past.

One of the most distinguished post-war writers, Carmen Martín Gaite,* also focuses on the stifling effects of patriarchal convention on women. Like Quiroga, she situates much of her narrative in a provincial society characterized by hypocrisy. Nonconformist individuals struggle against the limits imposed on them by the restrictive environment around them. *Entre visillos* (1958) conveys the stultifying atmosphere of a provincial capital (based on Salamanca) in post-war Spain through the dissident characters Pablo Klein, a German teacher, and Natalia Ruiz Guilarte, his star pupil who contests the prescribed role models for women through her desire to go to university. The main character of the novella *Las ataduras* (1960: *Bonds*), Alina, succeeds in escaping from a similarly smothering provincial existence to study in Madrid. However, to the disappointment of her father, she abandons her education, choosing the obligations of motherhood and married life with a French intellectual in Paris. In *Ritmo lento* (1962: *A Slow Rhythm*) the male nonconformist protagonist is an alienated intellectual, David Fuente, who is trapped not by family ties but by his reclusion in a mental asylum.

Martín Gaite returns to the issue of female development and the problems of growing up during the Civil War and post-war period in *El cuarto de atrás* (1978). The novel examines the strictures imposed on women through the moral and social codes of the regime exemplified in the work of the Sección Femenina and encapsulated in the phrase 'quedarse, conformar y aguantar' (1992a: 125) ('stay, conform, and put up with it') to which Martín Gaite opposes the attractive formulation 'salir, escapar y fugar' (125) ('go out, escape, and run away'). She subverts the regime's appropriation of figures such as Christ and St Teresa by emphasizing their transgressive abandonment of home and family. For the young narrator this escape to freedom is personified by the figure of the 'loose woman', the *locas* and *frescas* of the 1940s and 1950s epitomized by the singer Conchita Piquer whose song 'Tatuaje' ('Tattoo') comes to signify forbidden passion whilst elliptically evoking the betrayals and losses endured in post-war Spain. The narrator of *El cuarto de atrás* cultivates her ability to escape through her readings of a wide variety of texts drawn from both high and popular culture.[1] These texts bring us to the back room of the title which is both physical playroom and imaginative recess of the mind. When shortages caused by the war cause her parents to convert her playroom into a larder, the narrator turns to literature. She is initiated into the pleasure of writing by a friend and the creative process provides an escape into internal freedom for the two girls. In the novel it is the private space which is a liberating site of resistance for women.

In interviews Martín Gaite has stressed the importance of solitude for self-awareness and its productive potentiality for her work. However, in *El cuarto de atrás* the in-depth examination of self and narrative process is instigated through a dialogic process. The man in black with whom the narrator converses is instrumental in teasing out her thoughts. In order to break out of the stultifying silence of the post-war period it is necessary to engage in verbal communication. The importance of dialogue, spoken and written, is emphasized in Martín Gaite's essays on the narrative process, 'La búsqueda del interlocutor' (1973: 'The Search for an Interlocutor') and *El cuento de nunca acabar* (1983: *The Never-Ending Story*). Her earlier novel, *Retahílas* (1974: *Links*), also focuses on the need for a sympathetic interlocutor through a night-long conversation between Eulalia and her nephew Germán. The successful—and fruitful—communication in *Retahílas* and *El cuarto de atrás* can be juxtaposed with narratives written in the 1970s which focus on the failure of communication and resultant breakdown in relationships (primarily) between men and women. In narratives such as *Julia* (1969: *Julia*) and *Walter, ¿por qué te fuiste?* (1973: *Walter, Why Did You Go?*) by Ana María Moix, *Presente profundo* (1973: *Profound Present*) by Quiroga, and *Fragmentos de interior* (1976: *Interior Fragments*) by Martín Gaite female protagonists seem condemned to frustration, isolation, madness, and eventually suicide. The effects of a patriarchal discourse of compulsory heterosexuality and the primacy of family are also to be seen in the context of homosexuality in *Los delitos insignificantes* (*Insignificant Offences*) by Álvaro Pombo (1986). Here, Gonzalo Ortega, a middle-aged author, confronts writer's block, loneliness, and his sexual desire for a young, narcissistic

---

[1] The liberating potential of popular culture in the novel is discussed in Chapter 9.

opportunist who casually and cruelly accuses him of hypocrisy and self-oppression (prior to demanding money and forcing Gonzalo to have sex with him to validate this demand).

In the 1980s, the feminist theatre of Lidia Falcón* presents a similarly bleak picture of powerless characters trapped in impossible situations, with women struggling to challenge male discourses but dependent upon men who are prepared to use their economic, political, and physical power mercilessly in defence of their own position. Part of the problem is the lingering legacy of the Franco years (despite changes of the 1980s such as the legalization of divorce), but Falcón is interested above all in how patriarchy adapts to the new circumstances so that men retain control over money, over women's fertility and work, and over language. Women's voices struggle to be heard, trying to explain reasonably how they feel and what they want, in the face of violence, distorted logic, and immovable institutions.

¡Calle, pague y no moleste, señora! (1984: *Shut up, Pay up, and Stop Nagging, Madam!*) is a black comedy in which three different women seeking help from (male) authorities are received with the same patronizing indifference. Magda tries to report her husband for beating her up and throwing her out of the house. The police inspector drags his attention away from the football commentary just long enough to sympathize angrily with the husband—coming home tired after work only to be prevented from listening to the cup final by a whingeing wife and screeching kids: '¡Pero si es para matarlos a todos! ¡Poco le ha hecho!' (Falcón 1994: 149) ('It's enough to make anyone kill the lot of you! Think yourself lucky!'). Next, Margarita wants to divorce her husband, who has been conducting a blatant affair with his secretary María and has now gone on holiday with her, leaving his wife and children with no money for a month. The lawyer patronizingly dismisses all this as mere supposition and advises her to devote herself to her housework and to winning him back. Lastly, María arrives for a session with a psychiatrist, but gets only a disembodied voice from an answerphone outside the door. She complains of depression because her married boss has suddenly broken off their affair; the machine intones contradictory Freudian platitudes until her time is up. The dramatization and staging are simple, invested with structural interest in the form of ironic parallels between the three women. Each of them finds herself forced to look up to the man:

the inspector slouches behind a desk on a high platform; the lawyer also has a raised desk, in front of which Margarita has to sit on an absurdly small chair; María has to stand on tiptoes to speak into the psychiatrist's answerphone. Each of them leaves the interview humiliated and speechless. They are all victims of the same system, but although their paths cross repeatedly, at no point do they speak to one another or attempt to form a united front against it.

In *Tres idiotas españolas* (1987: *Three Spanish Idiot Women*) three women tell their stories of frustrated lives at the mercy of men's priorities. In recent years women's voices have frequently been dramatized in the form of monologues, usually with the implication that in dialogue they tend to be drowned out by men's voices and can only speak freely in solitude. Each of the three 'idiots' represents a different role for women at a particular time, characterized by distinctive codes of language, dress, and mannerisms: the 'mystique of femininity' in the 1950s, the 'liberated woman' of the late 1960s and 1970s, the working woman of the 1980s. They all find that they have no control over their roles, and that whatever they do, the relationships and institutions work against them, damaging their minds and their bodies.

In both these plays, Falcón's strategy seems to be one of deliberate provocation. The situations are exaggerated, virtually all men are egotistical oppressors, and the female protagonists are often annoyingly gullible and helpless, naively giving their men the benefit of the doubt, allowing themselves to be used and betrayed, with the result that neither male nor female spectators are offered characters with whom they can comfortably identify. They are encouraged to focus on the discourses and structures more than the individual experiences, and are challenged to change their own attitudes and circumstances even if the characters in the plays are unable to do so.

Paradoxically in 1981 Falcón, as a literary critic for the feminist magazine *Poder y libertad* (*Power and Freedom*), had lambasted Rosa Montero and Montserrat Roig for portraying strong men and weak women characterized by insecurity (1981: 23). However, as the above analysis of Falcón's plays demonstrates, texts mediate socio-historical circumstances through particular discursive practices. Whilst the novels criticized may not provide positive role models, they engage with the deconstruction of patriarchal codes. The uncertainty which pervades these texts is perhaps a reflection of the debates taking place around identity during the 1980s. There would seem to have been a generational crisis as young women rejected traditional roles for women but seemed unable to construct new models. Falcón (1981) also criticizes Montero and Roig for mediating women's economic and professional problems through sentimental preoccupations and it could be argued that the introspective, intimate nature of much contemporary writing by women may serve to reconfirm their exclusion from public, social discourse. In Rosa Montero's* narrative men repeatedly attempt to silence women or fail to listen. However, through the use of metafictive techniques in the novels *Crónica del desamor* and *La función delta* (1981: *The Delta Function*), she explores the construction of identity through textual means. Her female narrators break out of passive silence by taking up the position of writing subject. The focus is on the discourses and codes through which experience is structured and readers are challenged, as with Falcón's plays, to reconsider their interpretative strategies both inside and outside the world of fiction.

5.1.2. Challenging codes through fantasy

Whilst Montero, like Martín Gaite, values the acceptance of solitude by women as a tool for self-knowledge and awareness, it can lock women into a solipsistic inner world. This would seem to be the case in Adelaida García Morales's *El silencio de las sirenas* (1985: *The Silence of the Sirens*), winner of the 1985 Herralde Prize. As the title suggests, the narrative space—a village isolated in the mountains of Las Alpujarras—is marked by silence. The reclusive protagonist Elsa has withdrawn to this female space in which the reader only encounters older, village women and the schoolteacher María. Elsa is consumed by an obsessive passion for a man she barely knows. Agustín exists within her imagination and her intense dreams are recounted by the narrator, María, who articulates Elsa's desire through language. When Agustín does communicate with Elsa, it is to express indifference and perhaps fear of her eccentric seduction. However, the sirens of the title are not those who attempted to entice Ulysses. They are the silent sirens of Kafka, alluded to in the novel, who have renounced their seductive call to live outside the symbolic order of language.

Elsa's increasing estrangement from the material world is expressed through her inability to think or speak. When Agustín instructs her to stop writing to him, the tenuous link which binds her to life is severed. Paradoxically, by attempting to withdraw from the symbolic order into an elusive, magical space of female rituals, as personified by the village wisewoman Matilde, she fulfils the expectations proper to a long-standing literary tradition whereby the spurned female lover retreats into insanity and death.

In this novel then, it would seem that the attempt to construct an alternative female subjectivity outside the space bounded by patriarchal discourse fails. However, the fantastic has been taken up by a number of women writers as a contestatory mode of writing or transgressive space in which patriarchal social and cultural structures may be interrogated.[2] The parodic works of Paloma Díaz-Mas and Carmen Gómez Ojea expand upon quests for an alternative women-centred mythopoesis, in which the emphasis is on matrilineage and the female body, in texts such as *Os habla Electra* (1975: *Electra Speaking*) and *Argeo ha muerto, supongo* (1982: *Argeo's Dead, I Suppose*) by Concha Alós, and *O segredo da Pedra Figueira* (1985: *The Secret of Figueira Rock*) by María Xosé Queizán. In the highly intertextual novels *El rapto del Santo Grial* by Díaz-Mas and *Temblor* (1990: *Tremor*) by Rosa Montero, the classical hero myth of the quest is reworked through the simultaneous interrogation of patriarchal plots and proposition of alternative narratives of self. Whilst the setting of the former is clearly the Arthurian legend of the Grail, the latter is ostensibly set in a post-nuclear future. Science fiction may provide an especially fruitful forum for the critical examination of ideologies of gender through the speculative projection of future social and cultural structures. In texts such as *Consecuencias naturales* (1994: *Natural Consequences*) by Elia Barceló the relationship between humans and extraterrestrials is used as an extended metaphor through which contemporary gender stereotypes and codes are critically examined. The seemingly natural division between the sexes is called into question by encounters with alien species such as the Xhroll, who, whilst clearly humanoid in features, cannot be easily categorized by either sex or gender.

[2] For an extended discussion of fantasy and science fiction by Spanish women see Knights (1999).

Fantasy and science fiction are often perjoratively labelled escapist. Yet whilst these genres may be humorous or playful flights into the imagination, they can effectively criticize social and cultural paradigms. Spanish women writers of science fiction have been doubly marginalized as they are often omitted even from specialized anthologies or studies of the field. Saiz Cidoncha (1988) estimates that at any one time 5–6 per cent of authors have been women of which he makes reference to two: Alicia Araujo and María Guera, who co-wrote a series of stories in the early 1970s with her son Arturo Mengotti. Miquel Barceló only cites one work by a Spanish woman writer in his 1990 guide to science fiction: the collection of short stories *Sagrada* (1989: 'Sacred') by Elia Barceló. Indeed, Barceló is the only woman writer of science fiction in Spain to have been recognized by the science fiction establishment through the award of the Premio Ignotus (1991) and Premio Internacional UPC (1993). She has addressed issues of sexuality in stories such as 'Piel' (1989: 'Skin') and 'La Dama Dragón' (1981: 'The Dragon Lady'), and deconstructed patriarchal social and cultural paradigms through the construction of alternative cognitive scenarios in texts such as 'Sagrada' (1981) and *Consecuencias naturales*. These stories in which female protagonists break with the traditional gender stereotypes frequently perpetuated in science fiction have direct antecedents in the work of earlier women writers omitted from the studies of Saiz Cidoncha and Barceló (1990). By painstaking investigation through back issues of the science fiction magazine *Nueva dimensión* (*New Dimension*), of various fanzines such as *Kandama*, *Maser*, and *Zikkurath*, and anthologies of Spanish science fiction, Dolores Robles Moreno of the Biblioteca de Mujeres in Madrid has been able to catalogue the work of women writers of science fiction in Spain from the 1960s onwards. This enables readers to locate works such as Alicia Araujo's 'El hijo de la ciencia' (1967: 'The Child of Science'), a dystopic vision of the incursion of genetic engineering into childbirth, and Teresa Inglés's 'Complemento: Un hombre' (1970: 'Complement: A Man'), which uses parodic inversion to critique contemporary, patriarchal social structures by depicting future Earth as a matriarchy in which men have assumed traditionally feminine characteristics.

This critical silencing of women's voices is not restricted to science fiction but was noted in the editorial of a special edition of the literary journal *Quimera* devoted to twenty Hispanic women writers in 1994 (no. 23), and Catherine Davies (1994) gives numerous examples of masculinist bias in critical works, anthologies, and literary histories published in Spain.

5.2. CHURCH AND STATE

As has already been seen in Chapter 2, it was not only women's identity that was explicitly constructed and constricted through the discourses of the regime in the 1940s and 1950s. Assertive at every level of social activity—government, Church, family, home, school, workplace, leisure activities—a new grammar and lexicon of power was being established which not only intended to rename explicitly the elements of reality but also insistently effaced its 'political' qualities to assert itself as the 'natural' character of Spanish society as writing at many levels, including newspapers and officially sanctioned literature, decrees, broadcasts, and documents of Church and state, stressed the essentialist and unchanging, excluding and subsuming differences.

The Church also represented a visual and emotional language of power which found its way daily onto the pages of the press in the early years of the regime. Public manifestations of spirituality (processions and rallies) were unblushingly identified by the Catholic hierarchy with Franco's campaign, as is recalled, and rehearsed, in *Cataluña con Franco* (see Chapter 2). With its publication date proudly displayed in the traditional manner on the inside page back—27 abril, Festividad de Nuestra Señora de Monserrat (Festival of Our Lady of Monserrat, the Patron Saint of Catalonia, and sentimentally nicknamed La Moreneta, or The Little Dark-Skinned One)—the book emblematically recalls with horror the capture of the image of the Christ of Lepanto by 'Marxistas [que] odiaban lo hermoso, lo bello, lo tradicional ('Marxists [who] hated all things lovely, beautiful, and traditional') and notes with satisfaction the subsequent rescue and repair of the image on 5 March 1939 amid the joy of the crowds; similarly, the reinstallation of the image of 'La Moreneta' is a key moment of proof since the project, the authors note, was offered up and paid for by 'el pueblo catalán' ('the Catalan people'), the event itself buoyed up by 'el fervor popular' ('the fervent enthusiasm of the people') and by the fact that this was 'una de esas bellas ocasiones en que la espiritualidad catalana se aunó a la del resto de España' ('one of those beautiful occasions on which Catalan spirituality united with that of the rest of Spain') (Aguirre et al. 1984: 96). However, even as the relationship between Church and state appeared to be ever more solidly cemented, cracks of dissension continued to appear although most were censored or clandestine in the early years. The five Basque and Catalan bishops who refused to sign the episcopal letter of 1937—despite the widespread repression, including some killings, of priests in those regions by Republican forces— signalled the beginning of a series of oppositional interventions by both high-ranking and grass-roots clergy from these regions throughout the 1950s and early 1960s which fed into the open conflicts of the late 1960s and the 1970s fuelled by the Second Vatican Council.

5.2.1. What is Spain?

Early in the Franco years, nation was redefined as abstract entity above and beyond the people, and the meanings of Spain were altered, both by the immediate destructive past and by current politics, in a process bitterly recognized by writers such as Luis Cernuda in exile: '—¿España?', observes a guest at a gloomy tea party in grey springtime London in the famous and chilling poem of 1939 'Impresión de destierro' ('Exile's Impress'), 'Un nombre. | España ha muerto' (Cernuda 1984: 110) ('Spain? [. . .] A name; no more. | Spain has died'). For others, like Augusto Haupold Gay in 1941, the name of Spain could be constructed quite differently: 'cuando España sea una realidad | de casas levantadas y fábricas en marcha | [. . .] | ya será la Patria que soñábamos | cuando, contra el terror de la noche marxista | rompíamos la aurora de nuestro Arriba España' (in Rodríguez Puértolas 1987: 562) ('when Spain is a reality | with houses built, and factories running | [. . .] | then she will be Our Country as we dreamed | when we fought the dark Marxist night | and broke through to the dawn of this our Risen Spain'). Essayists within Spain took on the task of reconfiguring the name of Spain both directly and discursively. Then Falangist (and later anti-Franco monarchist) Pedro Laín Entralgo's *España como problema* (1949: *Spain as Problem*) picked up on the earlier Generation of 1898's ideas of decay, national essence, and regeneration, only to be rebutted by Rafael Calvo Serer's *España sin problema* (also 1949: *Spain as Problem-Free*), which saw the Civil War and current debates on the construction of an integrated, traditionalist, brave new Spain as the solution. The work of Julián Marías—an active presence still as this book goes to press—and José Luis López Aranguren—an iconic figure of liberalizing Catholicism in the late 1960s—attempted early on to open up Spain, its meanings, and its thinking, both to a past deliberately obliterated and to a European tradition in danger of becoming a victim of state politics and foreign policy. In exile, philosophical writings such as those of María Zambrano, the essays of Max Aub collected in *Hablo como hombre* (1967: *I Speak as a Man*), and on into the next decade the essays of self-exiled Juan Goytisolo all respond to the originary repressive impulses of the early years of the regime, returning again and again to interrogating, denying, reconstructing, and declaring the subject's proof, or 'signs', of identity (as Goytisolo's* famous novel *Señas de identidad* (1969: *Marks of Identity*) encapsulates it (see Abellán 1980b)).

It was not only the terminologies of geopolitics and social organization—Spanishness in those senses—which came under control and under the pressure of new or newly recuperated interpretations in the 1940s and 1950s in Spain. Crucially, and not surprisingly, more abstract ideas also needed changing. Gabriel Arias-Salgado, Secretary for Popular Education and National Delegate for Press and Propaganda in the Ministry of Information and Tourism until 1962, had these thoughts on liberalism and liberty:

Liberarse del liberalismo no es renunciar a la libertad, sino todo lo contrario, ponerse en condiciones de adquirir una libertad más auténtica. Esta libertad más auténtica no es la libertad contra el Estado, sino la libertad en un Estado independiente de los grupos de presión y de la presión de los partidos. (Arias-Salgado 1958: 65)

(To liberate oneself from liberalism is not to renounce liberty. On the contrary, it means to put oneself in a position to gain a more authentic liberty. This more authentic liberty is not freedom against the State, but freedom within a State that is independent of pressure groups and the pressures of party politics.

Liberty, in short, is upheld by authority.

5.3. ANSWERING BACK

From the 1950s to the end of the dictatorship power in its various forms was increasingly subjected to critical analysis. This was set against a continuing effort by the regime to establish the legitimacy and necessity of its role and discourse, and to construct identificatory strategies between itself and the subject interpellated, in Franco's own simplistic, unifying vocative, as 'españoles' ('Spaniards': the characteristic beginning to most of his public speeches).

5.3.1. Authority on stage

In the nonconformist theatre, whether the allusions to contemporary political circumstances are direct or indirect, and whether the focus is on an autocratic individual, an impersonal system of oppression, or the effect of tyranny on its victims, the primary concern is usually the relationship between language and power. Dramatic situations that are often enclosed or isolated, featuring a struggle for dominance or functioning as a microcosm of a hierarchical society, expose the manipulation of language and of other sign systems for exploitative or coercive purposes. Since one of the key sites of such power relationships is the family, some of the issues with which this chapter is concerned have been anticipated in Chapter 4. Here we focus more specifically on political structures and discourses.

Alfonso Sastre's* *Escuadra hacia la muerte* (1952: *Condemned Squad*, first published in 1957) sets up an enclosed, isolated location in which a small group of people is oppressed by a ruthless figure of authority and is driven to rebellion. Here the setting is somewhere in Europe during a third world war. The corporal in charge of a platoon of court-martialled soldiers imposes a brutal, single-minded form of military authority. To some extent he represents institutional power: he merely enforces the orders of remote, unseen superiors. However, although his squad is completely isolated, with nothing to do except wait for a holocaust to break out around them, he still insists on maintaining rigid discipline and pointless routines despite the futility of their suicidal mission (to give early warning from the front line of enemy advances). He evokes a mystique of military values clearly reminiscent of the fanatical conviction of Franco and his collaborators that the ruthless purification and disciplining of Spanish society needed to be pursued well beyond the defeat of the Republican armies. The language combines, in knowing clichés, discipline, *machismo*, asceticism, sacrifice, penitence, and a contempt for intellectualism: 'Un soldado no es más que un hombre que sabe morir [. . .] Es lo único que os queda, morir como hombres' (Sastre 1987: 72) ('A soldier's just a man who knows how to die [. . .] It's all you've got left, to die like men').

A psychological dimension to the corporal's fanaticism emerges, for he too has been court-martialled (for losing control and killing a reluctant recruit in training), and his obsessive authoritarianism seems to serve in part to avoid facing up to the responsibility for murder, which has profound implications for any analogy that may be drawn with the dictatorship: a regime founded on executions displaces its guilt onto the population as a whole. In view of implicit associations such as these, the play's generally hostile treatment of the military, and the soldiers' violent murder of the corporal halfway through, it is perhaps surprising that its première was authorized at all in 1953. The impact was short-lived, however: the production was banned after the third night.

Important as such topical references are, *Escuadra hacia la muerte* explicitly invites broader analogies, beyond the immediate conflict, which itself is not unique; on the front line the men are constantly aware of a huge invisible threat hanging over the entire continent—the possibility that not only they but millions of people could be annihilated at any moment. The frustration of a generation growing up in a country suffering hunger and repression is combined with the fear and hopelessness generated by the Cold War and a general sense of existential anguish, as is expressed by the despairing Javier:

¡Un, dos! ¡Un, dos! Una escuadra hacia la muerte. ¡Un, dos! Lo éramos ya antes de estallar la guerra. Una generación estúpidamente condenada al matadero. Estudiábamos, nos afanábamos por las cosas, y ya estábamos encuadrados en una gigantesca escuadra hacia la muerte. (95)
(Left, right! Left, right! A squad marching towards death. Left, right! That's what we were even before the war broke out. A generation heading stupidly for the slaughterhouse. There we were, studying, chasing after things, and we were already lined up in a gigantic condemned squad.)

However hopeless the metaphysical outlook may be, action is possible in the social sphere. The men rebel against their little dictator and collectively murder him. Revolution is liberating but immediately problematic, since they prove to be incapable of agreeing on a common strategy for dealing with the new situation. Authority held them together and gave them a collective sense of purpose of a kind, but it crushed their individuality and was prepared to sacrifice them without compunction. This necessary rebellion against tyranny is only the beginning: each of the men must seek his own answers to the problems of being, of surviving in a hostile world, and of constructing meaningful relationships with others.

5.3.2. Parodies of power

In the New Theatre* of the 1960s and early 1970s, the peculiarly personal nature of Franco's regime and the absurdity of its rhetorical extremes give rise to satirical caricatures of authority and comic interrogations of the obsessions and contradictions of dictatorship. Many of these pieces were banned or restricted to minority venues, since the references they make to the *Caudillo* or to the structures and ideology of his regime are not very subtly coded. In any case, the point of symbolic or allegorical modes of representation was usually less to do with camouflaging political opposition or direct attacks on the regime than with deliberate provocation and an aspiration to construct universal metaphors of power.

José Ruibal's* *El hombre y la mosca* (1968: *The Man and the Fly*, first staged in New York in 1974) is an elaborate allegory of absolute power's obsession with self-perpetuation. The set itself is of primary symbolic importance: an impregnable glass dome built amid a devastated landscape by a dictator as a monument to total victory, resting on the skulls of his defeated enemies. The dictator turns a younger man into his double to succeed him and perpetuate the system, but the double turns out to be incapable of inspiring the fear that has sustained the regime. The kind of manipulation carried out by Franco's regime of terms such as *Patria*, peace, revolution, and reconciliation is hilariously parodied: 'Por eso yo defiendo violentamente la paz. ¡Corrocotocó! Palomas, palomitas con pistolas al cinto. Una paloma dentro de un tanque. ¡Corrocotocó! Una paloma con una granada en el pico, ¡corrocotocó!' (Ruibal 1977: 53) ('That's why I defend peace with violence.

Coo cooo! Doves, little doves with pistols in their belts. A dove driving a tank. Coo cooo! A dove with a grenade in its beak, coo cooo!'). This power is highly personal, but at the same time is shown to be an elaborate ideological system.

One of the most complex theatrical explorations of the discourses and obsessions of political, patriarchal, and religious power is the extraordinary *El desván de los machos y el sótano de las hembras* (*Males in the Attic, Females in the Basement*, 1974) by Luis Riaza.* Don, feudal lord of an archaic domain with his crony Boni, constructs an elaborate set of myths, games, and rituals designed to celebrate, legitimize, and perpetuate his power. He uses his children—Ti Prans, the anaemic little prince under the bed upstairs, and Leidi, the female downstairs whose authentic fertility is the only threat to the regime—in repeated ceremonies of feigned marriage, birth, death, succession, and resurrection savouring his own eternal self-succession. The control of sexuality, reproduction, and gender identity, and the manipulation of their language and symbols, are shown to be essential parts of the functioning of power. The patriarch even takes control of childbirth, appropriating the roles of mother and creator—begetter and bearer of all beings, originator of all History, all myths, and of language itself.

In the context of a decay to which both Franco and his regime seemed blind, *El desván de los machos* can be read as a topical political parody. However, its deconstructive rampage through the psychology, mythology, semiotics, and even obstetrics of power is ultimately less concerned with the immediacy of a coded attack on the dictatorship than with relationships of political control and the manipulation of symbols.

5.3.3. *Painting the walls: graffiti*

Increasingly, as the Franco regime faltered and was superseded, language itself is constituted as a site of rebellion, with sets of terms and modes of representation being reclaimed (usually from the right by the left), and old rhetoric being interrogated and emptied out. This was happening, literally, on the streets as well as in print. In the wake of the events of 1968 language took more obviously political forms on the streets, as graffiti (or *pintadas*) inscribed on walls and doorways, and later, as marches and demonstrations became more possible, slogans on banners and flyers. The execution of Julián

Grimau, the Burgos trial, the '1001', the executions of 27 September 1975, and the assassination of Admiral Carrero Blanco all gave rise to outbreaks of what one member of the last Franco administration preferred to call, with euphemistic pomposity, 'expresiones gráficas' (graphic expressions), that is, graffiti. The authorized slogans of the regime, in their proper places, already existed all over Spain—FRANCO SÍ—COMUNISMO NO, VIVA FRANCO—ARRIBA ESPAÑA, JOSÉ ANTONIO PRESENTE (Franco Yes—Communism No, Long Live Franco—Spain Onwards and Upwards, José Antonio [Primo De Rivera] Present among Us)—alongside the lists of the fallen Nationalist heroes of the locality. Before 1975 these might simply be erased or defaced by those in opposition (though at considerable personal risk). Once walls began to be written on, the state and local authorities, along with ultra-rightists, also made use of the strategy of erasure; and the right and ultra-right were able to build on their heritage: ARRIBA FRANCO—LA ETA AL CARAJO (Franco Onwards and Upwards—ETA Straight to Hell), CURAS ROJOS NO (No to Commie Priests), FRANCO PRESENTE R.I.P. (Franco Present among Us, R.I.P.). A long tradition of Noes and Yeses is of interest too: NO A LA DICTADURA VATICANA (No Dictatorship by the Vatican), NO MÁS MUERTOS (No More Deaths) on the one side; and no to reform, change, political parties, and yes to the army on the other side; and, metaphorically astride the wall, REY SI PERO NO (Yes to the King, But No) (Sampere 1977: 154–64). As well as constructing a direct language of resistance through their contestatory content alone—and their calls for amnesties, freedom, rights, and consultation—the left and the alternative left modified publicly displayed texts large and small (alterations to advertising hoardings, the addition of the word Libertad to No Right Turn signs, crossing out the Free/Occupied labels on toilet doors to leave just Free, crossing out rightist slogans and crossing out crossings out, writing in Basque and Catalan, and resurrecting long-suppressed terminologies and ideas (54–86)). The alternative left added a new vocabulary altogether, with sources in liberal Europe and the USA: CULTIVA TU PROPIA HIERBA—A LA MIERDA LOS INTERMEDIARIOS (Grow your Own Grass—Cut out the Middle Man); FOLLA PERO SEGURO—UTILIZA ANTICONCEPTIVOS (Screw, But Safely—Use a Condom); FOLLEU, FOLLEU, QU'EL MON S'ACABA (Screw, Screw, For the End of the World is Nigh); and LIBERTÉ, ÉGALITÉ, Y STRIPTEASE. Or, with the sharp value-reversing ironic humour of specific political moments, in wry satisfaction at Franco's death, DIOS EXISTE (God Exists); and, in an echo of the right-wing bourgeois lament that things were better under Franco, but also a comment on continuing poor standards of living, CON FELIPE II VIVIAMOS MEJOR (Things Were Better under Felipe II) (176–8).

5.3.4. Power in print: non-literary publications

New contestatory languages in print were the immediate consequence of Manuel Fraga Iribarne's desire, through his liberalizations leading up to the Press Law of 1966, to find '[los] cauces idóneos a través de los cuales sea posible canalizar debidamente las aspiraciones de todos los grupos sociales, alrededor de los cuales gira la convivencia nacional' (in Barrera y Barro 1995: 96) ('[the] ideal channels through which appropriately to direct the aspirations of all social groups, and around which to articulate a national consensus'). The Christian humanist language of non-rightist Catholic publications of the 1950s (¡Tú!, or Ecclesia), and discourses around the term 'normalización' (appearing frequently, for example, in the opinion columns of Pueblo from the mid-1950s to the mid-1960s), had already begun to stand against the legacy of the hegemonic language of the national Falangist newspaper Arriba, as had, from another perspective, the monarchist ABC. In an echo of the layering of erasure and reinstatement on the streets Cuadernos para el diálogo's progressive Christian Democrat stance and incorporation of the debates of the Second Vatican Council provoked the issue in May 1968 (of all times) of a short-lived (Falangist) rival Cuadernos para el monólogo (Sketchbook for Monologue) and an editorial headline from Arriba in March 1969 'Cuadernos para el garrotazo' (substituting 'garrotte' for 'dialogue'). The inclusion in the magazine's first editorial (in March 1963) of the word 'distintas' ('different') applied to beliefs, feelings, and ideas added more than just a drop to the flow of pluralism in the channels of Fraga's diffuse metaphor; Spain was placed, once more, in European and Latin American intellectual and cultural contexts; being a Catholic was a matter of the 1960s, not of the 1940s, nor of the imperial Golden Age.

Cultural and literary supplements, and regular columns on abstract or small-scale topical issues in the daily press, played crucial roles both on the one hand in blocking the flow of new ideas and on the other in further opening Spain's reading classes to ideas from outside, and, in the second half of the 1960s, from exile returnees. The columnists of the conservative press had frequent recourse to the cosy, clear, yet stultifying details of life in the (often gingerly and briefly visited) villages of Spain or of middle-class leisure (as indeed still do many of the columnists of the once progressive *El país*: regular contributor Manuel Vicent is especially, though not uniquely, prone to superfluous rhapsodies on menus and sunny days).[3] Literary review pages, not least perhaps because prominently serviced by university professors, looked backwards and inwards, and when outwards usually with the chief concern to re-identify world classics and to mark anniversaries with due *politesse* and display of cultured sensibility. On its own terms, the most intellectual of the conservative press, *ABC*, has maintained in its cultural pages a powerful—for some still the authoritative—framework of values for the testing of ideas and literary works along the lines just described; but in the 1960s it, the more liberal *La vanguardia de España*, and the newspapers of Editorial Católica had to contend with the phenomenon of a leftist cultural press of ever-widening readership and genuinely new ideas. *Informaciones* was especially influential in addressing the impact and potential of new theories (semiotics, structuralism), disciplines (sociology, psychoanalysis), and genres (fantasy, science fiction, magic realism, the thriller), as well as the literatures of Catalonia, Galicia, and, to a lesser extent, the Basque Country.

5.4. AGAINST THE PSOE

From its victory of 1982 and in a context of hegemony, the PSOE constructed its own distinctive discourses of power and control. From the unorthodox right Sánchez Dragó (1995: 15) sought to revive an old debate:

¿España, por enésima vez, como problema? Pero, sí [. . .] Y más que nunca, caballeros [. . .] Son ellos—los ilustrados, los felipistas, los putisocialistas,

---

[3] For a selection of revealing pieces in this and other styles from *ABC* in the 1940s and 1950s see Balleste (1955), particularly Rafael Calvo Serer on Orihuela and its surrounds (better than anywhere in Europe and uniting past and present), Francisco de Cossío on Toledo (ineffable and eternal), and Víctor de la Serna on Madrid (as essentially a peasant city) (72–5, 106–8, and 435–8).

los modernos, los europeizantes—quienes nos han conducido a este callejón del gato aparentemente sin salida.
(Spain as a problem, for the umpteenth time? Well, yes [. . .] And more so than ever, gentlemen [. . .] It is they—the enlightened intellectuals, the Felipe-ites, the socialist lab-whore-ites, the moderns, the Europeanizers—who have led us up this apparently blind cat-piss alley.)

More continent, but more damaging, were dissenting voices in columns in the liberal press by writers such as Vicente Molina Foix, Antonio Gala, Rosa Montero, and Francisco Umbral who were able—in the cases of Montero and Umbral thanks to an apprenticeship in subversion under Franco—to parody and oppose the themes, tactics, and buzzwords of post-Francoism. Comparing Prime Minister Felipe González's mode of speech with the impersonal and impenetrable language of all institutions, Umbral (1996: 92-7) wryly suggests that his long-windedness and cultivation of Andalusian pronunciation and turns of phrase means that 'estamos siendo gobernados por un acento regional. La gente sale emocionada' (94) ('we are being governed by a regional accent. Everyone is left deeply moved'): truth and deceit cease to matter, emotion is all, and opposition leader José María Aznar with his dry, curt Castilian way of speaking cannot compete (94). But institutional language persists, and González's contribution, towards the end of the PSOE's last mandate, has come to nothing: 'no trata de convencer. Trata de fascinar [. . .] renovó las palabras de la tribu, pero nada más. La tribu hoy ya no le vota' (97) ('he does not try to convince. He tries to fascinate. [. . .] He gave new life to the language of the people, but no more than that. And the people are no longer voting for him').

Rosa Montero* is one of a number of influential journalists associated by the public with the development of a democratic press during the Transition through her work with *El país* as both a writer and editor. From its inception in 1976 *El país* was seen to have a pro-PSOE editorial line. However, in the early 1990s she was openly challenging the discourses of democracy invoked by the PSOE to legitimize their position and defend themselves against accusations of corruption. She accused the PSOE of an anti-democratic abuse of power and of looking to the ghosts of the past instead of constructing a valid future for Spain (Fontradona 1995: 32). In particular she singled out their demonizing of two institutions she deems fundamental to a democratic system: an independent judiciary and press.

These issues are clearly engaged with in her most recent novel to date, *La hija del caníbal* (*The Cannibal's Daughter*), which won the Premio Primavera de la Novela in 1997. In this blackly comical thriller the failures of the left in both past and present come together through the interwoven stories of the kidnapping of Ramón, a civil servant, in the present day and the narration by Félix, an anarchist in his eighties, of his youthful (mis)adventures with Durruti in the 1920s. The three main protagonists, Ramón's wife Lucía and her neighbours Félix and Adrián, meet a variety of marginal characters involved with criminal activities, primarily in Madrid, but also in Amsterdam. The kidnapping turns out to be an elaborate scam involving corrupt civil servants, government ministers, and police officers which is being investigated by the seemingly incorruptible judge María Marina. None of the characters is innocent and it becomes increasingly difficult to decipher what is real in a novel in which the main narrator, Lucía, openly admits to deliberately lying to the reader and characters repeatedly swap or conceal their identities. It is a novel of betrayal and maturity which examines how a forty-something comes to terms with a loss of ideals. Lucía's situation is comparable to that of a generation of Spaniards who had identified with the progressive, oppositional ideology of the PSOE now being rocked by a series of corruption scandals and revelations implicating leading PSOE figures in the activities of the GAL counter-terrorist death squads.

In *Tonto, MUERTO, BASTARDO e invisible* (1995: *Stupid, DEAD, ILLEGITIMATE, and Invisible*) by Juan José Millás, the criticism of contemporary socialist values is more direct in the frequent, corrosively sarcastic attacks on 'socialdemocracia' by the first person narrator, Jesús. Social democracy is equated with standardization to a corporate model in which individuals no longer smoke or take milk and sugar with their coffee; corrupt government ministers encourage privatization, and profit from EC subsidies and cheap Third World labour; older executives are discarded to make way for ambitious youths for whom stress is a competitive advantage. To summarize, it is a hypocritical ideology which is characterized as 'la única filosofía de la vida que permite hacer todo lo contrario de lo que predica en nombre de lo que predica' (Millás 1996: 219) ('the only philosophy which allows you to do the opposite of what it preaches in the name of what it preaches'). When Jesús loses his job after devising the perfect employee profile which unfortunately he does not fit, he gradually transforms the world around him into an oneiric, interior universe in which he takes on the characteristics of the title—originally attributed to the character Olegario in the bedtime stories he tells his son—in multiple versions of himself. Everyday life becomes an artificial imaginary construct which he had previously assumed as a 'social democratic prosthesis' (1996: 176). The novel continually calls into question what is real by focusing on how individuals are interpellated through a set of ideological practices. As it concludes the narrator draws attention to the constructedness of his own account which is teasingly dismissed in the final line as possibly no more than an elusive mirage, a drug-induced hallucination whilst he enjoys a 'dose of reality' (1996: 241) by screwing an Oriental hooker who is simultaneously in Malaysia and Madrid.

The monolithic power structures and their languages of the Franco era had given way, then, not to a new era of liberation but to new configurations of power and rhetoric. Just as the old alliance of Church and state had been undermined, initially covertly, through a range of textual strategies and clandestine organization, and later in open rebellion, so the new regime's promises of democratic empowerment were questioned in a now nominally free press and new forms of writing (which will be discussed in greater detail in Chapter 8). By the 1990s, however, power is understood less as a relationship of oppression and resistance than as a complex network of self- and social construction in which the discourse of resistance may itself be complicit in reproducing the dominant order.

Further reading

Brooksbank Jones (1997); Brown (1991); Davies (1998); Gracia (1996: 9–67); Pérez (1988).

6
Languages of Silence

6.1. KEEPING IT QUIET

The preceding chapters have examined ways in which dominant discourses are imposed, exposed, or transcended. This chapter begins by looking at the silences and suppressions that lie behind them during the Franco years, and in particular examines the peculiar workings of official censorship and its effects on writers and publications at different moments in this period; but the chapter is concerned, too, with other forms of silencing and exclusion and writers' responses to these. Although the transition to democracy brought the recuperation of previously silenced voices and the return of exiled writers, many forms of writing were initially implicated in tricky processes of negotiation and compromise; under the PSOE, controls of certain media (Anson et al.: 1996) and the formation through policy of a dominant cultural discourse brought their own suppressions; and by the 1990s an appearance of openness and pluralism is contradicted by voices which remain stifled, ignored, or without an instrumental language as well as by those which paradoxically challenge through silence.

Juan Goytisolo's* powerful essay 'In memoriam F.F.B.', dated 25 November 1975, uses legal, penal, psychological, and medical terminologies to make clear the extent of the effects of the regime of Franco ('F.F.B.'), who is, in the essay, '[un] personaje cuya sombra ha pesado sobre mi destino con mucha mayor fuerza que mi propio padre' (Goytisolo 1997: 306) ('[a] character whose shadow has hung over my destiny with more weight and force than my own father's'):

Junto a la censura promovida por él, su régimen creaba algo peor: un sistema de autocensura y atrofia espiritual que ha condenado a los españoles al arte sinuoso de escribir y leer entre líneas [. . .] Por experiencia propia sé que me fueron precisos grandes esfuerzos para eliminar de mi fuero interior un huésped inoportuno: el policía que se había colado dentro sin que aparentemente nadie le hubiera invitado a ello. (305)

(As well as the censorship which he promoted, his regime created something worse: a system of self-censorship and spiritual atrophy which has condemned Spaniards to the squirming art of writing and reading between the lines [. . .] I know from my own experience that I had to make great efforts to eliminate from the domain of my own self an inopportune guest: the policeman who had slipped in without, apparently, anyone inviting him to do so.)

Self-censorship is something 'incluida en el mecanismo del alma' ('embedded in the mechanisms of the soul'), a mutilating Super-Ego, relieved of which Spanish writers will one day feel a vertiginous, disturbing sense of freedom (305).

6.1.1. Antonio Buero Vallejo and Alfonso Sastre: posibilismo *and* imposibilismo

The prickly debate that arose in 1960 between the playwrights Antonio Buero Vallejo* and Alfonso Sastre* offers interesting insights on the different strategies adopted by writers to deal with the stifling effects of censorship. Sastre published an article in *Primer acto* responding to suggestions that his work was *imposibilista*—deliberately provoking censorship but thereby condemning itself to sterility. In it he characterizes Buero as advocating 'un teatro posible' which accepts the need to make certain sacrifices in order to say as much as is possible within the prevailing system, and Alfonso Paso—a former fellow experimentalist now turned commercial success—as engaging in a pact with a conservative public and the rules of the theatrical establishment which, though comfortably pragmatic, prevented the playwright from contributing from outside the mainstream to the struggle for positive change in the theatre and in society at large. Sastre's message to Buero is that the distinction between *posibilismo* and *imposibilismo* is false; to enter into dialogue with censorship is to accept its legitimacy, and no sacrifice or compromise for the sake of accommodating oneself to the system is worthwhile, since the system itself is contradictory, unpredictable, and bound to change: while there is no such thing, therefore, as 'impossible theatre' since the definitions keep shifting, nevertheless, 'hay, eso sí, un teatro momentáneamente "imposibilitado" ' (in García Lorenzo 1980: 113) ('What certainly does happen is that theatre is "made impossible" at particular moments').

But what Buero means by *imposibilismo* is the deliberate selection of language, images, or subjects likely to be banned—to make a tactical point rather than because they are essential to the work in hand. Writers must operate in the real world and communicate with real audiences, aiming to make 'impossible' theatre possible (121). Pushing at the limits of what is possible is more constructive than uncompromisingly provoking the suppression of one's work. Finally, Sastre emphasized the subtleties of the problem by postulating, along the lines of the dialectical method of 'Socratic ignorance', a kind of 'ironic freedom': 'No hay esa libertad, pero hagamos de algún modo como si la hubiera, con lo que podemos llegar a saber en qué medida no la hay y, de esa forma, luchar por conquistarla' (129) ('There is no such freedom, but we should behave in some sense as if there were, so as to be able to determine the extent to which it does not exist and be in a better position to struggle to achieve it').

Inevitably, Sastre's plays were regularly banned (but enjoyed a kind of underground cult status), while Buero became a master of the art of negotiating with the censors to get his plays onto major stages with as much of his wording as possible retained. His first play, *Historia de una escalera* (1949: *Story of a Staircase*), is a model of significant understatement. The setting is dingy and confined, the action is banal, the only important events occur offstage; twenty years pass between the second act (set in 1929) and the third, yet little has changed and no one directly mentions the war. While the mere fact of suggesting, however tentatively, that contemporary Spanish society was dominated by tedium, deprivation, and frustrated aspirations was important, the play's impact in 1949 also had a great deal to do with its silences, with what is not said out loud. The tensions, disillusionments, and repetitions that dog the relationships between the characters are implicitly related to developments in society outside, yet these links are never made explicit. Under the surface of the mundane drama of failed personal relationships, there is a whole society that ends up frustrated and inarticulate. The form of the play is a crucial component of the way in which the text itself embodies the difficulty of speaking openly. Its setting, characters, and tone initially suggest the very familiar conventions of the *sainete* (a one-act comic play, often with music and usually set in a working-class environment), yet these expectations are overturned: there is little comedy, no tidy resolution or happy ending, and the historical perspective, however underplayed, is uncharacteristic of this essentially ahistorical genre. The implication seems to be that the predictable formula of the *sainete* is the only permissible means of expression, used self-consciously and as if in despair: it cannot be transformed into anything radically different, but the refusal to fulfil the normal expectations of the genre constitutes a subtle form of defamiliarization, prompting the audience to ask themselves what the ultimate point is. The censors who approved the text for performance in 1949 assumed that the mismatch between apparent genre and actual content could only be seen as a failure by most spectators and were unable to foresee how successful and influential it would be (Neuschäfer 1994: 328).

Twenty years later, Buero's prestige was such that censors had to take into account the fact that banning any of his works was likely to attract unwelcome attention. The records of their lengthy deliberations on *El sueño de la razón* (*The Sleep of Reason*, approved in December 1969) show the discourse of censorship becoming more sophisticated, weighing up the consequences of its actions in terms of public relations. The play is based upon a conflict between Francisco de Goya and King Fernando VII. The Black Paintings on Goya's walls are interpreted as oblique but powerful symbolic expressions of despair, isolation, and protest, the product of circumstances in which freedom of expression is severely restricted as well as of the deaf artist's own struggle to communicate. The monsters that emerge when reason sleeps are (politically) the horrors of despotism and (psychologically) the ravings of a madman, but they are also the creative discoveries of genius, made more powerful by the very obstacles they push against. The censors in 1969 were alert to the possibility of analogies being drawn between *El sueño de la razón* and the political circumstances of the present, but concluded that a ban would only be likely to validate and draw attention to such parallels (Neuschäfer 1994: 332). There was one occasion on which Sastre, frustrated at the banning of several of his works, successfully camouflaged a politically sensitive play—and apparently regretted it. *La mordaza* (1954: *The Gag*) is a powerful protest against censorship itself, represented as the product of the need of tyrannical power to conceal the guilty secrets of its origins. However, various details of plot and setting deliberately obscure possible analogies with post-war Spain. The text was approved for performance without amendments and generated little controversy, leaving the author disappointed that the disguise had been so successful. The protagonist, Isaías Krappo, presides over his household with a mixture of brute force and contempt for the others' weakness. When a stranger—a former collaborator—arrives in the middle of the night threatening to avenge the deaths of his wife and daughter in the war, Isaías Krappo murders him without compunction. His daughter-in-law (Luisa) witnesses the murder and informs the rest of the family. Isaías becomes even more tyrannical, bullying them all into silence, regarding the killing as equivalent to those everyone was obliged to carry out in wartime, legitimized by victory.

Sastre's plays often show that oppression works only for as long as its victims are intimidated or persuaded to put up with it. The significance of this family conflict as an analogy for a nation living in fearful silence, not daring to denounce the continuing violence on which an unjust peace is founded, is made clear by Luisa:

Hay silencio en la casa. Parece como si no ocurriera nada por dentro, como si todos estuviéramos tranquilos y fuéramos felices. Ésta es una casa sin disgustos, sin voces de desesperación, sin gritos de angustia o de furia . . . Entonces, ¿es que no ocurre nada? [. . .] Esa mordaza nos ahoga y algún día va a ser preciso hablar, gritar . . ., si es que ese día nos quedan fuerzas. . . Y ese día va a ser un día de ira y de sangre . . . (Sastre 1987: 173)

(There's silence in this house. It's as if there was nothing happening here at all, as if we were all calm and happy. No one upsets anyone else in this house, no one voices their desperation, no one cries out in anguish or rage . . . Is that it then, is nothing happening here? [. . .] The gag's suffocating us and one day we're going to have to speak out, to shout . . ., if we've still got the strength when the day comes . . . and that day's going to be a day of blood and fury . . .)

Finally, Luisa denounces the old man to the police and liberates the family. However, as in all Sastre's plays, the overthrow of tyranny is not a definitive solution in itself. Liberation is problematic, difficult to deal with individually and collectively. Luisa, the mother, and her sons are left feeling relieved but guilty and start to imagine a new life without the patriarch, a simple normality based on co-operation and mutual respect, working and living together 'como si la vida hubiera empezado hoy' (191) ('as if life had just begun today').

6.1.2. José Ruibal: refusing to co-operate

Sastre was not alone in arguing against making compromises for the sake of ensuring publication or performance. Some of the playwrights of the avant-garde *nuevo teatro* (New Theatre) made a virtue of the marginalization imposed on them by censorship and the conservatism of the theatrical establishment. In any case, alternative means of disseminating their work (of less concern to the censors since audiences were usually small) were opening up: a circuit of theatre festivals and prizes, the loose network of the *teatro independiente* (Independent Theatre) seeking different audiences and trying out new venues and working methods, a few productions in US universities. José Ruibal, writing in 1976, recalls that from the beginning (the mid-1950s) he was aware that his work would be rejected in Spain, both 'administratively' and by conventional companies and audiences. He makes clear that this has not been primarily to do with direct reference to current political realities, a function he attributes to a 'testimonial' (usually realist) type of theatre, banned when it is most relevant, then irrelevant when it is no longer banned. His symbolic approach was not merely a means of encoding political protest during the dictatorship in the hope of fooling the censors; if this had been the intention, greater deviousness would have been required. Since the aim is to construct 'poetic' representations of processes and discourses which remain meaningful beyond a particular set of historical circumstances, a certain distance—partly enforced and partly self-imposed—from those circumstances and from the theatrical mainstream is artistically productive (in Ruibal's case, the distance has also been physical—he has worked in Argentina and the USA). Thanks in part to interest in his work from outside Spain, by the late 1960s Ruibal had become sufficiently well known to receive a commission for a new play from the Ministry of Information and Tourism (in a liberalizing mood under Manuel Fraga), but he could not resist kicking the gift horse in the mouth. In the event, *La máquina de pedir* (1969: *The Begging Machine*) was not staged, partly because Fraga was replaced by the hard-liner Alfredo Sánchez Bella and partly because of the nature of the play: wildly extravagant staging (a huge octopus giving birth to petrol tankers, robots, video screens), bizarre language and symbolism, and cryptically subversive messages about capitalism and authoritarianism.

6.1.3. Cinco horas con Mario *(1966): a silence more eloquent than words*

It is arguable that the pressures of censorship could indeed in some cases have the effect of stimulating creativity and sharpening expressions of dissent, with subterfuge turning out to be a more effective form of resistance than open confrontation, as in the case of *Cinco horas con Mario* (1966: *Five Hours with Mario*) by Miguel Delibes (see Neuschäfer 1994: 12, 100–15).

Delibes's novel looks back over the life together of a frustrated and mismatched couple: Mario, a schoolteacher and aspiring writer with liberal opinions and an interest in the new socially conscious Catholicism of the 1960s, and Carmen, unquestioningly traditionalist in her religion and her attitudes towards marriage and social class. The most interesting and distinctive structural feature of the text is that it consists largely of a monologue spoken by Carmen to her dead husband. It is therefore the voice of the conformist that predominates, while the tentatively dissident Mario remains silent throughout. Delibes has stated that he originally intended to have both characters express their own points of view but decided against this when he thought of the obstacles that would be put in the way by the censors (Neuschäfer 1994: 327). What began as a compromise turns out to be a brilliantly effective literary device, since the more than two hundred pages in which Carmen pours out her reminiscences, recriminations, and confessions give her world-view more than enough rope with which rhetorically to hang itself. Through a mass of received ideas and half-understood fragments of National Catholic ideology, she and the Spain she represents are exposed as small-minded, selfish, bigoted, hypocritical, and reactionary, while her crudely caricatured versions of Mario's ideas ironically allow an alternative discourse to emerge—open-minded, humane, progressive, scrupulous, and idealistic. The censor's report recommending approval shows little sign of awareness of this fundamental irony and appears to take Carmen at face value: 'Representa la conciencia de su clase social modesta y sana' (Neuschäfer 1994: 327) ('She represents the mentality of her modest, wholesome social class'). Although on balance the text implicitly invests Mario with moral superiority, the opposition between the two world-views is not a simplistic one. Carmen can be seen as a frustrated victim of her upbringing, and is appealing as a literary construction: the language of her monologue is vividly colloquial and often unintentionally funny; repetitive and full of clichés yet paradoxically inventive. Mario emerges as rather dull and earnest, perhaps unrealistic, perhaps intellectually arrogant. At the end, their son articulates a desire to supersede Manichaean divisions, to leave the past behind and look towards the future: '¡Los buenos a la derecha y los malos a la izquierda! Eso os enseñaron, ¿verdad que sí? Pero vosotros preferís aceptarlo sin más, antes que tomaros la molestia de miraros por dentro. Todos somos buenos y malos, mamá. Las dos cosas a un tiempo' (Delibes 1977: 290) ('The good people on the right and the evil people on the left! That's what they taught you, isn't it? But you prefer just to accept it, rather than taking the trouble to look inside yourselves. We're all good and bad, mum. Both things at once').

6.2. POETRY OF EXILE AND ABSENCE

If on the one hand, for some sensibilities, exile and its concomitant introspections was to exacerbate a reclusive and 'pure', anti-realist strain in Spanish poetry (as in the cases of Juan Ramón Jiménez and Pedro Salinas), or an elegiac mode, as in the case of Emilio Prados, on the other hand, the realities of survival in exile, the amplifying effects of political and personal frustration, and new perspectives on the problems of Spain afforded by contact with foreign cultures militated against disinterested introspection, aestheticism, or abstraction. It is worth bearing in mind for a moment, however, the persistence of the non-committed voice in poetry, and its formative power. The posthumous publication in 1964 of an extended re-edition of Jiménez's *Dios deseado y deseante* (*God Desired and Desiring*: first published in 1949)—a bridge to the Spain that was—may have seemed to mark the end of the long and brilliant elaboration of Spanish *poesía pura* (abstract writing with its focus on ideal forms and intense, refined emotional response), but elements of it persist in (and beyond) poems in the period by José Ángel Valente, and (within Spain) Carlos Bousoño and Francisco Brines (although these latter two inject more pain and anecdote than Jiménez ever would). Some poets, back in the late 1930s, had left Spain in verbal fighting spirit suddenly to find imposed—or simply find inside—a voice more personal than public, like Rafael Alberti, with the war poems of *Capital de la gloria* (1939: *The Capital of Glory*) behind him and a turn to elegiac, nostalgic poetry in front of him (at its peak in *Retornos de lo vivo lejano* (1952: *Distant Lives Return*)). Others found the tone of resistance and the topics of exile thrust upon them and were still, in some senses, 'pure' poets. Cernuda's elegiac tone in *Las nubes* (1940: *The Clouds*)[1] is pointed up by anger, restricted (and thus intensified) images of violence and death, and a striking (because isolated) directness: 'Ellos, los vencedores | Caínes sempiternos, | De todo me arrancaron. | Me dejan el destierro' (Cernuda 1984: 126) ('The victors, | those eternal Cains, | ripped me away from all I knew. | And leave me exile.'). An earlier Surrealist style and the continuing metaphysical and philosophical strain in his writing are both disrupted by the events and state of exile and in subsequent volumes (forming part of *La realidad y el deseo, Reality and Desire*: in four expanding editions to 1964), recollection, a sense of rupture, and the 'traces' as Ugarte (1989: 179) puts it, 'of things from another time and place' are a constant, if not of course the only, feature of Cernuda's writing, as Harris (1973) for one makes clear. One such set of traces is the cultural, and particularly the liberal literary, production of the past. This is evoked in the poem 'Díptico español' ('A Spanish Diptych') from *Desolación de la quimera* (1964) and represents a better, ideal Spain, paradoxically 'Más real y entresoñada que la otra' ('More real and more dreamed of than that other'): 'No ésa, mas aquélla es hoy tu tierra' ('It's not the latter but the former which today is home to you') (Cernuda 1984: 158). The destiny and task of the poet is to register the effects of the paradoxical positioning both inevitably within and irremediably outside Spain; but not only Spain, since what Cernuda is also, and perhaps principally, concerned with here is the larger issue of being, as Villena has put it (1984: 30), 'no sólo un desterrado de su país material, sino un exilado en el mundo [. . .] porque todo poeta [. . .] pertenece a un orbe más perfecto y más alto, a un mundo más puro' ('not only exiled from his physical homeland but in exile from the world [. . .] since every poet [. . .] belongs to a higher and more perfect sphere, a purer world'). Thus for Cernuda the

[1] For English translations of selected poems see Gibbons (1977).

personal circumstances of exile are subsumed into Romantic and proto-Platonic notions of the unattainability of and yet faith in a metaphorical place, a place of language or forms or images, where wholeness, purity, and belonging are sealed together by the fulfilment of spiritual desire, as has long been the theme of critical writings on him. Yet art, idealizations, and books do not bridge the distance or heal a divided self: in the same volume, Cernuda feels cut off from—or wishing to be cut off from—contemporary Spanish writing which, he says, he never reads (just as what he writes is never read, or properly read, by the countrymen the poem 'A mis paisanos' is dedicated to):

> soy, sin tierra y sin gente,
> Escritor bien extraño; sujeto quedo aún más que otros
> Al viento del olvido que, cuando sopla, mata. (208)

(With neither homeland nor a people, I | am indeed a strange writer; left more exposed than others | To the wind of oblivion which, when it blows, kills.)

For León Felipe, on the other hand, despite his vivid awareness and muted representation of the violence of the Spanish conflict and the divisive cruelty of war and injustice—all epitomized in the title as well as played out in the texts of his pessimistic *El hacha* (1939: *The Axe*)—there is the brave and challenging affirmation that the exiled poets had taken with them poetry, 'the song', itself, thus leaving those behind in fact the marginalized and disempowered ones. Later, in 'Ángeles' (1965: 'Angels'), the power of poetry is still located, though from a different historical perspective, among the exiled. The poet forcefully notes the change from one manner of writing to another (in similar terms to the Chilean Pablo Neruda in his post-Spanish Civil War period): refuting he was ever a 'romantic poet', Felipe insists he is, rather, 'mezquino' ('meanspirited'), continuing to be indebted to 'todos; | los ilustres e innominados refugiados españoles | muertos en el destierro' (in Rubio and Falcó 1981: 168) ('all | you illustrious, unnamed, Spanish refugees, | dead in exile').

The processes of grief in the wake of the Civil War, involving personal loss through violent death, the loss of ideals, territorial exile, and ruptures within communities and families, find memorable encapsulation and perpetuation in poetry of the 1940s and 1950s. Dionisio Ridruejo's *Elegías* (*Elegies*: 1945) offer a rare example of inner exile on the right (he had written in July 1942 to Franco expressing his total disagreement with his policies and also resigned his political posts and membership of the Movement) and forge a strong sense of lost opportunities and of a wide-ranging poetic voice cut off from its sustaining contexts. Leopoldo Panero's *Escrito a cada instante* (1949: *Written at Every Moment*) has poems (some of which appeared in *Escorial* and *Espadaña* among other journals) where quiet, solitude, shadow, and prayer are recurrent; solitude is, as for Blas de Otero, the absence or incomprehensibility of God in 'Tú que andas sobre la nieve' ('You Who Walk the Snow') or 'Casi roto de ti' ('All But Broken for You'); or, in a long poem to Federico García Lorca, 'España hasta los huesos' (Panero 1973: 199–207) ('Spain in the Very Bones'), solitude is a way of connecting with the dead poet, his quest for the impossible truth, his celebration of 'la soledad hermosa | de España' (204), and 'la luz, la fresca luz de tus palabras, | tan heridas de sombra . . .' (207) ('the light, the bright fresh light of your words, | words so cut through by shadow'):

> El dolor español de haber nacido;
> la pena convencida y española
> de abrir los ojos a la seca brisa
> que cruje en la memoria. (201)

(The Spanish agony at being born; | the fully felt and Spanish grief | of opening ones eyes to the dry breeze | which crackles in the memory.)

6.2.1. *Purity and impurity*

In poetry in the 1950s and 1960s a symptomatic debate arose between writers stung into social and political commitment by the particular historical circumstances of Spain (like Blas de Otero, gradually developing from a quietly religious poetry into an angrily prophetic mode), and those defending the right of poetry to represent subtle feeling, moral rather than social complexities, transcendent values, and the autonomy of the individual. In Madrid in 1950, in the literary journals *Ínsula* and *Espadaña* a set of aphorisms by Vicente Aleixandre had famously made the linkage between poetry and communicability (Riera 1988: 151–2), recapitulating a debate which in the years immediately preceding the Civil War had crystallized briefly around notions of pure poetry (the refined elaboration of subtlety, aesthetic values, and a dialogue with the legacies of European Symbolism) and impure poetry (tapping raw mental energies, constructing a politics of writing, and entering into dialogue with Marxism and Surrealism). In the contexts of metropolitan and middle-class Barcelona, a related debate around the origin and aims of poetry, and whether these were sited in 'conocimiento' or 'comunicación' ('knowledge' or 'communicability'), brought into focus the finer detail of difference and sameness in strategies of silence and resistance. The apparent polarities of social and private, political and 'artistic', 'conocimiento' and 'comunicación' are soon revealed to be highly provisional and flexible in journalistic interventions and speeches by Jaime Gil de Biedma, Carlos Barral, Enrique Badosa, and, into the 1960s, José Ángel Valente and Claudio Rodríguez (Riera 1988: 158–62). Gil de Biedma's* poetry of the 1950s and 1960s has an everyday realism, attention to sharp personal memories and feelings, and a tone which is at once acute and colloquial; and yet it communicates knowledge of a world made strange and senseless by time's destructive passage (Jiménez 1998: 113), as in the poem 'Noche triste de octubre, 1959' ('Sad October Night, 1959') where the cruel rain washes grain, old shoes, and protest petitions all together down to the sea (Gil de Biedma 1998: 43–4). When Barral published in the journal *Laye* in 1953 a piece entitled 'Poesía no es comunicación' ('Poetry is not communication') it was to defend 'la autonomía del momento creativo' ('the autonomy of the creative moment') from ignorance and neglect at the hands of talk about intelligibility (Riera 1988: 152–3); his *Metropolitano* (1957) is hermetic and highly allusive poetry (some of it requiring the poet's own notes for its elucidation), but he was also famed for his friendships and connections with such straight-talking dissenters as Gil de Biedma, Juan Marsé, and Ángel González.

The term 'comunicación' had anyway come from a poet, Aleixandre, of considerable verbal obscurity and affective complexity and had already acquired a set of connotations which led beyond mere plain speaking (which corresponded more to the aspirations of the 'social' poets*). In 1952 a seminal essay by Carlos Bousoño, *Teoría de la expresión poética* (*A Theory of Poetic Expression*), talked of poetry as '[la] comunicación establecida con meras palabras, de un contenido psíquico-afectivo conceptual, conocido por el espíritu formando un todo, una síntesis' (in Riera 1988: 152) ('the communication through mere words of a psycho-affective and conceptual meaning which is recognized by the spirit and formed into a whole, a synthesis'). This adventurously anti-rational, provisional, semi-definition can be heard to have resonance in Bousoño's own poetry, as also in that of Francisco Brines—another member of what Olivio Jiménez (1964) decisively named the group of *Poetas del Tiempo* (Poets of Time). The elegiac yet sensual existentialism of *Las brasas* (*Embers*) published in 1960, and the classicizing discourse of *Materia narrativa inexacta* (*Inexact Material for a Story*) of 1965, carefully construct, along traditional post-Romantic lines, a set of approximations to an ideal, textualized, ultimate Truth based on the contemplation of (often fictionalized) personal experience. Brines may be seen as a heroic rebel, yet serene, resigned, and controlled, confronting the transient world with the written word (Jiménez 1964: 20–1, 454–5). He places the accent on the work of poetry as an act of discovery, and on its transcendence (Debicki 1982: 9); this poetry, with its 'tendency to relate individual concerns to larger patterns of life, and not just to the issues of one society or one political moment' (11), represents a significant site of coalescence of the coded and the transparent, the evasive and the purposeful. In these writers a sharply contoured, alternative moral and emotional reality is carved meticulously out of the materials of intellectual life in Spain in spite of anger, frustration, and opposition. Addressing his fictional interlocutor, but also his reader, in 1966, in *Palabras a la oscuridad* (*Words into the Darkness*) Brines offers a justificatory epitome of this poetry of indirect communication founded on a knowledge more individualistic and philosophical than common and political:

> Tú me comprendes con dificultad,
> pero sabes también
> que es suficiente mi dolor,
> y por eso me lees.
> (Brines 1984: 60)

(You find me difficult to understand, | but you also know | that my pain suffices, | and so read on.)

6.2.2. *The poetics of silence*

In poetry of the 1960s to 1980s, using coded language and evasive forms takes on the proportions of an obsession, shifting attention from the socio-political to the aesthetic and linguistic sphere. Guillermo Carnero, Pere Gimferrer, Carlos Sahagún, and Jaime Siles produce, at various stages of their careers, a radically textual poetry which either homes in on the self-sufficient poetic sign with a minimum of reference to the unmediated material world or constructs a space as crowded with cultural allusions as it is conformed by elaborate patterns of sound, line, stanza, and blank paper. As much as it is a reaction to the *poesía social* of the preceding decade such writing is a return to the modernist cult of the image and the admiration for the complexity of certain manifestations of poetry of the seventeenth century (most famously, that by Luis de Góngora) which underlay the most prominent poetry of the Generation of 1927. It represents a continuation of an extremely refined style of self-reflexive, highly abstract poetic writing most arrestingly exemplified in two volumes first published in 1949, Jiménez's *Dios deseado y deseante* and Pedro Salinas's *Todo más claro y otros poemas* (*All is Clearer, and Other Poems*) (to which Gabriel Celaya's *De claro en claro* is in a way a riposte).

Guillermo Carnero's* poetry moves between two tendencies—the aestheticist and the minimalist—and as Bousoño has noted, is a continually self-questioning meditation on poetic language and on the distorting effects of words (1983: 62); more particularly, in the 1967 *Dibujo de la muerte* (*A Sketch of Death*) metalinguistic and metapoetic strategies are deployed rebelliously, along with a radical aestheticism, to challenge hegemonic discourses (or 'el Poder', as Bousoño has it: 27–8). Like Luis Cernuda before him and Luis Antonio de Villena after him, Carnero looks to canonical works of art and architecture, myths, and historical events of Renaissance or Imperial Rome for signs of precious beauty or melancholy and often perverse, violent symptoms of death and decline. Even the cathedral at Burgos is aestheticized and made subtly decadent: although 'Amanecer en Burgos' (Carnero 1983: 82) begins with 'el silencio de los claustros' ('the silence of the cloisters') and ends with 'el armonioso vuelo de la piedra, elevado | en muda catarata de dolor' ('the harmonious flight of stone, raised up | in a muted cataract of pain') (in conceits not far removed from those of the style of the official poetry of the early 1940s, as we have seen in Chapter 2), that 'muda catarata' is made perversely impure by the insistence in the body of the poem on the fascination of death, faded glories, rotting corpses:

Andrajos y oro
el esplendor revelan de los cuerpos antiguos.
Entre imágenes de lejana belleza, piadosamente se oculta
la carne muerta.

(Rags and gilding | reveal the splendour of those ancient bodies. | Amid images of distant beauty, the dead flesh | is piously concealed.)

This vision of the austere and historically coded place is in symptomatic extreme contrast to ex-Falangist Rafael García Serrano's later memories (1985: 85) of mass there in 1936, where the cathedral is 'viva, palpitante [. . .] confortante' ('living, palpitating [. . .] comforting'), the site of 'la fe sólida de la Edad Media' ('the solid faith of the Middle Ages'), where God and only God is perceived, and as such a place which is free of all thoughts of art and beauty.

Carnero's *Variaciones y figuras sobre un tema de La Bruyère* (*Variations and Figures on a Theme from La Bruyère*) of 1974, in its self-conscious and explicit emphasis on the analysis of poetic discourse, moves on from the dense textures of artistic and anecdotic allusion towards an abstract apprehension of emotional experience based around considerations of 'el posible objeto del poema: lo intratable | por otros formas de saber' ('possibly the poem's objective: that which cannot be dealt with | in other forms of knowledge'), of the poem as 'enigma', and of the way a word used in this venture gravitates 'no hacia el significado sino hacia el signo mismo' (Carnero 1983: 181) ('not towards the signified but towards the sign itself'). The poet 'camina por un tiempo vacío, | espectador de formas y volúmenes | entre presencias que no ve' (195) ('walks through empty time, | the spectactor of a show of forms and volumes | amid presences he cannot see').

Such anti-realist preoccupations with unsayability, invisibility, and ultimate meaninglessness persisted into the 1980s to become not now reactions to *poesía social* or *poesía de combate* (Poetry of Struggle) but a counterpoint to the extremely worldly and image-laden poetry of the *novísimos** and *posnovísimos*. The Catalan poet Pere Gimferrer* speaks arrestingly of how 'el tema de las apariciones | es el tema del yo' (in Palomero 1987: 305–6) ('this theme of apparitions | is the theme of the self') and of 'fulgores invisibles, | que siento en un vacío de visibilidad' ('invisible brilliances, | which I sense in a void of visibility') in a poem from the 1982 collection *Apariciones y otros poemas* (*Apparitions and*

Other Poems). Jaime Siles in *Columnae* (poems written between 1982 and 1985) is austerely exciting in his devotion to unknowability and ineffability. 'Palimpsesto' ends in 'sones, signos, emblemas | de sí mismos, lenguaje, | negación: el poema' (Siles 1992: 189) ('Sounds, signs, emblems | of themselves, language, | negation: the poem').

While the poets discussed above moved, largely, from the aesthetically heavily laden to a more austere language of silence or scepticism, the poetry of José Ángel Valente* shows a movement towards radical abstraction from a different starting point, that of a commitment to finding a controlled but colloquial voice in which to address others plainly but forcefully on issues existential, national historical, or spiritual—in *A modo de esperanza* (*By Way of Hope*) and *Poemas a Lázaro* (*Poems to Lazarus*) of 1955 and 1960 respectively. He moves towards a position, in his later writing—*El fulgor* (*Brilliance*) of 1984 and *Al dios del lugar* (*To the God of This Place*) of 1989—where 'La poesía no sólo no es comunicación; es, antes que nada o mucho antes de que pueda llegar a ser comunicación, incomunicación' (Valente 1992: 11) ('Poetry not only is not communication, it is before anything else or long before it can aspire to be communication, the lack of it'). In the original collection *Material memoria* (*Material Memory*) of 1979 the terse poem 'Palabra' ('Word'), dedicated to the literary philosopher María Zambrano, begins with the notion of

>   Palabra
>   hecha de nada.
>
>   Rama
>   en el aire vacío. (21)

(Word | made of nothingness. | Branch | in the empty air.)

Ten years on, in *Al dios del lugar*, comes the sense that,

>   Conviene [. . .]
>   no asomarse a la Historia con banderas
>   como si la Historia existiese en algún reino,
>
>   caer del aire, disolverse como
>   si nunca hubieras existido. (225)

(It is best [. . .] | not to come to History with flags to hand | as if History ever occupied a realm at all, | to fall from the air, dissolving | as if you never did exist.)

It was, though, possible to come to History from both the intimate, abstract and the extrovert, practical positions. Julia Otxoa* (perhaps with less time on her hands for metaphysics than the men) writes in *Centauro* (1989) poems which deplore violence, post-industrial greed, and ecological irresponsibility, but she also leaves aside social reference and collective concerns to assert that 'A veces, insistir en la razón no basta, | es necesario trazar un ámbito de fuego' (46) ('At times it's not enough to insist on reason, | you have to trace a boundary of fire'); 'Sólo se puede escribir con fiebre, | [. . .] | sólo unas córneas heridas, | en las que cabe el mundo, pueden' (47) (also in Benegas and Munárriz 1997: 176) ('You can only write in the heat of fever, | [. . .] | only the cornea wounded and with the world inside will serve'). The realm of blazing fire and a world which fits in the gleam of an eye are, as well as being (if obliquely and unintentionally) strong testimonies to feminism's exhortations to productive anger, the stuff of *poesía pura*. So too is the strategy, in the manner of Pedro Salinas, of writing erotic verse in which the human object of desire is intermittently confused with poetry (or the expression of beauty) itself. This is taken up in the poems 'Tú, el incendiado' (49) ('You, Set Ablaze'), 'Nadie te ha visto, ni conoce tu nombre' (51; also in Benegas and Munárriz 1997: 177) ('No One Has Seen You or Knows your Name'), and 'Como cascada de luz definitiva' (52–3) ('Like a Cascade of Defining Light').

In these various ways imposed silences become concentrations of contemplative power, and imagination flares up in acts of micro-resistance and the idealistic hopes of the pure poets of earlier years are unexpectedly fulfilled, their spheres of operation extended into proliferating political arenas.

Further reading

Abellán (1980b); Debicki (1982); Ilie (1980); Neuschäfer (1994).

7
Getting a Sense of Reality

7.1. POWER AND REALITY

Earlier chapters have shown the extent to which the Francoist state sought to control ideas and promote a permanent culture of conservatism, and have discussed writings that contribute to this project alongside others that resist it. This chapter will relate these processes to particular forms of representation: ways of perceiving and constructing reality. An important implication of the regime's insistence on authority, national destiny, and the supremacy of Catholic values was that 'reality' was not a category to be investigated or problematized, but to be defined and fixed by the authorities, directly through censorship and control of education and publishing, and indirectly through general pressure to conform to a conservative status quo. In such a context, the ideological implications of apparently purely formal questions come forcefully to the surface, sharpening aesthetic debates about realism, abstraction, and experimentalism.

7.2. VERSIONS OF REALISM

Until recently, conventional literary histories have tended to compress a wide variety of texts produced in the 1950s to mid-1970s into a putative evolutionary scheme, from an early tentative realism (1950s) to a more openly critical realism (late 1950s to mid-1960s) with a strand of initially revisionist and finally anti-realist writing (early 1960s onwards) giving way to yet another new realism in the 1980s. This picture—originally heavily dependent on the writings of the Catalan critic Josep María Castellet and writer-critic Juan Goytisolo—is one which now needs revision.

Castellet's interventions in the Barcelona review *Laye* (an official publication sponsored by the Ministry of Education), reworked and supplemented in what became the critical bible of the new realism—*La hora del lector* (1957: *Readers' Time*)—are the most visible sign of a theoretical debate which opened up a new space for discussion of realism and the role of writing in Spain in the 1950s. Instead of looking back at debates of the 1930s amongst committed writers like Sender*, César Arconada, and Andrés Carranque de Ríos around Soviet socialist realism, Castellet draws on the work of the French existentialist writer and philosopher-critic Jean-Paul Sartre *Qu'est-ce que la littérature?* (*What Is Literature?*: published in Spanish by Losada in 1950) in order to argue for a politically committed ('engagé') writing which would reveal social injustice in a pared down, 'objective' style which would supposedly permit readers the freedom to develop their own reaction to the situation depicted. This writing would move beyond what he unfairly characterized as the unselfconscious didacticism of nineteenth-century Spanish realists like Benito Pérez Galdós[1] and the unacceptable subjectivism of modernism. In Castellet's language, the writer becomes an 'obrero' (manual worker) who is paradoxically both crucial to the text in his active social concern yet self-effacing in narrative terms. Castellet also attempts to negotiate a further tension between the exhortation to 'modernize' and the appeal to a historical Hispanic realist tradition, invoking selected US realists (particularly Faulkner, whose profile was raised by his Nobel Prize in 1950 and who was more widely available in Spain than Hemingway or Dos Passos who had influenced the pre-war social novelists) and the Italian neo-realist Cesare Zattini (see Jordan 1990: 84–128). *Laye* was but one site of debate of these issues. Informal meetings, congresses, and dispersed interventions, many articulated by the Spanish Communist Party project known informally as 'Operación Realismo' ('Operation Realism') in which context the poetry of Gabriel Celaya and the essays of Alfonso Sastre should be read, were also important. The journals *Ínsula* and *Acento cultural* (of Falangist affiliation), and especially *Destino* and the *Revista española,* were all important focuses for the many-sided debates on what was becoming steadily fixed in the term 'realismo social' ('social realism'), an often misleading amalgam of neo-realism (in the roughest terms, non-political and looking back to Galdós) and social

---

[1] For a clear introduction to thinking on Galdós's realism see Labanyi (1993).

realism (more inflected by the political urgencies of the 1940s and 1950s in Spain and Europe). The *Revista española* gave particular impulse to a booming production of short stories, by Ignacio Aldecoa, Josefina Rodríguez, and Jesús Fernández Santos* (all discussed in Jordan 1990: 66–83), in which may be discerned both realist currents, while *Destino*, like *Ínsula*, was an important channel for explorations of North American realisms. The powerful moral explorations of recent and contemporary Spanish history and the dilemmas of the individual in Francisco Ayala's *Los usurpadores* and *La cabeza del cordero* (both 1949: *The Usurpers* and *The Sheep's Head*) brought further weight, from exile, to this renewal of a venerable tradition in Spanish literary history (Baquero Goyanes 1992).

One strand in a growing commercial market for narrative writing is represented by the short-story writers mentioned above, along with National Literature Prize winners Jorge Campos (for *Tiempo pasado* (1955: *Time Past*)) and Daniel Sueiro (for *Los conspiradores* (1959: *The Conspirators*)), Medardo Fraile, and Lauro Olmo; another (also exploited in the short stories) came out of the 1940s tradition of writing about the immediate, traumatic past, and that was the commercially less successful but intellectually more exciting new tradition of social realist writing. Although the clearest Spanish examples of social realism proper are usually considered to be a string of late 1950s novels such as Jesús López Pacheco's *Central eléctrica* (1958: *The Power Station*), Antonio Ferres's *La piqueta* (1959: *Demolition*), and, particularly, working-class Communist Party member Armando López Salinas's *La mina* (1959: *The Mine*), the broader termed 'novela social' ('social novel') is usually traced back to Jesús Fernández Santos's *Los bravos* (1954). Dubbed *novela social* or *cívica* partly to waylay the censor, this writing was promoted by Castellet in *La hora del lector* (*Readers' Time*) (1957), and by the publisher Carlos Barral. Both would later denounce the writers' failure to produce a 'proletarian' rather than 'anti-bourgeois' novel and their inability to play a role in stimulating new kinds of realism.

The *tremendismo** of the 1940s persisted in aspects of the highly successful bourgeois realist narratives of Juan Antonio de Zunzunegui and particularly in those of Ángel María de Lera (*Los clarines del miedo* (*The Bugle Notes of Fear*) of 1958 is a late sign of the persistence of this writing); at the level of even easier reading, in the news weekly *El caso* reports knowingly combine *tremendismo*, court-room drama, forensic police story, and plain prurience (see, for a classic example, *El caso* 1952). The continuing success in the 1950s of this mode of writing is due perhaps, as Barrero Pérez (1992: 62) suggests, to the need for the (moderate) thrill of a violence disallowed on stage (although the plays of Pemán do their best to oblige) and cinema screen. Further continuity with the immediate past is represented by narrative writing from a committed Catholic perspective shifting from the affirmative and sometimes triumphalist to an interrogatory, existential mode (as also in much poetry of the period, such as that of Blas de Otero): José Luis Martín Descalzo's *La frontera de Dios* (1957: *God's Frontier*), another Nadal Prize winner, mingles a pared-down, sporadically semi-experimental narrative of poverty on the land with an account of the role of faith (including the cult of miracles) and of a non-doctrinaire, humane ministry in small communities.

An important strand of humanist narrative whose authors began publishing in the 1940s, enjoyed critical and market success in the 1950s, and are still selling today includes the rural Catalonian novels of Sebastián Juan Arbó (who won the Nadal Prize in 1949) and Miguel Delibes's* (b. 1920) existentialist-inflected writing which celebrates rural culture and questions urban notions of progress, while exposing poverty and injustice; he shifts in this decade from the overtly didactic narration (reminiscent of nineteenth-century realism) of *La sombra del ciprés es alargada* (1948: *The Long Shadow of the Cypress Tree*) (the 1947 Nadal Prize winner), through the dialectical narration of *El camino* (1950: *The Road*),[2] to a progressively purified and lyrical style in which the narrator virtually disappears, as in *Las ratas* (1962). Delibes's *Los santos inocentes* (1982: *April Fools/The Holy Innocents*) frequently makes it into the top 100 most read books in the newspaper surveys. Existentialist traces persisted in urban writers like Cela* and Laforet,* whose *La familia de Pascual Duarte* and *Nada* had indirectly challenged the regime's version of reality in the 1940s, the first in a subtle reworking of the picaresque tradition, with complex levels of narration, the second in its rewriting of Gothic and fairy-tale romance, contrasting versions of key events

---

[2] For an English translation see Delibes (1961).

and the dual narration of the younger and older Andrea which challenged the monolithic vision of the regime with regard to truth and history. Both were subsumed at the time under the label of *tremendismo*, although Laforet's *Nada* bears little resemblance to its main features. Cela mockingly rejected the label as applied to *La colmena* (1951: *The Hive*),[3] despite the fact that the novel, actually completed in 1945, is stylistically closer to his earlier work. In that *tremendismo* was likened to the nineteenth-century Naturalism of Zola and his imitators (denigrated as coarse neo-realism in comparison to complex and ironic works of Spanish writers like Galdós, Pardo Bazán, and Clarín) as well as to the *esperpentos* created by Valle-Inclán, to the *picaresque* tradition, and to Francisco de Quevedo's satires, traces certainly remain on Cela's text.

7.2.1. *Urban and rural realities:* La colmena *and* Los bravos

Sex, starvation, and a climate of suspicion are the ingredients which earned *La colmena* the moral opprobrium of both government and Church censors, but, circulating clandestinely, it quickly gained critical approval from figures like Dámaso Alonso. Set in 1942, it represents post-war Madrid as a grim, alienating 'beehive' in which most of its characters, drawn from the working classes and a bourgeoisie fallen on hard times, struggle to scrape or hustle a living, through prostitution, black marketeering, speculation, menial or tedious jobs with rare moments of pleasure or escape. Tuberculosis, exacerbated by miserable living conditions, orphans brought up by the oldest sister, desperate solitude juxtaposed with the stress and exhaustion of family life on the poverty line appear in brief vignettes (ranging from a third of a page to just over a page in length) like the cells of a beehive, communicated through snatches of dialogue, sardonic narration, with frequent interventions by the narrator and dark humour. The compressed, mostly anonymous spaces (doña Rosa's cafe and the house of Suárez, a homosexual character, are exceptions which bring some of the disparate figures together) and timescale (three or four days and nights) contribute to the claustrophobia generated by raw memories of the war (some characters have been in prison or had relatives

---

[3] For an English translation see Cela (1953).

who were killed by firing squad) and a general climate of fear which flares up in the face of sudden political insults or threats. The domineering café owner, doña Rosa, calls her waiters 'rojos' (literally 'reds': 'Communist pigs'); a client in the café threatens to reveal how another one voted in 1936. Influenced by Dos Passos's attempts to portray collective protagonism (in novels like *Manhattan Transfer*) to break with the individual heroes and heroines of bourgeois realist forms, Cela creates a vision of post-war Madrid seething with life: the novel is unique, in its time, for attempting to represent a collective protagonist with its multiple micro-portraits of post-war citizens of Madrid, most of them impoverished. Even the few more well-to-do and powerful figures who relish their position are, however, submerged in 'abulia' (apathy) and atomized conformism, only rarely relieved by examples of affection, loyalty, and love. The ending brings, nonetheless, both unexpected solidarity (as several characters try to warn the writer Martín Marco that he is in danger), and a surprisingly upbeat coda from Martín. While *La colmena* is credited with inaugurating a trend in novels with collective protagonists—beginning the following year with Luis Romero's *La noria* (*The Waterwheel*)—and of inspiring a range of writers grappling with the desire to represent the realities of Francoist Spain, stylistically his impact was less important than that of a novel published three years later by the then unknown author Jesús Fernández Santos, one of a group of friends, including Carmen Martín Gaite, Ana María Matute, Rafael Sánchez Ferlosio, and Ignacio Aldecoa, who met while at university, discussed their work in *tertulias* (informal literary gatherings), and gradually gained a profile in the 1950s.

Neither a great commercial nor critical success in its time, Fernández Santos's *Los bravos* (1954: *The Brave*) is nonetheless important in the development of the so-called *novela social* (social novel) in a number of ways. Shifting narrative away from the war, it focuses on the hardship of daily life in rural Spain; its sparse, objectivist narration has minimal action and is free of any picturesque *costumbrista* touches. Drawing on Fernández Santos's experience in the Escuela Oficial de Cine, it eschews chapter breaks and its narrative is sequenced like a film, a narrative trend which would intensify in Spanish writing in the late 1950s and 1960s. Set in an unnamed Leonese village on the border with Asturias, it centres on the displacement of the landowner by a young doctor from the city who eventually occupies his house and establishes a love affair with his mistress. Alienated from the other villages when his medical ethics lead him to treat and protect an itinerant swindler, he becomes an ambivalent figure: does he represent a more progressive new order for the village or a new form of oppression? Ultimately this unresolved issue is less important than the skilful individuation of its range of rural characters, the subtle, indirect critique of social injustice, and its contextualization of current hardship in the references to more prosperous times when villagers would migrate (to Mexico) not merely to survive but to make their fortune. The novel therefore goes beyond the supposedly simple, apolitical, presentation of reality to avoid censorship which still characterizes literary historical categorizing of this whole group of writers (Martínez Cachero 1997: 172–3).

If we ignore these labels, we can see very different kinds of writing in two other novels published in 1954. *Pequeño teatro* (*Minor Drama*), by Santos's fellow group member Matute,* set in one of the peripheral spaces—here, a Basque fishing village—which characterize her writing, uses the trope of the *commedia dell'arte*, a dramatic denouement, and heightened, lyrical language to explore the struggles of individuals in oppressive social relationships, particularly the ambivalence experienced by the female protagonist Zazu at the loss of self which she attributes to heterosexual love as opposed to the autonomy of her (implied) sexual promiscuity. The second, *Juegos de manos* (*Sleights of Hand*), by a member of a new generation, Juan Goytisolo, actually addresses the issue of political commitment directly in its storyline and is an attack on the bourgeoisie rather than a portrait of working-class conditions. Jordan (1990: 131–7) points out the complete lack of the verisimilitude which was considered key to the social novel and the relative complexity of its fragmented structure and frequent time-shifts, accentuated in his following novel *Duelo en el paraíso* (1955: *Duel in Paradise*).[4] This makes significant demands on the reader, although they barely presage the turn his writing would take in the late 1960s.

7.2.2. *Beyond the kitchen sink:* El Jarama

The kind of realism represented by *Los bravos* can be traced instead to a text which brings together rural and urban reality,

---

[4] For an English translation see Goytisolo (1958).

although its own status in the 1950s as the epitome of objectivist narration has been critically modified in important ways, Rafael Sánchez Ferlosio's 1955 Nadal prizewinning *El Jarama* (1956: *The Jarama*). The novel, savagely criticized by the influential critic Juan Luis Alborg (1958: 312) as 'una epopeya de la vulgaridad' ('an epic of the commonplace') and denounced in the Barcelona newspaper *Solidaridad nacional* as an insult to the heroic Hispanic narrative tradition (Martínez Cachero 1997: 193), received a warmer response from other writers and the reading public in its efforts to represent the lives of both working-class urban youth and a primarily older generation of rural dwellers, largely manual workers, small businessmen, or unemployed. Influenced variously by Italian neo-realist cinema, the French *nouveau roman* and North American writers like Faulkner, *El Jarama* offers a complex reading experience in which 'generational and communicational gaps [. . .] are the means by which the novel probes certain themes: the nature of class society in post-Civil War Spain as well as the role of popular memory and the value of historical consciousness' (Jordan 1990: 162–3). While the textual predominance of skilfully rendered dialogue and almost total confinement of the narrative to what is seen or heard suggests the neo-Naturalist 'objetivismo' (objectivism) theorized by Castellet and Juan Goytisolo amongst others, this is undercut in a number of ways. The novel opens with 'Describiré' ('I will describe'), a statement which cannot be attributed to any character in the novel, thus foregrounding the act of narration. Furthermore, much of this passage and the one which closes the novel is extracts from a geography manual, and the stark contrast at the end between the emotions of both young and old at the death by drowning of Luci, one of the group of Madrid friends out for a day by the river, and the dispassionate tone of the geographer suggests a further subtle questioning—whether conscious or unconscious—of objective realism.

While the geographical text provides authority for the novel's claims to realist authenticity of setting, it also creates a sense of the novel as 'but an insertion [. . .] in the interminable life-cycle and historical flow of the river' (Jordan 1990: 163). This itself evokes a long Hispanic tradition of writing from the fifteenth-century poet Jorge Manrique's famous couplets on the death of his father to Antonio Machado's *Campos de Castilla* which has interpreted the Heraclitan vision evoked in the quote from Leonardo da Vinci which prefaces the novel. Thus Luci's death in the river might set readers searching for further, symbolic meaning (Riley 1976: 124), form part of the creation of a mythical discourse which subsumes the historical (Labanyi 1989: 47–8), or, more simply, bring together the older generation which fought in the Civil War and the alienated working-class youth of Madrid, for whom the deaths at the bloody battle waged in February 1937 during Franco's bid to take Madrid now take on a historical and a personal meaning which shocks them out of the eternal present in which they are locked (Jordan 1990: 168).

Moreover, the resignation, political indifference, and anxious pursuit of brief pleasures to break the monotony of the work-driven existence of the majority of the young daytrippers, the fatalism of the older, rural characters, the bureaucratic approach of officialdom to Luci's death, all give way to a tentative renewal of optimism and struggle in the figure who has embodied the embittered, sceptical observer throughout: Lucio. An unemployed Republican who was imprisoned in the Ocaña concentration camp just after the Civil War and was then cheated by his business partner, he spends most of the novel seated in the same spot but ends it deciding to go for an opening as a part-time baker, the profession he pursued before the war, and gains physical and symbolic release in prolonged urination, counterposing the human flow of History to the mythic timelessness of the river. Rather than reproducing the stasis of Francoist Spain, out of a desire to maintain rural culture in the face of Francoist capitalist modernization, as Labanyi proposes (1989: 47), therefore, *El Jarama* both represents and critiques it.

7.3. FROM REALISM TO ANTI-REALISM?

Juan Goytisolo's *Problemas de la novela* (1959: *Problems of the Novel*), mostly published as separate articles in *Destino*, with its call for committed writing that would expose injustice, and Juan Benet's *La inspiración y el estilo* (1965: *Inspiration and Style*), which called on writers to 'inventar la realidad' ('invent reality'), are usually cited as signposts of an important shift in emphasis from realism to anti-realism during this period. Yet, as we saw above, Goytisolo's* early writing focuses not on the socially, economically, and politically marginalized but on the (albeit disaffected and quietly traumatized) children of prosperous Nationalist families in *Juegos de manos* and *Duelo en el paraíso*. However, *La resaca* (1959: *Aftermath*) focuses on the Andalusian migrant underclass in Barcelona whose poverty and deprivation is represented as impelling them to take refuge in fantasy, narrated in the documentary form advocated by Goytisolo at the time, while the hypocrisy of the Catholic Church and the Catalonians' bigoted and uncharitable treatment of the Andalusians is critiqued through descriptive tone and situation rather than overt authorial comment. *La resaca* marked only a temporary move into a recognizable form of the 'social novel' since Goytisolo was already becoming aware of what he described in an interview as the impossibility of representing reality objectively. There are two further complicating overlaps in the flawed story of transition from realism to anti- or multi-perspectival realism: Alfonso Sastre published his own realist manifesto as late as 1968 when Goytisolo had already embarked on a radical stylistic and political adventure in a trilogy of new novels which we shall be exploring in Chapter 8; lastly, much of the writing of the 1950s—like *La colmena* itself, but particularly writing by women such as Laforet, Matute, Martín Gaite, Elena Quiroga, Mercedes Salisachs, and Elena Soriano—does not fit neatly into 'objectivism'. Moreover, as Jo Labanyi has argued (1989: 43–5), the realist aims of many writers in the 1950s are undercut by 'an underlying mythical vision' which, although it inverts the terms of the prevailing nationalist ideology, effectively paralyses the processes of Spanish history in cyclical patterns of an unchanging 'destiny', idealizing as 'Paradise Lost' that which the regime regarded as 'The Fall' (44).

While the theorizing of social realism gradually acquired critical hegemony, a number of texts were published during the decade which testify to the strong public demand for other kinds of writing. Two of the most successful writers were Ignacio Agustí and Zunzunegui, a contemporary of the Generation of 1927 who continued on the avant-garde narrative adventure of Ramón Gómez de la Serna, studding his texts with sharp, quirky, aphorism, but also producing novels in the bourgeois realist tradition of the nineteenth century and adapting the magic realism of the Italian writer Massimo Bontempelli. Zunzunegui had earlier dismissed *tremendismo* as 'muy vieja' ('old hat') (Martínez Cachero 1997:

147) and continued to tread his own path in the 1950s. Towards the end of the decade, Miguel Buñuel's poetic or fantastic realism similarly reveals the influence of Gómez de la Serna, with traces of Saint-Exupéry in the complex, playful, and lyrical *Narciso bajo las aguas* (1959: *Underwater Narcissus*) while Juan Perucho and Álvaro Cunqueiro continued to produce fantastic texts, with Cunqueiro receiving the Critics' Prize for *Las crónicas del sochantre* (1959: *The Chronicles of the Cantor*). Finally, a less popular but pivotal novel, Luis Goytisolo's *Las afueras* (1958: *City's Edge*), is notable in making a complex (anti-realist) structure underpin the representation of a progressive rural alternative to the capitalist development undertaken by the Francoist regime, without either condemning rural culture to obliteration or freezing it in a nostalgic evocation of the past, thus avoiding two pitfalls of the decade's dominant narrative forms.

7.3.1. The empire strikes back: the Latin American 'boom'

A further element which challenges the conventional notion of evolution in Spanish writing of the 1960s is the impact of a renewed interest in Latin American writing in a process in which the publisher Barral and Spanish literary prizes, particularly the Biblioteca Breve, played a crucial role in the promotion of what became known as the Latin American 'boom'. In reality, rather than a sudden boom, this was an intensification of long-standing intellectual links, in sustaining which *Cuadernos hispanoamericanos* among others played a key role, and a development of publishing interests which had existed in both France and Spain throughout the century. Only a selection of writers became household names in Spain in the period between the publication of Vargas Llosa's *La ciudad y los perros* (1963: *The City and the Dogs*; Biblioteca Breve Prize 1962) and the peak of the boom in the 1970s, partly due to the influence of Barral's taste, partly to the unconscious remnants of the status of Latin America as a colonial possession, constructed as an exotic 'other' to a supposedly rational, ordered European Spain. While this difference now worked to the advantage of some writers, whose linguistic ebullience and intense subject matter was contrasted by critics, in reviews like *Ínsula* and *Destino*, with the aesthetic limitations of Spanish objectivist writing, it also locked Latin American writing into a 'magic realist' ghetto, sidelining the cerebral short stories of Borges, for example, or the laconic narratives of the Uruguayan Onetti whom Antonio Muñoz Molina (1994: 11) would later cite as an important influence in the development of his own brand of neo-neorealism.

In the more liberal and left-leaning reviews such as *Cuadernos para el diálogo* and the recently liberalized *Revista de Occidente,* a number of critics read the stylistic flourishes of this writing in political terms, shifting the Spanish realist debate away from the monopoly of objectivism towards a plurality of appropriate styles so long as the content was properly social, whereas *La vanguardia de España* invoked a new Hispanic literary brotherhood against the market success of literatures in translation (Sánchez López 1998: 112). Mexican writer Carlos Fuentes's *La nueva novela hispanoamericana* (1969: *The New Hispanoamerican Novel*) added a further twist to the critical process by incorporating Juan Goytisolo in his canon of writers whose revolutionary style was supposedly effecting a cultural revolution. The 'boom' was barely beginning, however, when a local text was heralded as a new departure for Spanish narrative: *Tiempo de silencio* (*Time of Silence*).

7.3.2. *Time for a change:* Tiempo de silencio

The publication of *Tiempo de silencio* by Luis Martín-Santos in 1961[5] is generally regarded as the turning point for the originality of the narrative techniques employed which seem to mark a clear break with the tendency towards objective realism. However, by the mid-1950s Elena Quiroga had already published works such as *Algo pasa en la calle* (1954: *Something's Happening in the Street*) and *La careta* (1955: *The Mask*) which are striking for their combination of socio-political critique and innovative techniques such as multiple perspectives, stream of consciousness narration, existentialist framings of time, and linguistic experimentation. *Tiempo de silencio* can also be related to the subjective realism of turn-of-the-century novelist Pío Baroja. The story (set in 1949), in which a young medical researcher, Pedro, loses his position when he gets involved in an illegal abortion in a shanty town on the outskirts of Madrid, is reminiscent of Baroja's *El árbol de la ciencia* (1911: *The*

---

[5] For an English translation see Martín-Santos (1964).

Tree of Knowledge), as is the panoramic view of a variety of social strata filtered through an individual conscience. However, whilst there are clear echoes of the writers of the 1898 Generation and of the related work of the philosopher essayist José Ortega y Gasset, their principal tenets are incorporated into the novel in order to be ironized and satirized; in particular, the appeal to a mythical, national character which became the basis of Francoist historiography as discussed in Chapter 2. This national character is defined by stoicism or the submission of the people to a higher authority which embodies the national 'project'. The novel subverts this ideology based on notions of destiny by suggesting the inverse: the people have been crushed—like the helpless masses in Goya's paintings (Martín-Santos 1989: 157)—into passive submission by the vertical hierarchy of the fascist state. Ortega y Gasset's advocacy of the need for a ruling elite is derided in the scenes involving the 'muchedumbre culta', the pretentious literati who gather together in cafés to talk endlessly without listening. The unnamed philosopher, 'el Maestro' (the Master), who delivers a condescending lecture on perspectivism using an apple—which is later parodied in a brothel scene by a madam holding a tomato—is clearly recognizable as Ortega y Gasset himself. His importance for the Nationalist essentializing of history is mocked when his path is blocked by a profusion of luxury cars and he fails to extract 'ninguna valoración eficaz del momento histórico' (161) ('any useful valuation of the historic moment').

The racial determinism associated with Ortega y Gasset is ironized throughout the novel when characters blame their problems on fate or describe themselves as martyrs, Pedro's very name suggests petrification into stone. It is perhaps most sarcastically refuted in the descriptions of the shanty town as a settlement in the aftermath of an atomic bomb in which the newly arrived migrants provide food for the worms (70). The causes of death are specified as disease, violence, and hunger enforced by the slum-dwellers' exclusion from the city with which they maintain a parasitic relationship. This exclusion cannot be justified through racialist argument for Spain is unfortunately unable to attribute class divisions to the 'accident' (71) of skin colour or any other biological difference. This is just one of the instances in the novel where Martín-Santos's political stance—he was on the executive committee of the illegal socialist party, PSOE, from 1961 until his death in a car crash in 1964 (Labanyi 1989: 54) — is evidenced despite the lack of explicit socio-political idioms in the text.

The description of the shanty dwellers as parasites suggests that the 'Spanish problem' is a disease similar to the cancer which Pedro is investigating. His aim is to discover whether this apparently hereditary strain is actually affected by environmental factors. Extrapolating to society as a whole, racial factors are therefore not sufficient to explain Spain's situation. However, neither are the socio-economic factors focused on by social realist writers. Whilst Martín-Santos obviously shares their concern with contemporary social conditions, his narrative differs notably in both content and form. The collective working-class protagonists of the social realist novel are strikingly absent in the variety of social strata explored and the text is focalized primarily through an alienated, middle-class individual. The resulting concentration on psychological factors can be related to Martín-Santos's work as a psychiatrist. As an existential psychiatrist he considered the basis of neurosis to be the denial of the possibility of change. Thus the regime's ideological 'project' becomes a willed falsification of meaning or a Sartrean act of Bad Faith. This monological mythification is contested through the shifting narrative perspective employed in *Tiempo de silencio*. The authoritative, invisible narrator of objective realism has been replaced by a first or third person narrator, sometimes anonymous and unidentified (particularly in the case of interior monologues), sometimes identified with a character. These abrupt shifts serve to disorient the reader and challenge notions of referentiality. The characters' points of view are clearly subjective and meaning is therefore neither evident nor static.

The language used shifts between a wide variety of registers such as street slang, Latinisms, scientific and technical language, literary allusions, and abundant neologisms. There is a high degree of formal experimentation in the text: syntax is distorted, punctuation and articles suppressed, orthographic rules disregarded, words recombined in agglutinative strings, there is repeated use of anaphoric constructions, prevalence of the gerund verb form, seemingly chaotic accumulation of adjectives and adverbs. The richness of the figurative tropes employed provokes comparison with baroque techniques: the artificiality and complexity of the language used palpably demonstrates its lack of transparency and reliability and can therefore be used to conceal as much as to reveal. The exaggerated idealization in the description of the shanty town leads the reader to suspect a reality far worse than that which could be conveyed by literal statement: '¡Cómo los valores espirituales que otros pueblos nos envidian eran palpablemente demostrados en la manera como de la nada y del detritus toda una armoniosa ciudad había surgido a impulsos de su soplo vivificador!' (1989: 52) ('How our spiritual values envied by other nations were palpably demonstrated in the manner in which from out of nothing and detritus a whole harmonious city had emerged, driven by their life-giving breath!'). The text's pervasive irony serves to undermine absolutist, hegemonic discourses with their claim to truth. Its basis in ambiguity and contradiction exposes the distortions and limitations of mythification as a way of dealing with historical progress. As the novel concludes Pedro reflects that in a time of silence protest is anaesthetized by a suffocating society where silence kills more effectively than the crude methods of yesteryear (1989: 291). Whilst he would seem to accept his fate, as the novel closes, by choosing to conform in silence despite being clearly aware of the destruction of his career which he describes in terms of castration, history itself has not been frozen. It progresses in the rhythmic motion of the train he is journeying on conveyed through onomatopoeia, 'tracatracatracatracatracatracatraca traqueteo tracatracatracatracatraca' (292).

In *Tiempo de silencio*, then, it would seem that Martín-Santos's wish to create a 'dialectical realism', which demonstrates the fundamentally contradictory nature of both the individual and society, and the dynamic nature of the process of alienation, is realized (Labanyi 1989: 83). Thus if *Tiempo de silencio* marks a new departure it is not as a rupture with realism but as an anticipation of the renovation of realism that would come in the narrative of the late 1970s and 1980s.

7.4. ESCAPISMS AND REALISMS IN THE THEATRE

Many forms of realist writing bridge the gap between literary and popular cultures, promote accessibility, and give voice, as we have been seeing, to rural and urban working classes. Yet the immediate theatrical context, at least as far as commercially viable (and thus, in the end, visible) dramatic production was concerned, seems, at first, not propitious for a new theatrical realism.

7.4.1. Avoiding reality: escapist comedies

There is little sign of serious engagement with contemporary reality in mainstream theatre of the 1940s and 1950s. One of the dominant trends was a successful genre of light comedy by authors such as José López Rubio and Víctor Ruiz Iriarte, in which characters seek escape from tedious existences in romance and fantasy, making avoidance of reality a constant source of humour and sentimentality. In the hands of Miguel Mihura and Enrique Jardiel Poncela, on the other hand, escapist comedy takes on more problematic dimensions.

Mihura is best known for *Tres sombreros de copa* (1932: *Three Top Hats*), which was not performed until 1952, when it began to acquire something of a cult reputation as a precursor of the Theatre of the Absurd, reinforced by Eugène Ionesco's praise for the Paris production of 1958 as a liberating exercise in 'intellectual gymnastics' (Ionesco 1959: 64). The protagonist (Dionisio), on the eve of a very conventional bourgeois marriage, is tempted to run off with Paula, a vivacious showgirl. A tender, childlike fantasy of a life of freedom with Paula and the troupe of entertainers is contrasted hilariously with the rigid, meaningless clichés of decent society. Paula brings Dionisio back to reality: true independence takes greater strength of spirit than Dionisio possesses. While Mihura's later plays do not have quite the same satirical edge, they continue the strategy of gleeful defamiliarization of social normality by means of absurd situations and dialogue that exposes the arbitrariness of language. In *Ni pobre ni rico sino todo lo contrario* (*Neither Poor Nor Rich But Exactly the Opposite*, written in 1939 in collaboration with Tono and first staged in 1943), the cliché of social difference as an obstacle to true love is turned inside out, and social conventions and the language in which they are constructed are emptied of significance with a light, whimsical touch.

The characteristic tone of Jardiel's theatre is elegantly cynical, disdainful of respectability and predictability. The creation of *lo inverosímil* (lack of verisimilitude) is as inventive as Mihura's, but less radically absurd in conception. Jardiel's implausible situations and bizarre characterization are the product of coincidences and emotional crises rather than expressions of a fundamentally illogical view of life. His plays are peopled by elegant socialites bored by conventional models of romance and marriage, eccentric older ladies and gentlemen obsessed by traumatic past experiences, and servants patiently playing the straight man to their employers' antics. *Eloísa está debajo de un almendro* (1940: *Eloïse is under an Almond Tree*) has become central to Jardiel's reputation thanks to a revival by the Centro Dramático Nacional in 1984. A web of mysteries, coincidences, and misunderstandings is woven around colourful and contradictory figures inhabiting a world of glamour and fantasy, which is contrasted with the prosaic existence of the lower-class patrons of the dingy suburban cinema in which the prologue is set.

Jardiel and Mihura both achieved commercial success, but were never fully accepted by the theatrical establishment and were even considered dangerous by some right-wing critics, although they denied their work had any ideological importance, and generally disparaged all forms of 'thesis' or experimentation in the theatre (see Miguel Martínez 1979: 215–19, 237). The reality from which their characters seek to escape consists of little more than the stifling effects of middle-class respectability, which is represented in much the same way in texts of the 1940s and 1950s as in those written before the war. There is a vague sense of despair implicit in the absurdity of these plays, but nothing of the anguished nihilism usually considered the defining feature of the Theatre of the Absurd (as exemplified by Ionesco, Beckett, or Arrabal). Their comedies are unapologetically escapist, simply offering unusually clever entertainment to a public in dire need of intelligent diversion. Yet it is not entirely reassuring, since it constitutes not an easy escape from reality but an uncomfortable refusal to accept its logic. The pursuit of *lo inverosímil* constitutes a plea for creative freedom and a questioning of Manichaean oppositions.

7.4.2. *Buero Vallejo* and Sastre**

Although *Historia de una escalera* (discussed in Chapter 6) and *Hoy es fiesta* (1956: *Today's a Holiday*) can be seen as inaugurating an apparently straightforward mode of social realism new to post-war Spanish theatre (characterized by detailed recreation of working-class locations, everyday colloquial language, linear plots, and convincing, ordinary characters), Buero Vallejo's work as a whole constitutes a sophisticated exploration of the nature of individual and collective perceptions and the uncertain boundaries between reality and fantasy. Even these two 'kitchen-sink' plays suggest an ironic awareness of the inevitability of comparisons with the traditional *sainete*, and contain elements of symbolism and structural patterning that conspicuously draw attention to form. Other early plays rework bourgeois domestic drama—*Madrugada* (1953: *Until Morning*)—and combine dreams and fantasy with everyday reality—*Irene o el tesoro* (1954: *Irene, or the Treasure*). From the beginning, then, Buero's texts reveal themselves as self-conscious exercises in theatrical form as well as meditations on social and metaphysical issues. Each play constitutes a solution to a technical challenge: the enclosed, dispiriting space of *Historia de una escalera*; the precise matching of fictional time with real performance time in *Madrugada*; the interpretation on stage of paintings by Velázquez and Goya in *Las meninas* (1960: *The Maids of Honour*) and *El sueño de la razón* (1970: *The Sleep of Reason*). The division of the stage into multiple spaces first employed in *Un soñador para un pueblo* (1958: *A Dreamer for the People*) becomes a trademark of Buero's theatre, allowing fluid use of sets combining realistic detail with stylized, schematic structures and lighting.

Buero ambitiously defines his work as tragedy, reworking the classical ideal of catharsis in the light of modern political and cultural developments. The vision of concrete social and historical realities is generally negative—dominated by injustice, human weakness, and the frustration of progress—and is represented in ways designed to strike spectators as believable and to provoke an emotional response. However, disaster is always tempered by a glimpse of hope for a better world, and catharsis is complicated by dramatic structures that keep audiences' emotional involvement and conscious analysis in tension. The increasingly elaborate theatrical strategies designed to achieve this balancing of Aristotelian identification and Brechtian distancing are commonly referred to by critics and Buero himself as 'efectos de inmersión' ('immersion effects'), a term coined by Ricardo Doménech in 1973 (updated in Doménech 1993: 58–66). These are striking devices that oblige spectators to share the experience of key characters in a direct way, yet at the same time draw attention to themselves as elements of stylization that disrupt the illusion of stage reality: a complete blackout in *El concierto de San Ovidio* (1962: *The Concert at Saint Ovid*) which momentarily makes the audience as blind as the hero; the silent mouthing of their lines by the actors in

El sueño de la razón when Goya is on stage; the gradual metamorphosis of the set in *La fundación* (1974: *The Foundation*) from a luxurious research institute into a prison as the protagonist's self-deception is stripped away; shifts from colour into black-and-white vision in *Diálogo secreto* (1984: *Secret Dialogue*) as the secret of the art critic's colour-blindness is revealed. *El tragaluz* (1967: *The Basement Window*) transforms a moving drama about the legacy of the Spanish Civil War into a complex metatheatrical exploration of the relationship between spectators and performance, encouraging the real contemporary audience to imagine that they are a virtual audience of the future, who in turn are invited to imagine themselves as people of the twentieth century. The real spectators, drawn into the game but disconcerted by the multiple layers of fiction and the mixing of 'real' action with memories and hallucinations, come to see that they and their society are the subjects of the 'experiment' carried out by the researchers of the future, the point of which is that they learn how to recognize themselves.

For Alfonso Sastre too the key challenge of realism is to maintain a productive tension between passive catharsis and active analysis, illusion and self-awareness. While the main emphasis in Buero is on individual moral responsibility, Sastre's work focuses more specifically on art's potential contribution to social change and the deconstruction of ideologies. Provocative declarations made in the 1950s such as 'lo social es una categoría superior a lo artístico' (Sastre 1973: 28) ('the social is a higher category than the artistic') may have been based on an overestimation of the practical relevance of theatre to political action, but Sastre's model of social realism has never lost sight of the inseparability of form and social function: 'Sólo un arte de gran calidad estética es capaz de transformar el mundo' (Sastre 1973: 28) ('Only art of the highest aesthetic quality is capable of transforming the world'). After an early phase of experimentation with existentialist symbolism (in 1946–8), Sastre's whole output of plays, theoretical texts—especially *Anatomía del realismo* (1965: *Anatomy of Realism*)—and practical initiatives amounts to a systematic investigation of realism, a project theorized as a dialectical process of synthesis. 'Realismo profundo' ('deep realism') is to be arrived at by superseding the 'surface' realisms of earlier periods—the familiar conventions of bourgeois drama, Naturalism's fetishistic concern for detail, the falsification of working-class experience in 'popular' theatre—and assimilating the creative shock of the avant-garde as well as the analytical techniques of Brechtianism. Sastre uses the phrase 'vanguardia realista' ('realist avant-garde') to emphasize the experimental thrust of this project, and proposes the notion of 'tragedia compleja' ('complex tragedy') as his version of the ideal form of theatre that combines emotional power, philosophical significance, social relevance, and aesthetic impact (Oliva 1989: 297).

Although Sastre remains best known for the relatively straightforward realism of *Escuadra hacia la muerte* (1952: *Condemned Squad*) and *La mordaza* (1954: *The Gag*) (discussed in Chapters 5 and 6 respectively), the search for 'tragedia compleja' since the mid-1960s has produced inventive, richly intertextual, and metatheatrical works such as *La sangre y la ceniza* (1965: *Blood and Ashes*), *El camarada oscuro* (1972: *The Unknown Comrade*), and *Jenofa Juncal la roja gitana del monte Jaizkibel* (1983: *Jenofa Juncal, the Red Gypsy of Mount Jaizkibel*). In its ironic playfulness, its self-conscious appropriation and deconstruction of theatrical languages, there is something postmodernist about Sastre's work — yet it retains its political seriousness and its faith in the social importance of theatre.

7.4.3. The Realist Generation

The term *Generación Realista* has often been used as a broad label to embrace Buero, Sastre, and a number of dramatists taken to be following in their footsteps, but is most usefully employed to refer to a smaller group born between 1922 and 1927, who began writing plays in the late 1940s or early 1950s but did not come to prominence until the early 1960s: José Martín Recuerda, Lauro Olmo,* José María Rodríguez Méndez,* and Carlos Muñiz. Although they have never declared any common artistic programme, they have frequently referred to their work as the product of shared historical circumstances and cultural roots (Rodríguez Méndez 1987: 4–14). Distancing themselves from Buero and Sastre, they refuse to theorize 'realism' and characterize their approach as simply speaking out in the face of the suppression of uncomfortable truths: 'A mí me importa más dar una "respuesta" que construir algo retórico y sometido a ciertas reglas' ('Lo poco que yo puedo decir', in Rodríguez Méndez 1968: 16, 18)

('I'm more interested in making a "response" than in creating a rhetorical construction subject to particular rules'). Rodríguez Méndez and Martín Recuerda in particular claim to express an authentic, passionate Spanish cultural identity summed up in the term *iberismo* (Iberianism): 'Piel de toro al rojo vivo, surgido de la tierra en que hemos nacido' (Martín Recuerda 1969: 32) ('Like the bull's hide of the Peninsula glowing red hot, straight out of the land of our birth'). *Iberismo* claims deep roots in history, geography, popular culture, and theatrical traditions. Although this echoes right-wing nationalism, it is proposed as a form of dissidence— aiming to reclaim Spanishness from Francoism, then to revive it in the 1980s and 1990s. Cultural and historical specificity is offered as an antidote to the technological, economic, and political forces of the modern world which promote mass conformity and passivity (*masificación*) ('El teatro como expresión social y cultural', in Rodríguez Méndez 1968: 87–92).

The texts that most obviously defined the Realist Generation at first are examples of a straightforward, naturalistic kind of realism. Every component of Olmo's* *La camisa*—the dingy setting, the action revolving around chronic unemployment, the convincing development of the main characters complemented by careful attention to minor ones, the everyday dialogue—contributes to a doggedly convincing picture of ordinariness and hardship, making a direct emotional appeal to the audience's sympathies, and texts by the other three *realistas* have a comparable flavour. Yet already in 1960 Muñiz's *El tintero* (*The Inkwell*) approached similar subject matter in a strikingly different style, representing the dehumanizing effect of bureaucracy by means of grotesque exaggeration and expressionist techniques. The most interesting texts by these writers date from the years between the mid-1960s and the mid-1970s, as they incorporate more flexible staging, more dynamic dramatic structures, and more sophisticated explorations of the relationship between stage and audience. Olmo's experimental pieces grouped under the title *El cuarto poder* (1963–7: *The Fourth Estate*) use projections, mime, and puppetry, and draw on various traditions of theatre and popular entertainment. Martín Recuerda's history plays such as *El engañao* (1972: *The Dupe*) aim to involve the audience in a wild, very physical *fiesta española*. Rodríguez Méndez's *Flor de otoño* (1972: *Autumn Flower*) is a spectacular romp through the sleazy sub-cultures of the Barcelona of 1930.

However, this expansion and diversification of realism never abandons the preoccupation with colloquial language, popular cultural identity, and concrete historical circumstances.

7.4.4. Realism in the Transition

If the last ten years of the dictatorship saw the creation of Buero's, Sastre's, and the Realist Generation's most exciting texts, most of them (except Buero's) were banned by the censors, remaining unpublished and unperformed. This suppression was made up for to some extent by a series of high-profile productions in the late 1970s and early 1980s, including Buero's *La doble historia del doctor Valmy* in 1976, Sastre's *La sangre y la ceniza* in 1977, Rodríguez Méndez's *Bodas que fueron famosas del Pingajo y la Fandanga* in 1978, and Martín Recuerda's *El engañao* in 1981. However, this belated recognition was not continued after 1982, and productions of new work by the *realistas* have been few and far between, only Buero maintaining a regular presence in mainstream theatre.

As in other literary genres, it is possible to identify something of a 'return to realism' in the work of younger dramatists emerging in the 1980s, but in no sense does this constitute an organized movement or declared agenda. José Luis Alonso de Santos is perhaps the playwright who most consistently maintains a realist aesthetic, notably in the highly successful *Bajarse al moro* (1984: *Going down to Morocco*),[6] in which frank but light-hearted handling of drugs and sex is matched by lively streetwise dialogue. He suggests in an interview that the contemporary world is such a confusing labyrinth of mirrors that theatre has an important role in helping to 'give people back their identities': 'Estamos tan alejados de la realidad ahora mismo que necesitamos recuperarla, volverle a mirar el rostro' (in Cabal and Alonso de Santos 1985: 156) ('We're so far from reality right now that we need to recuperate it, to find a way of looking it in the face again'). Realistic treatment of settings (often urban), characters (often young and single), dialogue (usually colloquial), or plot structure is deployed selectively by a number of playwrights, including women writers such as María

---

[6] Published in a translation entitled *Going down to Marrakesh* in O'Connor (1992: 313–79).

Manuela Reina and Paloma Pedrero, simply as part of the range of representational strategies available. Fermín Cabal's pragmatism echoes comments made by members of the Realist Generation twenty years earlier: 'A mí me importa un bledo [. . .] hacer un teatro realista o no hacer un teatro realista. Yo hago el teatro que de una forma natural me sale, el teatro que me apetece, intuyendo que en ese teatro hay grandes dosis de realidad, pero que aún así es turbio y fangoso como todo el arte' (Cabal and Alonso de Santos 1985: 177) ('I don't give a damn [. . .] about setting out to produce realist theatre or not to produce realist theatre. I make the kind of theatre that comes naturally to me, the kind of theatre I like, aware all the time that if there are heavy doses of reality in my theatre, it's still blurred and muddy like all art').

7.5. NEW REALISM IN POETRY

Although the early 1960s are generally accepted as marking the end of the boom in socially committed poetry in Spain (despite the after-echoes of anger from exiled poets, discussed earlier), debates around realism and the civic role of poetry remained an important cultural force, and a significant set of poets beginning their careers in the 1950s found themselves speaking more 'colloquially' than 'poetically', more to a community of readers than to one reader, to God, or just themselves. Poetry became, in short, an important tool in clarifying the blur and muddiness of 'art' and crystallizing 'reality'. On the one hand a clear break with *poesía social** is represented by the density and the often contemplative nature of the poetry of José María Caballero Bonald, José Ángel Valente, and Claudio Rodríguez, and not least the lyrically charged psychological realism and strong philosophical and classical foundations of Francisco Brines and Carlos Bousoño. These poets of the 'Generation of 1950' established a new tradition for the 1960s of preoccupation with language which has carried on powerfully into later years. On the other hand, the committed and plain-speaking tradition of *poesía social* finds a certain continuity when, in the 1980s and 1990s, poetry returns to ancient roles as chronicle and analytic history, as in the cases of Andrés Trapiello, Julio Martínez Mesanza (constructing an epic, cumulative work, *Europa*), and new women poets (discussed below).

A Sense of Reality

Jaime Siles has suggested (1994: 16–17) some characteristic emphases of Spanish poetry in the 1980s and 1990s which move away from the abstractionism that he himself once espoused in the elaboration of a poetry of silence: attention to everyday experience, emotion, perception, and intelligibility, and an interest in urban and contemporary themes. In some ways, for Siles, this is a return to the traditions of the Generation of 1950 (a consideration which needs to be set against any tendency to view more recent Spanish poetry as playfully anti-realist, as conventionally with the *novísimos*, or concerned with pure form). In two poets of, or coinciding with, the Generation of 1950, Valente* and Gloria Fuertes, the meanings of critical realism were still being extended in the 1980s. Fuertes— whose frequent appearances at poetry readings all over Spain gave her the same sort of popular profile as Alberti — uses a self-deprecating, anti-poetical mode to interconnect poetry and the everyday: at least writing poems has not been in vain, she says, 'he distraído | a los chicos de mi barrio. | Algo es algo' (Fuertes 1981: 267) ('I've kept | the local boys happy. | Something's better than nothing'). She also, though, deploys this in tactics of micro-resistance, toning down—perhaps sharpening—the rhetoric of Celaya and Neruda (a clear influence, as is perhaps also another Chilean, Nicanor Parra):

> Hay que hablar poco y decir mucho
> hay que hacer mucho
> y que nos parezca poco:
> Arrancar el gatillo a las armas,
> por ejemplo. (120)

(We must talk little and say much, | do a lot | and deem it little: | such as plucking triggers off guns, | for example.)

Valente* uses formal aspects of both *poesía popular* and *poesía pura* to distil his sense of poetry's more oblique relation to history in *Breve son* (poems of 1953–68): 'perdimos la verdad, | perdimos las palabras | y el cantor y el cantar' (Valente 1980: 258) ('we lost the truth, | and lost the words | and the singer and the song'), where the archaic term 'cantar' quietly elicits associations of Antonio Machado and his own use of the epic past to construct possible futures for Spain. In the 'Segundo homenaje a Isidore Ducasse' ('A Second Homage to Isidore Ducasse'), however, there are more direct statements on the inextricability of aesthetic and ethical concerns: 'Un poeta debe ser más útil | que ningún ciudadano de su tribu [...] La poesía ha de tener por fin la verdad práctica. | Su misión es difícil' (294–5) ('A poet must be more useful | than any citizen of his tribe | [...] Poetry must have practical truth as its only end. | Its mission is difficult').

In 1973, Carlos Bousoño—for many years the contemplative, difficult, word-refining poet *par excellence*—had acknowledged a debt to the social poets (to whose style and aims he nonetheless remained opposed): 'el poeta ha aprendido en ese realismo un cierto lenguaje: nexos que antes se consideraban exclusivamente prosísticos' (in Brines 1995b: 344) ('poets have learned from that form of realism a particular language: articulations which before were considered the exclusive property of prose').

Formative variations on the theme of productive prosaism are to be seen in the poets of the *Escuela [o grupo] de Barcelona* (The Barcelona School [or Group])—Jaime Gil de Biedma, José Agustín Goytisolo, and Carlos Barral, whose preoccupations—urban, historicized, and socio-critical—can be read off from the titles of collections: *Diecinueve figuras de mi historia civil* (Barral, 1961: *Nineteen Motifs from my Life as a Citizen*), *Años decisivos* (Goytisolo, 1961: *Decisive Years*), *Moralidades* (Gil de Biedma, 1966: *Moralities*). One obvious strategy for making poetry more directly 'communicative' and a useful tool for the 'tribe' (in Valente's term) is to deploy the rhythms and attitudes of something approaching ordinary speech. Gil de Biedma[7]—a poet much admired by writers of slightly later generations such as Ana María Moix and José María Álvarez, Luis Antonio de Villena and Luis García Montero— is exemplary in this regard. He speaks of life in Barcelona and of himself in the tones of an ironic and studiously ordinary observer: his famous 'Contra Jaime Gil de Biedma' of 1968 begins by asking,

> ¿De qué sirve, quisiera yo saber, cambiar de piso,
>   dejar atrás un sótano más negro
>   que mi reputación —y ya es decir—,
>   poner visillos blancos
>   y tomar criada,
>   renunciar a la vida de bohemio
>   si vienes luego tú, pelmazo,
>   embarazoso huésped, memo vestido con mis trajes [...]?
>   (Gil de Biedma 1998: 80)

[7] For a detailed analysis of this feature in Gil de Biedma, Goytisolo, and Barral see Riera (1988: 264–308).

160 A Sense of Reality

(What, I'd like to know, is the point of changing flats, | and leaving behind a basement darker | than my reputation—and that is something—, | putting up lace curtains | and taking a maid, | giving up on the free and easy lifestyle | if then you turn up, great lump, | unwanted guest, a fool dressed in my clothing [. . .]?)

Gil de Biedma's writing—which is both intensely intimate and sardonic enough to stand back from solipsism—has debts both to Cernuda and to the Guillén of *Clamor* in its rigorously ethical and invigoratingly clarifying language. As such it stands, in the late 1960s, in extreme opposition to the far from sober poetry of a parallel new group of writers clustered *post hoc* around the term *novísimos** and more concerned with art (high and otherwise) than with a quietly measured philosophy of experience.

7.5.1 Poetry and real lives in the 1980s and beyond

La poesía es útil porque puede reconstruir estéticamente [. . .] las experiencias de nuestra realidad, ayudándonos a comprenderlas [. . .] Es importante que los protagonistas del poema no sean héroes, profetas expresivos, sino personas normales que representen la capacidad de sentir de las personas normales. (Garcia Montero 1993: 35–6)

(Poetry is useful because it can reconstruct aesthetically [. . .] our own experiences of reality, helping us to understand them [. . .] It is important that a poem's protagonists are not heroes or expressive, prophetic voices, but normal people representing normal people's capacity for feeling.)

These words, delivered in a Madrid lecture in 1990 by the poet Luis García Montero, have striking resonances of the idealistic, responsibly didactic discourses of the left on poetry in the 1950s, but for the balanced inclusion here of two key concepts—the aesthetic (which moves García Montero back into the post-1970s mainstream in Spain) and the sentimental (that 'capacity for feeling'). García Montero is one of a group of poets who from 1983 were associated with the notion of 'la otra sentimentalidad' ('the new sensibility'); one, that is, which distances itself from bourgeois notions of the central sensitive self, yet leaves room for 'real' feelings. Consequently, he dramatizes personal experience—hurt and longing—in the figure, for example, of 'El viajero' ('The Traveller'):

> acepta que la vida se refugie
> en una habitación que no es la suya.
> La luz se queda siempre detrás de una ventana.
> . . . .
> Sabe que le resulta necesario
> aprender a vivir en otra edad,
> en otro amor,
> en otro tiempo.
> Tiempo de habitaciones separadas.
> (García Montero 1994: 12)

(he accepts the fact that life has taken refuge | in a room not his own. | The light always comes from the other side of the window. | [. . .] He knows he must learn now | to live in another age, | another love, | another time. | The time of life in separate rooms.)

There are, of course, less quiet despairs to narrate and give aesthetic form to. In Clara Janés's *Libro de las alienaciones* (1980: *The Book of Alienations*) images of violent death, mutilation, imprisonment, and endless pain construct a discourse of despair at the material world, or more particularly the world of destructive urban materialism:

> Lo que mata es el cerco
> de absurdos objetos,
> la miseria del alma,
> el aire enfermo,
> tuberculoso,
> que irremediablemente
> nos envuelve.
> (Janés 1980: 93–5)

(What kills is the siege | of pointless objects, | poverty of the soul, | the sickly air | which surrounds us, tubercular, | irredeemable.)

There is a strong eco-political strain in poems of *Centauro* (1989: *Centaur*) by Julia Otxoa.* It is difficult for readers to distance themselves from the expected specificity of the 'Basque problem' in the poem 'País o fiera que me matas' (Otxoa 1989: 18–19) ('Country or beast which kills me'), or when confronting a declaration such as 'Vengo de un Pueblo clavado en mi costado, | un tiempo sitiado, | [. . .] | El lugar de la ira' (17) ('I come from a People hilt-deep in my side, | a time of siege, | [. . .] | The place of rage'), or from the clear political sympathies of the poem 'Larga sombra de intolerancia sobre julio' (22) ('Long Shadow of Intolerance over July'), which links Wagner, Nazism, Vietnam, Nicaragua, and the death of Lorca to the 'shadow' of the July 1939 victory of the Nationalist forces (174–5); but, as with the writings of male poets in the 1950s, this 'rage', if activated by particular circumstances, spreads wide across personal and collective experience and is a response to an intricate crisis of hope and faith. For Otxoa, 'hemos hecho de la depradación | costumbre, | y al cabo, falta aire, | y sobran piras funerarias' (13) ('we have made a habit | of depredation | and in the end, there's no air to breathe, | but funeral pyres to spare').

Though it can learn from 1950s versions of realism poetry may still sustain its age-old role of resistance to banality, to the imaginatively deadening—to construct, indeed, alternative realities in the spirit, though never again quite in the manner, of the pure poets starting out in the pre-Civil War years.

Further reading

Asís (1990); Colección Visor (1998); Jordan (1990); Labanyi (1989); O'Connor (1992); Oliva (1989); Ruiz Ramón (1989); Sastre (1973).

8
New Writing: New Spain?

8.1. PROBLEMS OF CATEGORIZATION

The attempt by critics to categorize the novels of the 1950s and 1960s through the constrictive binary opposition of realism and anti-realism breaks down over the course of the following decade as a period of intense experimentalism gives way to the explosion of *nueva narrativa* characterized by its diversity. It is this plurality which has led to considerable disagreement about whether *nueva narrativa* as such exists and, if so, how it can be categorized. There is, however, consensus that the principal change since 1975 has been a return to a problematized realism.

8.1.1. Gender and literary histories

A number of interesting and innovative women writers are still marginalized within the major literary histories, despite the growing body of serious scholarly work to draw on.[1] Elena Quiroga is an important example since her literary development parallels that of Juan Goytisolo in a number of ways, in its movement from recognizably realist to more experimental writing and engagement with critical theory, and she has achieved the distinction of being the second woman elected to the Real Academia Española (Royal Spanish Academy), in 1983. Yet despite winning both the Nadal Prize in 1951 for *Viento del norte* (*Northwind*) and the prestigious Critics' Prize for *Tristura* (Galician for *Sadness*) in 1960, she subsequently failed to receive critical attention to the extent that the feature story on her election in *Cambio 16* was entitled 'Elena Quiroga, la olvidada' (Llopis 1983). Tackling taboo subjects such as the problematic situations created by the Francoist regime's

---

[1] Detailed bibliographies can be found in Davies (1998); Brooksbank Jones (1997). A panorama of writers and useful biographical information is available in Brown (1991) and Pérez (1988).

outlawing of divorce, including the invalidation of divorces granted during the Republican period in *Algo pasa en la calle* (1954: *Something's Happening in the Street*) and, later, in *Escribo tu nombre* (1965: *I Write your Name*), what Pérez describes as the first direct depiction of female sexuality in writing by Hispanic women (1988: 130); many of her novels are set in Galicia (although written in Castilian), which may be another factor in her exclusion from the heavily Madrid- and Barcelona-centred literary histories.[2] Given that her early style is more polished than Goytisolo's, if we compare the fluidly executed, shifting, and fragmented perspectives of *Algo pasa en la calle* to the stilted dialogue and sometimes clumsy cutting which mars an otherwise complex narrative strategy in *Juegos de manos* (*Sleights of Hand*) in the same year, or note her skilful use of stream of consciousness in two novels published in 1955, *La enferma* (*The Sick Woman*) and *La careta* (*The Mask*), we can see why some critics created a separate category of 'psychological realism' for this style of writing. After all, Quiroga was one of the first writers to examine the psychological aftermath provoked by the Civil War through a family narrative, anticipating other texts which have proved difficult to categorize such as Matute's trilogy *Los mercaderes* (*The Merchants*) published between 1960 and 1969. Yet *Algo pasa en la calle*, for example, precisely because of its shifting, fragmentary perspectives, demands greater reader involvement—one of the major tenets of Castellet's and Goytisolo's 1950s theorizing of realism—in reconstructing the fate of the dead protagonist than anything by Goytisolo prior to *Señas de identidad*, while *La careta* is more sophisticated in its existentialism. Finally, they are infinitely more interesting in their complex, detailed representation of women, both peasant and upper-class, while still producing some extraordinary male protagonists, like the alienated Moisés in *La careta*, the ageing bullfighter in *La última corrida* (1958: *The Last Bullfight*), and the unwitting bigamist, Ventura, in *Algo pasa en la calle*.

Similarly, the emphasis placed on the urban chronicles of figures like Cela and Goytisolo has sidelined writers like Dolores Medio,

[2] This lack of attention also extends to the censors. Quiroga believes that *Algo pasa en la calle* was passed because they did not actually read it, perhaps assuming that it would be similar to *Viento del norte* (Zatlin 1991: 45).

whose *El pez sigue flotando* (1959: *The Fish Keeps Floating*) constructs a microcosm of Madrid through the lives of the inhabitants of ten flats in an apartment block, with thumbnail sketches of their difficult lives, their financial pressures, isolation, and emotional responses. Another of her indisputably 'social' novels, *Funcionario público* (1956: *City Employee*), is credited with resulting in a pay rise for communications workers (Pérez 1988: 123), the only tangible impact of a movement which its major theorists would pronounce a failure in the late 1960s, because it had neither produced authentically proletarian novels nor helped to bring about social change. In the same decade, Concha Alós produced a series of socially concerned novels, exposing and overtly denouncing inequality and injustice, particularly in relation to women, but encompassing Civil War refugees and village life in Mallorca. Her shift into more psychological analysis in the 1970s produced *Os habla Electra* (1975: *Electra Speaking*), a complex narrative exploration of Freudian theory superimposing different timescales in a fragmentary dreamscape which represents a struggle between matriarchy and patriarchy in which Electra struggles for an androgynous identity (Ordóñez 1980: 38–49).

Even commercially successful, prizewinning writers with high public and critical profiles like Matute and Martín Gaite are slotted into ill-fitting categories drawn up from the analysis of male novelists in this period.[3] Matute's extraordinarily suggestive and often dramatic novels with their marginal settings (islands, villages), layered explorations of stifling social structures, and the disruptive power of sexual desire have still to receive the kind of psychoanalytical reading they surely invite, although a more complex critical analysis can be found in López (1995). Both Matute and Martín Gaite produce writing which in its introspection and its sense of identity as performance, drawn from existentialist notions of authenticity but particularly Simone de Beauvoir's feminist insight that 'You are not born a woman, you become one', prefigure, from a woman-centred perspective, the later male-focused interest in subjectivity and explorations of performative identities in writers like Juan Goytisolo and Juan Marsé.

---

[3] López (1995: 189) points to both the inadequacies in this respect of a male critical tradition and problematic aspects of some Anglo-American criticism.

8.1.2. History from below: Juan Marsé

If gender continues to be a deeply problematic issue in literary histories, both in the categorization of writers and in the analysis of individual texts, the narrow class base from which most writers, including the women, emerge also requires critical attention, particularly in periods when one social class attempts to represent another in its writing. Marsé is one of the few leading contemporary Spanish writers brought up in a working-class district, in Barcelona, who left school to work at the age of 13. One important effect of this noted by Labanyi (1989: 135) is that he differs in the kind of discourses he deploys from Martín-Santos and Benet, both given a classical education. Where they require their readers to be familiar with classical mythology, Marsé draws on the films (especially Hollywood), comics, and pulp fiction that he grew up with in the 1940s. His early writing, however, dwells more on a fairly sympathetic critique of the young Catalan bourgeoisie rather than the marginalized barrios of his own youth. In *Encerrados con un solo juguete* (1960: *Shut Inside with Only One Toy*) and *Esta cara de la luna* (1962: *This Side of the Moon*) the bourgeois youth lacks ideals, in the latter the initially revolutionary protagonist is reintegrated into bourgeois society, and can only find satisfaction through love or sex (the toy in the first title). In 1962, following his rapprochement to the Catalan Communist Party, Marsé declared to the French review *Lettres françaises* that he supported the role of literature as an 'arma política' ('political weapon') (in Corrales Egea 1971: 62), in terms which echo Castellet, yet he was soon satirizing *La hora del lector* in *Últimas tardes con Teresa* (1966: *Last Evenings with Teresa*) (Amell 1984: 68) which critiques the inauthenticity of the privileged bourgeois youth whose revolutionary ideals seem to be linked more to the thrill of transgressing social boundaries than to ideological concerns. In *La oscura historia de la prima Montse* (1970: *The Murky Story of Cousin Montse*) Marsé's satire extends to the institutionalized conventions of traditional bourgeois society, particularly false piety and charity.

Marsé's *Si te dicen que caí* (1973: *If They Say I Fell*),[4] published in Mexico and banned in Spain until 1976, became one of the best-

---

[4] For an English translation, see Marsé (1994). Vicente Aranda's film version of the novel, 1989, brought it vividly back to prominence.

New Writing: New Spain? 167

sellers of the democratic period and, although not devoid of Manichaeistic simplifications, counters the monolithic image of the *vencidos* with a collective and often contradictory oral history narrated from the point of view of the defeated and the marginal. Marsé claimed that many readers would have been disappointed by a novel whose blaze of post-censorship publicity would have raised expectations about a text which 'no es más que una evocación nostálgica de un hermoso y repelente paraíso perdido: mi infancia, mi verdadera patria' (in Martínez Cachero 1997: 365) ('is no more than a nostalgic evocation of a lovely yet loathsome lost paradise: my childhood, my true homeland'). However, the childhood evoked here is far from innocent and, despite the author's suggestion that it is not specifically a political novel, or even about the Civil War (Martínez Cachero 1997: 365), it does offer a complex, shifting, and often brutal history from below, concocted in the 'aventis' (tales) of the 'golfillos' (street kids) who hang out in the marginal areas of Barcelona, sons of imprisoned, exiled, or dead Republican fathers. The boys' relationships with orphan girls from the local home are forged within sadomasochistic scenarios which dramatize traumatic events of the Civil War, and paint a sordid picture of post-war Barcelona. Central to the main tale told and retold by Java (Daniel Javaloyes) and his friend Sarnita is the figure of Aurora-Ramona, her movement into prostitution, and her murder. The final piecing together of her life and death coincides with Java's definitive absorption into the sphere of the post-war victors as he becomes another of Marsé's 'trepadores' (social climbers), escaping the relentless misery and incessant persecution of 'the enemy within'. Torture, death in hiding, the payment of women and young boys to perform degrading sexual acts for a hidden voyeur (the fascist Conrad, a director of amateur dramatics), are layered onto finely observed details of the daily experience of poverty, hunger, and subjection to the vigilance of both the Falange and pious local Catholic women. As in earlier novels by Marsé, the Church plays a largely negative role. Although a priest sympathetic to the terrorist resistance is one of those tortured in a central scene, others affiliated to the Church (such as those who run the orphanage) are represented as hypocritical or perverse.

The retrospective narrative, focalized through Java's friend el Ñito/Sarnita, is an ambiguous blend of mythical and realist depictions of a cruel and violent society, at times reminiscent of that depicted in the *tremendista* novels of the 1940s, which engages in corrosive social critique whilst experimenting with form through the use of multiple perspectives and temporal dislocations.

8.2. EXPERIENCE AND EXPERIMENTALISM: JUAN GOYTISOLO* AND JUAN BENET

This mix of corrosive critique and experimental technique is extensively developed in the work of another writer from Barcelona, Juan Goytisolo. In Goytisolo's travelogues *La Chanca* (1962: *La Chanca*) and *Campos de Níjar* (1968: *The Fields of Níjar*), his commentary on poverty is joined by a growing appreciation of Spain's Moorish heritage and the cultural difference of the 'hot' 'south' (Mediterranean/Caribbean) against the 'cold' north, in part deployed as a counter-discourse to the denigratory use of 'africanos' (Africans) by some Catalonians for the Andalusian immigrant workers. This multiple—cultural and literary—metamorphosis bore its first fruit in the subjective narration of *Señas de identidad* (1966: *Marks of Identity*). The protagonist/alias Álvaro Mendiola struggles to put some order into both his family history—whose wealth is based on sugar plantations and slave labour in colonial Cuba—and that of Spain, working from a chaotic patchwork of fragmentary memories, official documents and other papers, and photographs. The reader shares in his disorientation as well as in the gradual piecing together of a meaningful picture and in his desire for a better social order than the monolithic Francoist regime, with its triad of oppressive state, reactionary Catholic Church, and the inequities of bourgeois capitalism in which he has been educated. As Álvaro shifts his attitudes and behaviour over the three novels of which *Señas de identidad* is the first, so the writing metamorphoses. A radical shift can be detected from an initial subjectivism and lingering nostalgia for order to a vision in which constant flux in individual and cultural identity becomes desirable (Lee Six 1990: 36). In *Reivindicación del Conde don Julián* (1970: *Count Julian*), all order is oppressive (seen across the trilogy in startling reworkings of the Catholic trope of martyrdom) and atrophying (constructed of images of human beings as crustaceans, social strata as geological strata, elements which cannot mix) (Lee Six 1990). More dramatic than the imagery, however, is the shift in narration which accompanies the author's embrace of the Maghreb—or at least his vision of it—as a creatively disordered society. In *Juan sin Tierra* (1975: *Juan the Landless*) the break with Spain is figured in the violently disorienting structure, imagery, and multilingualism accumulated over the three books (paratextually commented on by the author as part of a recuperation of radical Anglo-Saxon modernist narrative and a break with ruling Spanish conventions): finally, triumphantly but disturbingly, Arabic breaks through phonetically then graphically. In *Makbara* (1980) the search for identity focalized through marginalized outsiders, a transvestite fallen angel and Arabic immigrant, is again combined with radical textual experimentation. As suggested by the end of the Mendiola trilogy, Goytisolo's ideological, social, and political critique is not confined to Spain. It is the whole of Western consumer society that comes under attack, along with Christian and Marxist dogma, as all are placed in opposition to a sensual vision of the Arabic world in which liberation would seem to be achieved through sexual love. However, the language and structure employed, like the shifting sands of the desert repeatedly referred to, resist fixed interpretations and the text is marked by contradiction, ambiguity, and ambivalence.[5]

The tendency towards dissolution of the individual subject in discontinuous narrative can be found in the work of writers as diverse as Goytisolo, Cela (*San Camilo 36*, 1969), and Alfonso Grosso (*Inés is Coming*, 1970). However, it is the narrative of Juan Benet that is most often isolated as an antecedent for the intense experimentalism that was to follow in the 1970s. It is perhaps a measure of the hegemony of the *novela social* in the 1950s that Juan Benet, credited as a theorist of anti-realism and the aesthetic autonomy of literature, should have begun by publishing a neo-realist play, *Max*, in *Revista española* in 1953 (although he excluded it from his collected plays, published in 1971). *Nunca llegarás a nada* (1959: *You'll Never Get Anywhere*), begun in the mid-1950s, already prefigures some of the trademarks of his later writing including the trope of the inevitable but destination-less journey. It also introduces the fictional space of Región in which the majority of his novels have been set. While he was working on *Volverás a Región* (1967: *You'll Return to Región*) Benet published

---

[5] For English translations see Goytisolo (1977, 1981).

a collection of essays, *La inspiración y el estilo* (1965: *Inspiration and Style*), which attacked the *costumbrista* and realist traditions, including 1950s politically committed literature, arguing for the centrality of style over content in literature and the superiority of the 'poet' (the writer of fictions) over the historian (the latter merely reconstructed what was already there while the poet had to 'invent' reality). *Volverás a Región* is a very complex, layered narrative, which provides a minimal framework for readers—and no plot—through the interplay between third person narration and pseudo-dialogues of indeterminate time-frame and status between the two main characters, Dr Sebastián and a woman known always as 'Gamallo's daughter'. Gradually their memories and speculations, interspersed with the narrator's comments, allow the reader to reconstruct the fragmented history of the ruined Regi between the two main characters, Dr Sebastinovel represents an ironic deployment of myth that reveals it as one among many failed attempts to impose ordered structure on an unstable, entropic history (Labanyi 1989: 134); on the other (Herzberger 1991: 225) the deconstruction of both myth and history offers a model for a more pluralist history to be constructed in the future. Certainly the minute detail with which Región is constructed, prompting Ricardo Gullón's famous response (1973: 3) that it seems so 'real' that it sends you straight to the atlas to look it up, highlights the ways in which realist writing presents its fictions as reality to its readers but conversely the text produces poignant moments of loss and suffering which point beyond textuality to the experience of history.

8.2.1. Metafictions

If the Región novels have been read largely as demythifying inadequate representations of truth and reality through fiction, they simultaneously draw attention to the ways in which fiction itself is constructed and can be linked to a developing metafictional tendency which has been much studied in writers like Goytisolo and Martín Gaite,* but can be detected earlier in the writing of Gonzalo Torrente Ballester. His *Don Juan* (1963) centres around a chance encounter in Paris between the narrator and Leporello, the fictional don Juan's servant. The narrative complicates this play on fiction and reality as it evolves into an attempt by the narrator (fictional, of course, but within the reality of the text the 'real' character who encounters the fictional Leporello) to become the author of his own story. Leporello's response is effectively a Barthesian vision of the intertextual nature of fiction and of authorial control as an illusion, given the polysemic nature of language: 'La escribió porque . . . una fuerza superior le obligó a hacerlo. Pero no se le ocurre presumir de haberla inventado. La historia no tiene nada suyo, usted lo sabe. Ni siquiera las palabras le pertenecen' (Torrente Ballester 1963: 255) ('You wrote it because . . . a force superior to you forced you to do it. But don't think for a moment that you invented it. The story isn't yours at all and you know it. Not even the words are yours'). This synthesis of reality and fiction is developed in *La saga/fuga de J.B.* (1972: *The Saga/Escape of J.B.*) in which the excessive accumulation of experimental techniques — including the multiple perspectives of a series of J.B.s, a mix of first and third person narration, typographic experimentation and graphic elements such as tables, illustrations, and split columns, fragmented syntax, and suppression of punctuation—emphasizes the literary artifice of a text in which linguistic play serves to both humorously parody social structures and ironize the act of writing (Moral 1999: 506–7). The metafictional and ludic impulses of this text are carried through *Fragmentos de apocalipsis* (1977: *Fragments of Apocalypse*), subtitled *Como escribir una novela* (*How to Write a Novel*), and *La isla de los Jacintos Cortados* (1980: *The Island of Cut Hyacinths*), subtitled *Cartas de amor con interpolaciones mágicas* (*Love Letters with Magic Interpolations*), which complete Torrente Ballester's 'fantastic trilogy'.

The self-referential interrogation of discursive structures, found in authors such as Juan and Luis Goytisolo, Martín Gaite, and Torrente Ballester, is combined with the influence of the French *nouveau roman* ('new novel') and structuralist theories of language in the extremely 'writerly' texts of a group of narrators, including Mariano Antolín Rato, José María Guelbenzu, Javier Marías, José María Merino, Vicente Molina Foix, Germán Sánchez Espeso, and Pedro Antonio Urbina, who began publishing in the late 1960s and early 1970s and were promoted as a group by Barral from 1972 as the 'nueva novela española'* ('new Spanish novel'). The trend towards elitist intellectualism and often pretentiously erudite intertextual references, in texts in which plot all but disappears to be replaced by virtuoso linguistic play, culminates in the publication in 1983 of Julián Ríos's homage to Joyce, *Larva*. Whilst such extreme experimentalism would seem to have run its course, the equally self-referential pastiche of not only elite but also mass cultural forms in Marsé and Martín Gaite anticipated what would become a dominant trend in the 1980s in the work of writers such as Jesús Ferrero and Antonio Muñoz Molina whose novels are characterized by eclectic intertextuality. Muñoz Molina's overtly postmodern thrillers, *El invierno en Lisboa* (1987: *Winter in Lisbon*) and *Beltenebros* (1989), are marked by references not only to *film noir* (both were made into films) but also to jazz and pulp fiction.

8.2.2. *The* novela negra

This reworking of mass cultural forms into texts which cross the boundaries of high and low literature is a key feature of the phenomenally popular *novela negra*, which benefited from the existing demand for conventional detective fiction in translation which swelled further during the Transition. The form provided an ideal medium for the ironic critique of contemporary social and political conditions and the literary expression of the sentiment of disillusionment or 'desencanto' that was to come to characterize the transition to democracy (Colmeiro 1994: 211–17).

La verdad sobre el caso Savolta (1975: *The Truth on the Savolta Case*) by Eduardo Mendoza was the first such novel both to enjoy market and critical success and to have been credited with bringing high cultural respectability to the detective novel by garnering the prestigious Critics' Prize in 1976. Mendoza has also been credited with restoring to the Spanish narrative tradition the pleasures of storytelling and characterization, in advance of later developments (Alonso 1988: 21). Yet this difficult text is a far cry from conventional detective fiction or the realist narratives discussed in Chapter 7. It demands a complex process of narrative reconstruction from non-sequential fragments and is set in a multiple time-frame: the unspecified present from which the narrator-protagonist speaks; the context of the Barcelona workers' uprisings of 1917–19 (although Spires sets 1909 as the real historical referent) (Spires 1996: 76); the year in which the protagonist gives his testimony about the case to a New York judge; and finally the sequence in which the reader receives the narrative fragments. Playing on the conventions of the genre, the text throws up a series of enigmas but, for Spires, the point of them is not to solve them to get at a truth as in the classic deductive detective novel but rather to explore the possibility of plural identities at a time when the death throes of the Francoist regime still attempted to exert social control. In a sense the plot hinges on the revelation that everyone, whatever their initial claim, subsumes their ideals to a crass materialism which only Javier finally resists, suggesting an important element of social critique. Equally, this structuring allows the reader to look back critically on the polarized ideological positions of the workers' uprisings and, implicitly, other conflicts in Spanish history (Spires 1996: 85). The novel shares a concern with the self-referential novels by Martín Gaite, Goytisolo, and Benet about the nature of individual identity and the capacity for agency. However, whereas Gaite's exploration of the songs of Conchita Piquer sees them as permitting the self-expression of taboo emotions and pleasures at an unconscious level, and the writing of the papers which pile up in Gaite's novel is represented as a mysterious (unconscious) process, in Mendoza's novel, although Javier 'fluctuates from being subject to and subject of conflicting ideological forces' (Spires 1996: 84), he plays a major role in deciding the order in which events are read. The radical edge of the writing is ultimately more concerned with the issue of the subject and agency in its 'postmodern distrust for the totalizing picture' (Spires 1996: 87).

Probably the best known of the *novela negra* writers is Manuel Vázquez Montalbán, whose *Tatuaje* (1974: *Tattoo*) (another reference to Piquer) anticipated the phenomenal success and growth of this sub-genre in the 1980s and 1990s. He is most famous as the creator of Pepe Carvalho, the detective protagonist of a best-selling series which has run from 1972 to the 1990s. For Vázquez Montalban, the *novela negra* offered a fertile ground to reconnect with a realist narrative of social critique at a time when he judged that the novel had become self-involved, verbose, 'aideológica, apolítica, ahistórica' (in Macklin 1992: 51) ('unideological, apolitical, ahistorical'). Montalbán had proposed an oblique 'estética subnormal' ('subnormal aesthetic') to attack the lingering Francoist regime in a period of renewed social control—including renewed censorship—following the assassination of Carrero Blanco. This explicitly anti-realist aesthetics drawing on the absurd and Surrealism is exemplified in texts such as *Yo maté a Kennedy*

(1972: *I Killed Kennedy*) and *Cuestiones Marxistas* (1974: *Marxist Issues*). With *Tatuaje*, second in the Carvalho series, Vázquez Montalbán shifts to an ironic recuperation of realism inflected with self-reflexive intertextual pastiche. The Carvalho novels foreground the conventions of the *novela negra* genre, thereby underlining their fictional status. Montalbán retains the vanguardist technique of collage from his 'subnormal aesthetic' through the juxtaposition of a wide variety of social, cultural, and literary discourses, both high and popular, highlighting the ways in which reality is constructed. The role of coincidence and chance in the writing of both Mendoza and Montalbán marks a break with the centrality of deductive logic both to classic realism and the detective tradition of the nineteenth century and brings them, in this respect, within the bounds of postmodernism.

Juan Madrid, who published his first novel in 1980 and is now considered one of the best writers of the Spanish *novela negra*, also saw in the form 'la posibilidad de un nuevo discurso realista' ('the possibility of a new realist discourse') (in Macklin 1992: 51) but his accounts of the seedy underside of Madrid and how it connects to the official face of the city in its prostitutes, corrupt cops, and neo-fascists are reminiscent of Raymond Chandler's stylized realism and have none of the metafictional undercutting of Vázquez Montalbán's writing. His detective, Toni Romano, is a less extreme macho figure than the self-mocking anti-hero Pepe Carvalho, and Hart sees an evolution in his character from one novel to another (1987: 166), but it is in Jorge Martínez Reverte that we find the so-called 'soft-boiled' detective, Julio Gálvez. A journalist like his creator, his adventures are partly a keen satire of the Spanish press in the late 1970s but also of the corruption of corporate business in texts like his first novel *Demasiado para Gálvez* (1979: *Too Much for Galvez*). Unlike the ambiguous male detectives discussed earlier, Gálvez is a clear send-up of both the macho stereotype and its lingering realities in the supposedly professional spheres of press and business. The initially light-hearted tone gives way to increasing seriousness and violence as the investigation proceeds over a trail of corpses. Later novels trace Gálvez's bumbling attempts to deal with ETA—in *Gálvez en Euskadi* (1983: *Gálvez in the Basque Country*) the *etarras* are treated with greater respect than the capitalist villains of his first novel and the complex female character of Sara Goicochea, caught in the contradictions of capitalist commodification as a fierce businesswoman and her political commitment to an oppressed Euskadi, departs from the rather underdeveloped women of the rest of this group.

The only female author to try her hand at the genre during the Transition, however, is Lourdes Ortiz whose *Picadura mortal* (1979: *A Fatal Bite*), a light-hearted yet sometimes deeply violent text, is dominated by Barbara Arenas, the witty, hash-smoking, gun-toting detective who embraces some masculine stereotypes but also relies on a semi-ironic 'feminine intuition'. For Brooksbank Jones, she embodies 'both newly won protagonism [...] and the search for a point from where to exercise it' (Brooksbank Jones 1997: 164). Ortiz relates the negative portrayal of the police to personal experience in the 1960s when as a member of the Communist Party she took part in student demonstrations, was often detained, and knew many people 'who were beaten, burned by cigarettes and even [...] killed', but also to her generation's exploration of both past and present realities from which she feels they were often protected, 'wrapped in cottonwool' (in Hart 1987: 180). A more radical feminist reworking of the genre is María Antònia Oliver's *Estudi en Lila* (1987: *Study in Lilac*), in which the framework is used to investigate the consequences of rape.

8.3. A RETURN TO REALISM

If the defining characteristic of post-1975 narrative is a self-styled return to realism, with even Benet publishing a realist Región novel (*El aire de un crimen*, 1980: *The Air of a Crime*), the question remains of what is meant by realism. Whilst certain features of the classic nineteenth-century realist novel are recuperated, such as the attention to plot and location of the individual within social and family groupings, this narrative is distanced, and on the whole parodic, and interrogates notions of selfhood and identity through self-aware first person narrators or protagonists (Christie, Drinkwater, and Macklin 1995: 169). The millenarian existential malaise evidenced by turn of the century authors such as Miguel de Unamuno resurfaces as the twentieth century draws to a close and old belief systems and ideologies break down. However, crises of faith have been replaced by a more diffuse sense of unease described by Luis Landero as 'un malestar que la gente no sabe con qué ideas conectar, con qué principios, con qué referencias' (*Ajoblanco* 1993: 47) ('a malaise in which people don't know what ideas, what principles, what references to connect with'). This postmodern existentialist angst around notions of identity and selfhood can be traced in texts such as *Beatus ille* (1986: *Beatus ille*) by Muñoz Molina and *Papel mojado* (1983; *Wet Paper*) by Juan José Millás. In both these texts the investigative protagonist discovers himself to be a fictional creation of the very person he believed himself to be investigating. Likewise a pervading atmosphere of uncertainty and unease plagues the narrators of Javier Marías's *Todas las almas* (1989: *All Souls*) and *Corazón tan blanco* (1992: *Such a White Heart*), the protagonists of Soledad Puértolas's *Todos mienten* (1988: *Everybody Lies*) and *Queda la noche* (1989: *The Night Remains*), and Lourdes Ortiz's *Antes de la batalla* (1992: *Before the Battle*). The protagonist of Rosa Montero's* fourth novel *Amado amo* (1988: *Beloved Master*), César Miranda, suffers from acute anxiety brought about by his fear of failure within the highly competitive world of advertising. His insecurity manifests itself through physical symptoms such as insomnia, choking, and migraines which induce nausea and disturb his speech, thought, and vision. These sensations are reproduced in the fragmentary structure of the narrative which combines free indirect style with stream of consciousness. The use of parallelisms and repetitive structures serves to emphasize César's obsessive concern with 'Poder' (power) and 'Deber' (duty); notions which are no longer bound up with the state but with the multinational company for which he works.

The introversion of protagonists like César has led to accusations of solipsism being levelled at such personalized accounts. In Luis Mateo Díez's *La fuente de la edad* (1986: *The Fountain of Youth*) and Luis Landero's *Juegos de la edad tardía* (1989: *Games of Later Life*)—a spectacular return to the pleasures of the long and long-gestated novel—and *Caballeros de fortuna* (1994: *Gentlemen of Fortune*) characters escape the banality of mediocre everyday life through the creation of fantastic adventures or Cervantine imaginary worlds. Whilst it is true that characters such as Elsa in García Morales's *El silencio de las sirenas*, and Sergio Prim in Belén Gopegui's *La escala de los mapas* (1993: *The Scale of Maps*) prefer to relate to others through the imaginary and language, in other cases solitude or looking inwards is a way in which to reinsert the personal into the social. The protagonists of Muñoz Molina's *El jinete polaco* (1990: *The Polish Horseman*) and Julio Llamazares's *Escenas del cine mudo* (1994: *Scenes from the Silent Screen*) reconstruct the past from a series of photographs, grounding personal history in collective memory. This sense of community is central to Llamazares's novels *Luna de lobos* (1985: *Wolf Moon*) and the immensely successful *La lluvia amarilla* (1988: *Yellow Rain*) which recover a fast-disappearing rural Spain. For Labanyi it is the importance of the ordinary and community in the novels of Llamazares and Landero, despite the latter's postmodern concern with identity as fictional construct, which signifies a recuperation of history in the contemporary Spanish novel (1999: 161).

Arguably within writing by women a clear engagement with social and political issues is evident in texts of the late 1970s in which the tendency towards testimonial and quasi-autobiographic narrative runs broadly counter to the perceived move away from committed literature during that period (Brooksbank Jones 1997: 163). Novels such as Montero's *Crónica del desamor* represent collective experience. Its very title suggests a documentary-style chronicle of everyday life. It can be located spatially and temporally: Madrid in the early transitional years. The focus on feminist issues and debates, as well as Montero's occupation as a journalist, led to mixed reviews of the novel as bordering on propaganda. Certainly, its testimonial value is evidenced by the extraordinary success which the novel had with young women who identified with the protagonists to the extent that some wrote to Montero asking for personal advice as if she was some kind of agony aunt. However, whilst the novel is written predominantly in a realist mode and does focus on strategies of resistance and agency for women, it also incorporates self-conscious narrative techniques such as narrative commentary, multiple perspectives, and pervasive irony, through a metafictional framework to explore how experience is mediated through discursive practice in a postmodern critique of prevailing cultural paradigms.

8.4. WILD FANTASIES

In several writers not affiliated with the New Narrative equally significant departures were made. The rather staid, rooted, but socially committed tradition of the short story in particular found itself revolutionized. Luis Antonio de Villena uses the form to resist the dictates of compulsory heterosexuality and conformity in collections such as *Para los dioses turcos* (1980: *For the Turkish Gods*). Ana María Moix's collection *Las virtudes peligrosas* (1985: *Dangerous Virtues*) has an enlivening obliquity and a strong connection with European and American traditions of short fantasy fiction. Fantastic, uncanny, and Gothic are labels often attached to the short stories of Cristina Fernández Cubas—*Mi hermana Elba* (1980: *My Sister Elba*), *Los altillos del Brumal* (1983: *The Highlands of Brumal*), *El ángulo del horror* (1990: *A Terrifying Angle*), *Con Ágatha en Estambul* (1994: *With Agatha in Istanbul*)—which probe the relationship between self and other through the inner worlds of fantasy, fear, and desire. Such a relationship is frequently mediated through intertextual reference: thus Eduardo Haro Ibars's introduction to the stories which make up his *El polvo azul* (1985: *The Blue Powder*) acknowledges John Bart, *The Thousand and One Nights,* William S. Burroughs, Aleister Crowley, Jean Genet, and Juan Goytisolo (Haro Ibars 1986: 12–13), but the references are many more and much more fractured than this. The title story centres, sporadically, on 'El Polvo Azul, el burdel más famoso de toda la Vía Láctea' ('Blue Powder, the most famous brothel in the Milky Way'), owned by 65-year-old Bebé Solera (Barrel Baby/Barrel Drinker), last visited by the Prince de Guermantes, and equipped with 'holografías de los muchachitos y muchachitas y pulpos y amebas' ('holographic pictures of the [available] young boys and girls and octopuses and amoebas') (18). Although the story, which like many of the stories weaves in and out of English, consistently translates its own title with inappropriate primness, the other meaning of *polvo*—fuck—is far from suppressed. The dust is also a heroin-like drug inducing cinematic visions of characters such as the Toltec-featured 'Chico solar' (Sun Boy in *Intersecciones* (*Intersections*: 1991)). The resonances of Burroughs are strong, and the intertextual references diverse; set (sometimes) in 'Altazonia', home to Dr Mengele, aka Mengy, aka The Shaman Mengelius, it involves shape-shifting, technologically enhanced sadomasochism, sinisterly attractive Niños Salvajes de los Pantanos (Savage Swamp Boys), an Ambassador to Transexia, and a battle between a radical lesbian collective, The Witches, and the patriarchal Empire of the East.

On the only slightly less wild side of conventional science fiction Luis Eduardo Aute's 'Morir de viejo' ('Dying an Old Man') is a satirical, dystopic vision of late capitalist society written in (extremely) experimental verse; Carlo Fabretti's 'Sodomáquina' ('Sodomachinery') is a stab at sci-fi drama; and Ignacio Romeo's 'Gaziyel' is an essay in interplanetary transgender experience (in Santos 1982: 71–6, 113–32, 213–27). Such variety and adventurousness—deployed also by women writers of fantasy and science fiction*—underlie a mode of Spanish writing too frequently denigrated.

8.5. POETIC REWRITES

If in prose writing we read the story of a steady departure from fixity and certainty, in poetry, beyond the age of *poesía social*, aestheticist extremism and wild eclecticism asserted themselves. Luis Jiménez Martos (1989: 10), introducing the second of the influential Adonais anthologies, noted that Decadence, aestheticism, *culturalismo* (the high-profile deployment of mainly high cultural allusions), and indifference to social issues had been regularly cited 'since the 1960s' as the defining characteristics of contemporary poetry; not since the *modernismo* (a post-Romantic and sometimes politicized aestheticism in art and writing) of the turn of the nineteenth into the twentieth century had there been such a preoccupation with beauty in poetic writing (10). In a different direction the wild, near-Surrealist modes of Lorca in *Poeta en Nueva York* (written 1929–30: *Poet in New York*), Alberti in *Sobre los ángeles* (1929: *On the Angels*), and Cernuda in *Los placeres prohibidos* (1931: *Forbidden Pleasures*) had been echoed and updated by Carlos Edmundo de Ory, Juan Eduardo Cirlot, associated with the late-1940s to early-1950s movement *postismo* (Postism: coming after, or instead of, the trend towards straightforward reference to social and material realities), and poets of the next two decades such as Antonio Martínez Sarrión (in *Teatro de operaciones* (1967: *Theatre of Operations*)) and Blanca Andreu (*De una niña de provincias que se vino a vivir en un Chagall* (1981: *About a Girl from the Provinces Who Came to Live in a Chagall*)) carried that voice forward.

The dominant trend was against direct political reference, against simple speech patterns and obvious metres. It was even against Spanishness itself, in the sense that the grimy specifics of post-war living in the agricultural or new industrial communities of a hungry, dusty, and noisy Spain gave way to dreams of the past, dreams of far away, and thoughts of transcendence. Gabriel Celaya's* claim that poetry was a weapon loaded with the possibilities of the future began to sound a little belated or at least misdirected when voices were already being raised for a return to modernism, against the committed style of the unreconstructed left. Similarly, the 1965 publication of Leopoldo de Luis's *Antología de poesía social* is very much the marker of the end of an era when seen juxtaposed to the publication in 1966 and 1967 of Gimferrer's *Arde el mar* (*So Burns the Sea*) and Carnero's *Dibujo de la muerte* (*A Sketch of Death*), and to the beginnings of an influential new libertarian poetry more concerned with the politics of leisure (music, drinks, books, museums, travel, art, and television) and the pleasures and pains of language than with ordinary suffering and the politics of organized resistance. In both Carnero* and Gimferrer, for instance, social immediacy is conjured almost completely away in their early writing, persisting only as cultural reference contemplated at leisure albeit with intensity. While Spain is present in Carnero's poems 'Ávila', 'Castilla', and 'Amanecer en Burgos' it is as a cipher of history and an object of melancholy admiration. In 'Ávila' (Carnero 1983: 77–9) there is the modern sound of a record playing in a bar but it only accentuates '[el] sordo sonido de los siglos' (78) ('the muted sound of the centuries'); the contemporary world is eclipsed by the whispered traces of a past which is known to be full of vast significance but which is dead almost beyond redemption. Like Luis Cernuda,* in poems of *Las nubes*, Carnero is looking for an alternative Spain, crystallized in the literature and art of the past, a poetic gesture which has a number of interestingly conflicting effects. Even to attend to the Castilian theme is partly to side with a long-established official discourse; but to invoke tacitly Antonio Machado and the even more controversial Cernuda is to display and incite dissident sympathies. To overwrite the voice of the people such as it had been envisioned by Blas de Otero, for example, with such hushed echoes of the vague, dead, and distant past is to be profoundly anti-political; but to ignore the Falangist codings of these places—not least Burgos—is an act of rebellion quite as powerful as the emotion of the lines themselves.

Throughout the 1960s Spanish topographies could be drawn upon for more than mere nostalgic consolidation of the cultural ideology of the state. Juan Gil-Albert and Francisco Brines were able to find in the landscapes of the Levante (of south-eastern Spain), and more especially in northern Mediterranean cultures, symbolic spaces promising continuation and renewal. The bucolic and idyllic in liberal mode has strong representation too in the poets of the *Cántico* Group. However, the tendency which was to set the fashion for a decade was to eschew Spain and all things historically Spanish. The more or less moneyed elite, those with jobs abroad, and those who had occasional access to the spin-offs from either of the above travelled and wrote about it. Failing that they read about travel and wrote about that. And both groups frantically read foreign writers, watched foreign films, heard the new popular music from the United States and from Britain. In the poetry of 1965–75 foreign forms and references crowded in to construct alternative experiences.

8.5.1. *The fabulous world of words: the* novísimos *and others*

Introducing an anthology published in 1967, Enrique Martín Pardo (1967: 12, 14) judged Spanish poetry to be 'in a coma' and 'the world of language, the fabulous world of words' as still waiting to be discovered. It was just this sort of genuinely felt if extreme position that was being responded to in the stylistic eclecticism and cosmopolitanism of the poets who either were or could have been included in the (accidentally) seminal anthology *Nueve novísimos poetas españoles* (1970: *Nine of the Very Latest Spanish Poets*), which was to label a style of writing for the foreseeable future. Although the group was diverse (Debicki 1999: 195) and seen as a group only in retrospect, the *novísimos* are most commonly credited with introducing into poetry the new realities of urban living in the age of mass media; and more subtle analyses emphasize that it is not this alone which is of interest but the commingling of contemporary themes with—variously, though sometimes simultaneously—topics and techniques from the Classical Age, the European Decadence of the end of the nineteenth century, Hispanic *modernismo*, the German philosophical tradition, and *poesía pura*. By 1975, just as an era was about to open out in which new formations of social and political discourse would gain enormous urgency and momentum, poetry had, perversely, become famous in Spain for a radical turning away against direct intervention in political and social history. But their radical modernizing style meant that, arguably, these poets return closer to the world even than their increasingly isolated leftwing opposites: both the ivory tower and the streets of protest are abandoned in favour of ludic and closely detailed interventions in the reality of the culturally constructed and mediatized environment (as is clear in *Una educación sentimental* (1967: *A Sentimental Education*) by Manuel Vázquez Montalbán, one of the anthologized poets, which, like Terenci Moix's later prose autobiographical writing on the same era, is replete with popular cultural references of Spanish and foreign origin).

José María Álvarez, another of the anthologized Nine Poets, commenced his *Museo de cera* (*Wax Museum*) in 1960 and amplified re-editions of the work (the latest in the prestigious Visor series) and the publication of *El botín del mundo* (1994: *The World's Plunder*) have extended through more than thirty years certain of the powerful motifs of *culturalismo*: it reveals at one extreme a tendency to centre on the individual while at the same time insisting on a cultural reality constructed out of fragments. The poems are often intensely autobiographical and intimate yet kaleidoscopic in their fields of reference. 'Rebelión en el desierto' ('Rebellion in the Desert') fills the cultural desert with a real and imagined night out, combining different emotions and levels of experience (as well as using three literary epigraphs covering three countries and as many centuries). There is alcohol-softened contentment, the deliberate use of cliché to underline feeling, and the shock of sudden grief at the remembered death of a sister. There is sensory disruption, and yet also the micro-realism of documented sensations and impressions:

>Toca la orquesta 'Bésame, bésame mucho'
>Me sirvo un vodka. 'Como
>si fuera esta noche'.
>Bebo. 'La última vez'.
>Pequeña es la ciudad por los cristales.
>
>. . . . . .
>
>G. Swanson
>baja por la escalera.
>
>(Álvarez 1993: 222)

(The orchestra is playing 'Kiss me, kiss me hard.' | I pour myself a vodka. 'Like | tonight was.' | I drink. 'The very last time.' | The city looks small beyond the windows. [. . .] G. Swanson | comes down the stairway.)

Such a poem displays in exacerbated form the elite multiculturalism of much of the poetry associated with the *novísimos*. In his position statement in the *Novísimos* anthology, the poet Antonio Martínez Sarrión identifies, among the influences on these poets, the influx via Latin American publishing houses of previously unavailable (because banned) Spanish texts, the new Latin American narrative, knowledge of foreign languages, networking, travel outside Spain, and a special interest in non-literary cultural forms: film, folk music, blues, jazz, neo-Dadaism, pop art, and comics (in Moral and Pereda 1985: 69). Such inclusiveness was, of course, exclusive in more or less equal measure. In demonstration of the dependency of new publishing projects at the time on male-populated *tertulia* circuits, only one woman—Ana María Moix—was included in the *Novísimos* anthology, whereas Carmen Conde, Angela Figuera, and Gloria Fuertes were among a large number of women poets who were at the height of their far from reactionary powers. In its desire to react, like *postismo* before it, against a perceived prosaism in more socially oriented poets, and in its hunger for all that was non-Spanish, this poetry risked drowning out the established and dissident voices of Francisco Brines, Jaime Gil de Biedma, Ángel González, and José Ángel Valente, all of whom were moving through the 1960s towards a radical new poetry based in experience—experience understood in terms ethical and aesthetic and perceived at its clearest through intense poetic language.

Yet there was room within for just such a tendency. Pere Gimferrer's *La muerte en Beverly Hills* of 1968 gave readers America, and in *Arde el mar* (1966: *So Burns the Sea*) Montreux, Geneva, London, and, famously, Venice (the topic earned among the envious and the disapproving a nickname for this style *veneciano*). But although a poem like Gimferrer's 'Band of Angels' (Gimferrer 1968: 42) begins characteristically with a cascade of sensual images, in its figuring of love as a presence both human and abstract, both woman and poetry, it is in the tradition of Pedro Salinas's 'pure' love poetry of the 1930s; and it is written in limpid, time-honoured eleven-syllable lines: 'Ven hasta mí, belleza silenciosa, | talismán de un planeta no vivido, | imagen del ayer y del mañana | que influye en las mareas y en los versos' (42) ('Come to me, quiet beauty, | talisman of a planet never known, | image of the past and of tomorrow | with influence on tides and lines of verse').

There is, in fact, a powerful continuation of a more restrained, older, and extremely refined style to some of this writing too, that of the self-referential poetic mode of Jorge Guillén's *Cántico* (1950) and Salinas's poems of the 1940s and 1950s. The extreme close-up aesthetic of these two influential poets—an aesthetic whereby a droplet of water, or a pronoun, might be replete with the many meanings of the world—finds its way readily into the many otherwise rather uncontrolled poets, like Álvarez or José-Miguel Ullán, perhaps also by way of admiration for Pound and Stevens on the one hand, Greek epigrams and Japanese haikus on the other. Characteristic too was what at first seems a perversely contradictory attention to precision in formal systems, both as used in the composition of the line and stanza and as employed beyond poetry (in particular in music and geometry) or, in the case of Carnero's *Ensayo de una teoría de la visión: Poesía 1966–1977* (*An Essay on Theory of Vision: Poetry 1966–1977*), optics.

8.6. 'NEW' THEATRE: ABOLISHING THE PYRENEES

Around the middle of the 1960s, a new wave of dramatists was gradually making its presence felt, albeit in restricted circles. Some had been writing in obscurity since the 1950s, others were born in the late 1930s or early 1940s. Fernando Arrabal was already achieving cult status abroad, but his highly individual brand of absurdist-Surrealist-libertarian theatre has had little influence within Spain. By the early 1970s, a sense of the existence of a broadly defined avant-garde or 'underground' movement had coalesced (encouraged by interest from abroad, especially the USA—see Wellwarth 1972), coming to be known as the *nuevo teatro* (New Theatre). The term embraces a large number of playwrights developing a wide range of dramatic techniques, but implies a shared critique of realism as a restriction of creativity and a common desire to overcome the insularity of Spanish culture, absorbing influences such as Valle-Inclán, Jarry, Surrealism, Brecht, Artaud, the Absurd, the Living Theatre, and Grotowski.

José Ruibal* has articulated the most forceful critique of realism as a means of opposing oppressive systems or ideologies, arguing that any attempt to represent 'reality' in familiar ways implies an acceptance of the terms dictated by a 'system' that maintains itself by manipulating ideas and language. The only answer is to reject those terms, 'no considerarlos interlocutores válidos' (Ruibal 1984: 36) ('to refuse to recognize them as valid interlocutors'). Ruibal proposes a more radical assault on a dehumanizing modern world, exposing and subverting manipulation, irrationality, and alienation by exaggerating them: 'Mediante la dinamita de la manipulación poética del lenguaje llegar a la destrucción de la realidad, de esa realidad política que, al falsificarnos, nos niega' (Ruibal 1977: 112) ('By making use of the dynamite of the poetic manipulation of language, to achieve the destruction of reality, of that political reality that negates us by falsifying us'). The Spanishness and sociohistorical detail pursued by the realists are seen as limiting factors that privilege circumstantial content to the detriment of form and ideas, as well as falling into a 'trampa nacionalista' ('nationalist trap')—complicity with the right's insistence that 'Spain is different'. He proposes a 'teatro sin Pirineos' (104) ('theatre without Pyrenees') based on symbolic verbal and visual forms constituting 'un lenguaje universalmente válido' (117) ('a universally valid language').

Words, instead of functioning as transparent vehicles of communication between characters, become signifying elements to be decoded and recoded, exposing the ways in which reality and identity are constructed through language. The figures who utter these words are projections of concepts rather than independent personalities: 'Salen de la boca de sus palabras' (Ruibal 1984: 29) ('They come out of the mouths of their words'). All the resources at the playwright's disposal are elements of a 'totalidad poética' ('poetic totality') built around a central idea or symbol and creating its own autonomous reality (24). The objective is not necessarily complete abstraction, but artistic freedom: the freedom to play with words and images, explore the possibilities of theatre, transcend topicality through symbolism and uninhibited creativity, and jolt audiences out of their normal habits of spectatorship. Some of Ruibal's own texts have been discussed in Chapters 4, 5, and 6 and construct startling stage images: the dictator's dome founded on skulls in *El hombre y la mosca* (1968: *The Man and the Fly*), the couple crushed under a huge stone and a heap of household gadgets in *Los mutantes* (1968: *The Mutants*).

Luis Riaza* has more cryptic ways of describing his approach, advocating 'la destrucción de los atributos específicos de la representacíon teatral' ('the destruction of the specific attributes of theatrical representation') so as to disconcert spectators and cast them into a metaphorical shipwreck out of which they are forced to struggle to 'salvarse, por sí mismo, activamente, del maremágnum generalizado' ('Prólogo, in Riaza 1978: 115) ('save themselves—actively, participatively—from the havoc around them'). Pieces such as *El desván de los machos y el sótano de las hembras* (1974: *Males in the Attic, Females in the Basement*) and *Revolución de trapo* (1990: *Rag Revolution*) play obsessively with the same motifs: multiplicity of roles, interchangeability of genders, sets with multiple levels, elaborate intertextuality, and abrupt changes of register. Francisco Nieva (best known as a stage and costume designer) insists that theatre is nothing to do with practical reality: 'Es una ceremonia ilegal, un crimen gustoso e impune' (Nieva 1975: 41) ('It is an illicit ceremony, a crime committed with gusto and impunity'). He cultivates verbal and visual excess and an atmosphere of ritualistic, orgiastic anarchy in works such as *Pelo de tormenta* (1962: *Storm Hair*, premièred in 1997) and *La carroza de plum canned* (1971: *The Carriage of Hot Lead*). Jerónimo López Mozo's *Cuatro happenings* (1967–9: *Four Happenings*) is a series of three enigmatic, minimalist experiments in movement, repetitive gestures, and few words, together with a poetic piece based on Picasso's *Guernica*. Productions of some of Manuel Martínez Mediero's plays in the 1970s achieved greater success than the New Theatre were used to, combining allegories of power, cruelty, and sexual repression with relatively accessible comedy. Eduardo Quiles develops what he calls a 'teatro del personaje' ('theatre of characters') thoughtfully exploring memory and solitude, sometimes using large puppets in place of actors, as in *La navaja* (1985: *The Razor*). José Sanchis Sinisterra is not usually associated with the New Theatre since he did not become well known as a playwright until 1980, but he had begun writing quirky, challenging plays in the early 1960s. His most characteristic preoccupation is metatheatricality, explored most successfully in *¡Ay, Carmela!* (1986), which combines down-to-earth colloquial dialogue and humour with a complex structure of flashbacks, fantasy, and theatre-within-theatre.

The 1980s saw a great deal of experimentation in terms of

performance (by high-profile directors such as Lluís Pasqual and improvisational groups), stimulated by increased public subsidy under the PSOE government and the creation in 1984 of the Centro Nacional de Nuevas Tendencias Escénicas (National Centre for New Directions in Theatre), but little of this activity was based on texts by existing Spanish dramatists. Dramatists writing in Catalan, notably Salvador Espriu, Joan Brossa, and Manuel de Pedrolo, have also worked inventively in symbolic, Surrealist, and Brechtian modes, but before the 1980s their contact with and influence on theatre in Castilian was limited (see George and London 1996). A notable exception was Jordi Teixidor's *El retaule del flautista* (1968: *The Legend of the Piper*), a Brechtian version of the tale of the Pied Piper that was much performed in Catalan and Castilian by independent theatre groups. Since 1980, writers such as Josep Maria Benet i Jornet, Rodolf Sirera, and Sergi Belbel have more regularly achieved success with plays translated into Castilian.

Further reading

Christie, Drinkwater, and Macklin (1995); Colmeiro (1994); Debicki (1999); Fuentes Mollá (1991); Halsey and Zatlin (1999); Oliva (1989); Perriam (1999); Ruiz Ramón (1989).

9
Languages of Pleasure

9.1. THE PERSISTENCE OF ROMANCE

The removal by death of the dictator and subsequently of formal censorship facilitated experimentation from the second half of the 1970s with erotic and pornographic writing. Such was the compelling power of the drama of the death, and such the emphasis subsequently placed in popular speech and by a gleeful liberal and rueful conservative press on the phenomenon of *destape* (with the two meanings of 'release of pressure' and 'going topless'), that it is all too easy to entertain the misconception of a Spain under tight moral lock and key right up until the punctual event of November 1975. Whereas it is certainly true that with the relaxation of censorship nudity in the theatre and cinema (and not just, as it had been for years, on the smarter tourist beaches) and pornography in the news kiosks (and not just under the counter) were suddenly a presence, the process of acclimatization is one with no easy point of origin and with many trajectories. Although many literary narratives and dramatic works of and about the Franco years are concerned with the denial and repression of pleasures, other texts were able to construct alternative spaces in which to explore fantasies or pursue ideals (even within the domains of religion, as is clear from the sensual, religious poetic writings of Adriano del Valle appearing in *Vértice* in the early 1940s and, at the end of the decade, in the poetry of the *Cántico* group of poets).

9.1.1. *Popular romantic fictions*

While the reclamation of memory, a focus on personal space, and the subversive potential of domestic intensity can, in middle- to highbrow texts by women writers such as Quiroga,* Rodoreda, and Martín Gaite, constitute an authentic resistance to the dominant ideology, in texts with wider female audiences the same emphases may lead, at least at first, in quite different directions. The radio soap opera and *fotonovela Lucecita*—the 'enthralling story of a country girl'—ran on radio five days a week for ten months of 1975 accompanied by a weekly run of 200,000 storybooks and carried an extremely conformist message based on the values of sacrifice, blamelessness, and simple love using its focus on the individual heroine to erase considerations of class (Sempere 1976: 170). The output of 'Corín Tellado' novels (at one per week) and their graphic versions (fortnightly) was matched by the serial *Simplemente María* (which in 1972 sold 170,000 issues a week), with many competing publishing houses entering the fray (Amorós 1977: 12).

The popularity of formulaic, serialized, and romantic fiction remained undiminished after the transition to democracy. Indeed, the market would seem to have expanded, as the previously dominant Edimundo/Corín Tellado has been joined by Harlequin Ibérica, subsidiary of the multinational company Harlequin who have sales of 200 million books per annum worldwide. In 1994 Harlequin Ibérica's sales of 3.5 million books per annum made it one of the most successful presses in Spain (Cruz 1994). This success has affected the market share of *fotonovelas* which was drastically reduced until they too resurfaced under the aegis of an Italian multinational. The popular novels (some 120 of them) of Rafael Pérez y Pérez, at their apogee in the 1940s and 1950s but reprinted through into the 1980s (and still occupying considerable metres of shelf-space in the bookstores of the Corte Inglés) carry on into post-Franco Spain attitudes of other eras (including, in *El hombre de casco* of 1941, a heroic version of the fifteenth century deemed worth reprinting as late as 1980). *Amor y dinero* (*Love and Money*), of 1951, has on the cover of its 1981 fifth reprint a glamorous blonde with a distinctly non-1950s hairstyle and a lowcut white dress to signal the persistence of its appeal. The novel is the story of the pious and timid but lovely orphan María Rosa, at first sure in her relationship to the medievalist scholar uncle who finds he must take over responsibility for her once she is 18, but later revealed to have been left in the care of nuns by a mysterious sailor. She is horrified that the small-town Catalonian community she finds herself in will think her a treasure-hunting imposter, but is finally reconfirmed in her claim and lineage and finds love in the strong arms and against the wide chest of aristocratic Víctor, who alarmingly soon after meeting María Rosa declares, in an unexpected shift into sentimental discourse, that she must not fret about the uncertainty of her position: 'El amor tiene alas ..., alitas de seda. O de encaje. O de pluma. Volemos juntos a otras regiones ...' (82) ('Love has wings ..., little silken wings. Or wings of lace. Or feather. We are going to fly together to another realm'). Her betrothal—an event which is 'un cuadro castizo' (103) ('a picture of real Spanishness')—and eventual marriage—'no había doncellica que no evocara con suspiros nostálgicos la hermosa ceremonia' (216) ('there was scarce a pretty maid that did not recall with sighs of nostalgia the lovely ceremony')—are her only way out of destitution or perpetual enclosure in the convent, and they link her to all intents and purposes forever to this rambling young man, her dry and history-obsessed uncle, and a scenario of caricature.

Unlike the case of Ana Ozores in Leopoldo Alas's famed novel of 1885, the case of María Rosa is not one treated with irony by the author; nevertheless, for some of his readers—connoisseurs of soap and romance with long experience—part of the enjoyment of Pérez y Pérez's books may well be one of reclamation and reading against the grain, as Brooksbank Jones (1997) has argued for other texts. Such is also the case for the novels and short stories of Concha Linares-Becerra: the much reprinted *La extraña llamada* (1980: *A Strange Voice Calling*) begins with a disciplined, minute-by-minute account of protagonist Paula's flight from a claustrophic, remote village and the attentions of the landowner. When a young and handsome man on the train gallantly drapes his coat over her knees and brushes against her, though, she feels that her adventure is like the sort of natural disaster, an earthquake for example, which is followed by 'ciclos de desenfreno erótico' (23) ('cycles of uninhibited eroticism'). The second part of the novel, accordingly, becomes thematically and generically disinhibited and indulges in thick and numerous layers of allusion to times past. Paula and the man become involved in a kind of a thriller and quest narrative, take refuge in a sombre and ghostly old mansion in Segovia (source of the Strange Voice of the title and a mélange of the sixteenth century, the Gothic, and the 1898-style topos of the decline of grandeur), and eventually marry: the old house, previously, had induced a chill in Paula, but this time 'mi estremecimiento fue de gozo: el mismo que debe sentir la tierra en primavera al disponerse a dar frutos' (220) ('the shivers that ran through me were of joy: the same joy which the earth must feel in springtime when it readies itself to bear fruit'). Here, then, is a woman more or less in charge of her own narrative but whose body is in the throes of elemental reflex actions, subject to the threat of bestial attack and primitive hatred, and in flight towards nightmarish unreality. As for Pérez y Pérez's María Rosa, the only resolution is marriage, the domestication of strangeness.

9.1.2. Rewriting romance

The persistence of earlier discourses such as these finds an echo in the tendency by younger contemporary writers of the genre to maintain traditional characterizations of women, thereby minimizing the transformation in women's status that has taken place in contemporary society. This tendency is one which has been criticized by Spanish feminists concerned with issues of equality (Brooksbank Jones 1997: 170). However, novels by women writers have engaged with the ambivalent pleasure women may feel in reading romance. Martín Gaite's novel *El cuarto de atrás** (1978: *The Back Room*) foreshadows her discussion of the evasive pleasures of romantic texts for women in the restrictive post-war period in her study *Usos amorosos de la postguerra española* (1987: *Love and Courtship Customs in Postwar Spain*). The narrator C., closely identified with Martín Gaite herself, evokes a variety of popular cultural texts including romantic novels, Hollywood films, and *bolero* and *copla* lyrics of the 1940s and 1950s. However, these are not simply escapist texts. They offer resistant models of womanhood undermining the traditional roles promoted by the Church and Sección Femenina. In particular, C. admires the singer Conchita Piquer whose voice breaks through the anaesthetized silence of the post-war period to recount stories of marginality, loss, and pain.

C.'s ambiguous nostalgia for past pleasures is most keenly expressed in her attitude towards romantic fiction. On the one hand, she condemns texts such as *Cristina Guzmán* for propagating the ideals of the Sección Femenina, whilst on the other, she admits that she too wrote a *novela rosa* as a child. However, her heroine, Esmeralda (whose unusual name significantly begins with an 'E' serving to identify her with the author Elisabeth Mulder who signifies exotic cosmopolitanism for the narrator), despises wealth and does not aspire to the happy-ever-after ending of conventional plots. Nonetheless, there is an obviously strong, nostalgic pull for the narrator. There is even some confusion between her mysterious interlocutor, a tall, enigmatic stranger who appears on a dark, stormy night, and the hero of her sentimental novel, Alejandro. However, in *El cuarto de atrás* there is no typical romance ending, instead there is a great deal of unresolved sexual tension. Ultimately the narrator, like Andrea in *Nada* and the other protagonists analysed by Martín Gaite in *Desde la ventana* (1987: *From the Window*), is a 'chica rara' who does not fit in (see Chapter 4).

In *Te trataré como a una reina* (1983: *I'll Treat You Like a Queen*) Rosa Montero* uses the *bolero* as a focus for the romantic fantasies and dreams of a better life of a group of marginalized characters. The happy ending suggested in the title is shown to be an empty promise as each of the characters' fantasies is frustrated in turn, leading to acts of extreme physical violence. Indeed, the opening pages of the novel, which depict a brutal attempted murder, immediately debunk any romantic illusion the reader might have. Whilst the text obviously exposes the limitations of romantic fantasy, it also acknowledges the possibilities for resistance inherent in the genre which may serve as an outlet for characters' anxieties, frustrations, and dissatisfaction. In particular it provides solace and hope for the club singer, Bella, a middle-aged woman who had grown up during the Franco years. Bella and Antonia are 'mujeres raras' who, like the younger protagonists of the novels discussed in Chapter 4, are deemed abnormal because they have not followed the prescribed roles for women: marriage and motherhood. At different times in the text they are both deemed hysterical, Antonia for her passive resignation to her brother's harsh treatment of her which results in fits of tears, and Bella for her aggressive attack on Antonio after she discovers his role in destroying Antonia's relationship with a younger man. They are both described by men as being mad 'solteronas' (old maids) in keeping with the negative portrayal of single women in the press and popular writing of the 1940s and 1950s, which is when these characters were young.

Not all *bolero* lyrics shore up patriarchal ideology and glorify romantic love. Indeed, Bella's favourite singer Olga Guillot was famous for singing about deceived women who had had enough and these songs would seem to provide a method of negotiating an unpleasant present. However, despite her acknowledgement that it is better to live alone than to enter into a relationship for the sake of it, Bella allows her fantasies of going away to Cuba with Paco to blind her to his obsession with a younger woman. She converts him into a mysterious, romantic hero and dreams of escape in terms of marriage, the goal of conventional, romantic fiction: 'Quería llevarla a Cuba y unirse a ella atravesando un océano, que era cosa que sacramentaba más que un cura' (Montero 1983: 114) ('He wanted to take her to Cuba and bind himself to her by crossing an ocean, that was more of a sacrament than any performed by a priest').

The pessimistic conclusion of the novel, in which relationships break down and characters are assaulted physically and psychologically, would seem to suggest that breaking with traditional gender roles is not an easy process and will require a radical shift in the behaviour and attitudes of both men and women. *Te trataré como a una reina* was written at a time of disenchantment with the democratic process, perhaps felt most keenly by women who perceived the gap between the formal, legal measures brought in by successive governments to ensure equality and the damaging cultural substructures still in place in Spanish society.

9.2. EROTICISM AND SEXUAL LIBERATION

If the liberal, leisured middle classes in their theatregoing and novel-reading of the 1960s and 1970s were learning to be entertained and instructed by interrogations soft and hard of patriarchal structures, so too the intelligentsia were able to supplement their consumption of fictions with theoretical and empirical investigations in the middle- to highbrow political press from the mid-1960s onwards. In particular, as the decade turned, there was an intensification of debates around morality, sexuality, and relationships. The magazine *Triunfo* ran a series of special editions: on 'Eroticism in Spain' in September 1970; on women in November (tellingly entitled 'La mujer: Una frustración, un problema, una revolución pendiente': 'Women: Frustrations, Problems, and a Revolution in the Making'); and, in April 1971, on marriage, including pieces by Martín Gaite, Alcalde, and Falcón. This last was banned (*secuestrado*) and the magazine shut down for three months.

Meanwhile, the 1971 manifesto of the Frente de la Liberación Homosexual del Estado Español called for far-reaching measures to guarantee every individual's right to 'hacer con su cuerpo lo que quiera' ('to do with their own body what they wish') (García Pérez 1976: 41), a call taken up, for example, by Villena, not only in his poetry and short stories but also in an essay in a joint volume with Fernando Savater (Savater and Villena 1982: 87–157) in which the alternative traditions of the late 1960s are drawn on in an exploration of new affective, erotic, and family arrangements.

The first United Nations International Women's Year in 1975 had seen a flurry of articles on women's issues and special editions of *Urogallo* and *Cuadernos para el diálogo,* and by the late 1970s serious and wide-ranging debates around the body had begun to take place in *Argumentos* and in influential alternative magazines such as *Ajoblanco, Bicicleta,* and *El viejo topo* (albeit in a contradictory context of new socialist, old anarchist, and ecological politics, all filtered through an editorial system dominated by only half-reconstructed men: the humour of the last of these examples is often laddish and politically naive). During the late 1970s and early 1980s feminist magazines such as *Vindicación feminista* explored the possibilities for change through liberating sexual politics. However, various articles published in the feminist press of the time would seem to suggest that sexual liberation did not equate to women's liberation. Laura Freixas analysed the 'machista' discourse of supposed progressives, 'progres' (1979: 95), who she argued had developed a consumerist notion of sex in contrast to their Marxist or socialist ideological background. She concluded that the pill had been proffered as the magic key to women's liberation without the necessary revision of the patriarchal ideology which pervades attitudes towards sexuality. In contrast women writers explored sexuality from a female-centred perspective which had caused problems with censors in the past: for example Carmen Kurtz's novel *Al lado del hombre* (1961: *Beside the Man*) had difficulties due to the representation of an unpunished extramarital affair and Elena Soriano's 1950s trilogy *Mujer y hombre* (*Woman and Man*) was prohibited from circulation due to its female-centred eroticism and critical portrayal of marriage. Montserrat Roig and Rosa Montero have both examined the contradictory relationship between sexual and women's liberation. In her essay 'Nosotras las mujeres' (1981: 'We Women'), Roig discussed the role of the male gynaecologist in Spanish society and argued that it was to uphold the patriarchal order in much the same way as priests had done before them through controlling access to knowledge and manipulating a moralistic discourse of sexuality. In a study carried out by the sociologist Julio Iglesias de Ussel in 1983, gynaecological texts were found to prescribe not only what is to be considered biologically normal for a woman but also normative sexual, familial, and social behaviour. Subjects which were omitted from these texts or discussed as pathological abnormalities were those which would indicate an autonomous female sexuality, for example, masturbation, abortion, contraception, and homosexuality.

9.2.1. *Eroticism and female self-discovery*

In her 1979 novel *Crónica del desamor,* Rosa Montero confronted many topical issues which were still taboo or politically sensitive at that time. The novel is a collage of the day-to-day experience of a group of thirty-somethings, predominantly women, which is held together by the unifying thread of sexual politics in post-Franco transitional Spain. Montero aligns herself with feminists campaigning for change through her sympathetic representation of the problematic access to contraception and the consequences of having an abortion abroad or an illegal abortion within Spain. She also questions the reduction of women's liberation to sexual permissiveness through her swipes at so-called progressive men, particularly the gynaecologist who is portrayed as thinking in terms of male pleasure and privilege.

The transgressive portrayal of sexuality from a woman's point of view runs throughout Montero's narrative production, in which she not only critiques the sexual objectification of women but also addresses the issue of agency for women by depicting them as sexual subjects. This is particularly transgressive in *Te trataré como a una reina*, where the protagonists Bella and Antonia are middle-aged single women who cross social boundaries by engaging in sexual relationships with younger men. In the case of Antonia she is transformed from sexual object to subject in a graphic scene which combines masturbation, exhibitionism, and voyeurism. Initially she channels her sexuality through rape fantasies in which she is a passive participant. These fantasies, which allow her to deny her sexual agency, reflect the repressive prohibitions of her

Catholic upbringing, which fall by the wayside when she enters into a relationship with Damián. Initially his intrusion into her fantasy world—he watches her masturbate through a window and begins to masturbate himself—causes her shame but when she realizes that in fact he is the more embarrassed of the two she becomes increasingly aroused.

Damián, an orphan, suffers deep-rooted fears about sexuality, such as the fear of merging completely with Antonia and losing his identity. Despite his apparent confidence, Antonia's brother Antonio experiences similar anxieties. Whilst he publicly boasts about his conquests in crude terms and sets himself up as a romantic don Juan, in private he is terrified of not being able to perform satisfactorily. Montero juxtaposes his pornographic tales of his exploits with his inner fears of women as suffocating Gorgons, vampires, and bottomless pits, thereby exposing his discourse to scrutiny by the reader. This focus on constructions of women's sexuality in men's discourse is the key structural element of the text. It is framed by a male-authored article about Bella's attack on Antonio and punctured by the monologic transcriptions of male voices which were used to compose the article. Through the careful positioning of these accounts, the unreliability of the male witnesses interviewed and the possible distortions in any interpretation or reading of an event are clearly demonstrated. The ensuing emphasis on male sexual inadequacies and debunking of narcissistic male fantasy is also extensively developed in *Luis en el país de las maravillas* (1982: *Luis in Wonderland*) by Consuelo García. As a consequence of women's liberation, Luis's forty-eight women refuse to continue in the worship of his 'santa polla' (Holy Dick) and inform him that the sex wasn't that good anyway.

9.2.2 *Performing female pleasure*

For Judith Drinkwater (1995) writers such as Montero, Roig, and Esther Tusquets engage with erotic discourses of pleasure and desire as an integral part of the process of female self-discovery. Most female playwrights of the 1980s and 1990s have tended to avoid the feminist militancy of the texts by Falcón* in which beleaguered women never get the chance to express their desires. They resist being labelled as feminist writers, arguing that women writing about women should no longer be regarded as extraordinary.

While continuing imbalances of power in relationships and society associated with gender are not underestimated, there is a greater sense of confidence and assertiveness—in the female characters and in the tone of the writing itself. The women in their plays may not be getting everything they want, but they are being represented more often as independent beings prepared to say what they want.

Paloma Pedrero emphasizes her desire to achieve a sense of normality about women being represented as individuals, rather than being defined by reference to a man—as wife, mother, lover, or daughter. Her plays are about men and women tentatively negotiating relationships in a complex society in which men often have the upper hand but which is not defined primarily as patriarchal. Women and men are equally uncertain about their roles, although men are more likely to fall back on aggression and women more likely to fool themselves into believing that they have found love and to allow themselves to be taken advantage of, as in Montero's *Te trataré como a una reina*, a point made by Pedrero in the introduction to *Locas de amar* (1994: *Soft in the Heart*), 'Las mujeres [. . .] convertimos a veces las relaciones amorosas en dolorosas obsesiones, en masoquistas abrazos al desamor' (Pedrero 1997: 15) ('We women [. . .] sometimes turn amorous relationships into painful obsessions, masochistically embracing indifference').

Each of the short plays in *Noches de amor efímero* (*Nights of Ephemeral Love*, 1990–4) consists of a brief encounter at night between a man and a woman, an unexpected departure from routine which gives them an opportunity to experiment with gender roles. The language of each text—realistic, sometimes sexually explicit, with occasional delicate touches of lyricism—precisely maps the shifting balance of power in the games the protagonists play. The women tend to be the ones who consciously adopt and adapt roles, while the men seem to be less imaginative, less playful, taking their identity much more for granted. Pedrero's theatre is an effective blend of intelligent, ironic sophistication with candid sentimentality and occasional jagged edges of bitterness and violence. In general, the conclusions suggested are moderately encouraging: in a fluid, postmodern society, it is possible for men and women to redefine their identities and renegotiate their relationships, and for women in particular to begin to express what they want. Other recent texts by female dramatists suggest a similarly tentative but affirmative exploration of women's self-discovery. Ana Diosdado's *Camino de plata* (1990: *Silver Road*) is also about a rejected wife learning how to overcome her rage and dependence, and *Un maldito beso* (1989: *A Damned Kiss*) by Concha Romero, *De película* (1992: *Just Like in the Movies*) by Carmen Resino, and *Sólo lo digo por tu bien* (1993: *I'm Only Telling You This for your Own Good*) by Pilar Pombo all deal with women achieving independence and individuality in some way.

9.2.3. Tentative lesbian narratives

As already suggested, Esther Tusquets was one of the first women writers to focus explicitly on lesbian sexuality. The relationship between Clara and Elia in *El amor es un juego solitario* suggests tender fusion as the women communicate in a secret language unknown to men:

[M]ecidos los dos cuerpos en el ritmo suave que Elia, al volver a hablar, va creando con sus palabras, acunadas las dos por estas palabras dulcísimas que le brotan secretas y terribles a una Elia que Clara todavía no conoce, pero a la que acaso ha podido en sueños intuir, una Elia en cualquier caso de la que ni el marido ni los amantes ni mucho menos Ricardo han podido nunca saber. (Tusquets 1979: 103)

(The two bodies rocked by the gentle rhythm that Elia, as she begins to speak again, creates with her words, the two of them cradled by those so-sweet words which spring forth, secret and terrible, from an Elia that Clara does not know yet, but whom she has just been able to sense in dreams, an Elia in any case which neither the husband, nor the lovers, nor Ricardo have ever been able to know.)

In the disturbing close to the novel, these two women are forcefully reinscribed within a male-centred sexual discourse of violation. Ricardo, Elia's lover and Clara's classmate, attempts to rape Clara and then brutally sodomizes Elia who is deprived of her voice and reduced to a dribbling vagina on heat.

Lesbian voices, as in other Western cultures, have emerged more slowly than male homosexual ones in the post-1968 and post-Stonewall era and have been subjected to the familiar double silencing (misogynistic and homophobic), and even in the late 1990s continue to have a relatively low profile. In an article written in 1993 for *El país* in collaboration with Madrid's Lesbian Feminist Collective, Montero observes that whilst 'gay' culture has had a notable public presence, lesbian culture has remained invisible and largely ignored. In a study of *Julia* (1969) by Ana María Moix, Linda Gould Levine notes that critics have avoided alluding to the homosexual overtones of the novel (1983: 304). Over the course of a sleepless night the 20-year-old Julia recollects instances from her past as she lies in a hospital bed following a suicide attempt. Her intense physical aversion to men and recurrent obsession with a series of strong female figures would seem to stem from traumatic childhood experiences, including her rape at the age of 6 by a family friend and the emotional deprivation felt in the relationship with her mother. Her passion for her literature lecturer Eva is never explicitly recognized as lesbianism by Julia although the intensity of desire is evident. Moix's following novel *Walter, ¿por qué te fuiste?* (*Walter, Why Did You Go?*) is much more daring in its portrayal of lesbianism as well as other sexual taboos such as masturbation, sodomy, and bisexuality. Considering this novel was published in 1973, it is therefore not surprising to learn that the censor made forty-five cuts, sexual and political, before publication (Gould Levine 1983: 309). An intense relationship between two women—the narrator and Mar— is also central to the short story 'Mar' by Montserrat Roig, first written in 1980 but published in 1990 in the collection *El cant de la joventut* (*The Song of Youth*). Although the relationship is once more clearly transgressive, the anonymous narrator/protagonist again does not identify it as lesbian. It is reminiscent of the intense bond between Kati and Judit in *L'hora violeta* and likewise ends with the suicide of the more bohemian woman. Whilst the flowing, lyrical style brings to mind the pulsating language of Tusquets's trilogy which can be identified with a diffuse female eroticism, the narrator cannot break free from male-identified discourses of desire (Davies 1994: 87–92).

The perceived invisibility of lesbian relationships is perhaps what gives impact to the conclusion to Carme Riera's story 'Te deix, amor, la mar com a penyora' (1975) ('I Leave You, my Love, the Sea as an Offering'). Heterosexist assumptions are unsettled when the intense affair described is eventually revealed to have been between two women. As lesbian writing (or writing on lesbians) gains a higher profile in the 1990s such problematic, cautious subtlety is to a certain extent replaced by tactically sophisticated directness, and the comfortable world of Tusquets is superseded by more convincingly representative ones.

9.3. PLEASURE IN POETRY

In established poetry published by the mainstream houses in the 1970s and 1980s a similar picture emerges of the simultaneous revelation of same-sex desire and the disavowal of its disruptive power by means of a dense structuring of the text around established prosodic conventions and high cultural references. In the case of writing by men, there was, given lyric poetry's interest in love and relative lack of interest in marriage, an erotically dissident tradition to build upon, not only in poetry from abroad (perhaps most famously and influentially that by Pablo Neruda and Octavio Paz) but in the far from conventional love poetry of the Spanish Generation of 1927 (Luis Cernuda's *Los placeres prohibidos* (*Forbidden Pleasures*) of 1931, and *La destrucción o el amor* (1935: *Destruction, or Love*) by Vicente Aleixandre, brought back into focus by the publication in 1974 of Cernuda's *Poesía completa* and 1975 of an *Antología total* of Aleixandre's work). The outspoken and luxuriant poetry of Luis Antonio de Villena from the 1970s and 1980s, associated with and springing from the *novísimos* and the urge to open out to non-Spanish influences, made pleasure part of its rebellion against the drearinesses of Francoism and its domestic values as well as against the perceived prosaism of leftist social realism. It found more than room for aestheticism, decadence, the knowingly chaotic use of formal strategies, and themes taken from a wide, wild, variety of sources. The poems in *Hymnica* and *Huir del invierno* (*To Flee from Winter*) (1979 and 1981), with their emphases on high art, classical and Romantic beauty, and their complex investigations of usually homoerotic desire, mix sanctified traditions and radical new conceptualizations of sensory, imaginative, and intellectual experience.

There is a general turn, in the 1980s, to the pleasures of high cultural allusion, pleasures heightened by a perverse, often ludic, slant on the cultural values and materials plundered. This had begun in the 1970s: among the younger, neither politically nor canonically committed poets, Ana María Moix's *Baladas del dulce Jim* (1969: *The Ballads of Sweet Jim*) and *No Time for Flowers* (1971) and José Luis Jover's *Memorial* (1978) and *En el grabado* (1979: *In the Engraving*) offer examples, set at either end of the decade, of the imaginative empowerment which could come from combining heterodox eroticism with avant-garde poetic technique. Carrying on from the early poetry of Gimferrer, Antonio Colinas for one, in *Sepulcro en Tarquinia* (1975: *Sepulchre in Tarquinia*), worked into a fabric of extreme erotic submission elements of classical mythology, references to Renaissance and Romantic art, music, literature, scents, and colours.

Much of Ana Rossetti's *Indicios vehementes* (1985: *Signs of Vehemence*) is a parodic taking to extremes of traditional forms (of the seventeenth and late nineteenth centuries); baroque and *modernista* imagery, and in *Devocionario* (1986: *Prayer Book*) the iconography of Catholicism, facilitates and complicates a radical and ludic demarginalization of female sexuality and a deconstruction of masculinity as dominant. Men are set up, framed, looked at, manipulated, violated, and elevated—that is to say reduced—to mere icons: saints, sailors, lovely young men, boys in jeans and leather, pictures of desire. Thus, for example, a bare-chested male outside a Madrid club one night is endowed, variously, with archetypal, classicized beauty, and primitive luminescence which, though presented as unequalled, is in fact outshone by flashes of Golden Age-sounding verbal pyrotechnics in the writing (in the poem 'A la puerta del cabaret'). This is a joyful, flagrant rewriting of the old languages of power, both Spanish-specific (the Golden Age) and more generalized (an invalidated world-view where men make and control desire and its languages).

Luisa Castro uses poetic tradition to similarly transgressive effect. Her *Los versos del eunuco* (1986: *The Eunuch's Verses*), while doing what earlier Spanish Surrealism so rarely did—express women's desires—has echoes for its readers of Aleixandre, Lorca, and Alberti. The role and identity of the eunuch cannot be clearly ascribed here. At times this figure is the representation of an unsatisfactory and disempowering love or lover whose presence is a disruptive and ludic threat to both the practical and the creative tasks of the poet in her daily life:

Cuando en la calle todos supieron que me agitaba las faldas un eunuco ni en los hipermercados mantuve mi turno de derecho, los peores pollos, las peores frutas, la carne muerta de siglos comí durante años. [. . .]

Venía con los versos descolgándose a las ocho; con el pantalón lleno de versos incompletos, malherido venía a verme con los ojos de madera con un círculo en el centro negro y un alfiler para sujetar el verbo, la pupila. (Castro 1986: 14–15).

(When everyone in the street knew that a eunuch was tugging at my skirts even in hypermarkets I couldn't keep my place in the queue: the worst chickens, the worst fruit, meat aeons dead was all I ate for years. [. . .]

He turned up at eight with verses hanging ragged off him; his trousers full of unfinished lines, wounded he came to see me with his wooden eyes with a circle in their black centre and a pin to fix the word, or the pupil.)

At other times the eunuch is a malign and sadistic spirit at work within words themselves and inside the poet's head. In 'Una virgen se debate pulsando con martillos el cuerpo inquebrantable' (21–2) ('A Virgin Writhes Tapping her Unbreakable Body with Hammer Blows') hammer blows—'zas' ('crack')—punctuate the text and break up the bone structure of the discoursing virgin:

> Mi cuerpo [. . .]
>   Aquí está zas.
>   Se ve que odia con su nombre y
> un número próximo en la cola del dolor
> que pregunta zas una zas, dos horas zas
>   cuánto tiempo, cuánto tiempo (21)

(My body [. . .] | Here it is crack. | It's obvious he uses his name to hate and | the next number in the queue for pain | is asking crack one crack, two crack o' clock | how long, how long.)

This nightmare of torture and uncertainty in its preoccupation with numbers and times of the day calls upon the Peruvian César Vallejo as much as the Spanish Surrealists. As in Vallejo's *Trilce*, words take on a horrifying autonomy, seeming to solidify into obstacles thrown up in the path of the poetry: in Castro's writing this phenomenon becomes complicated with erotic frustrations. Early in the book the narrating 'yo' (ambivalently the eunuch and the poet) notes at the end of a sequence of oneiric experiences that 'Cuando volvemos las paredes están llenas | de palabras' (31) ('When we return, the walls are covered | with words') and five poems take the form of concatenations of strange, micro-narratives like graffiti or personal ads, printed in capital letters: 'SE PUEDEN PLANTAR ENREDADERAS EN ESA VENTANA [. . .] SE DEBE ESCALAR HASTA LA LAMENTACIÓN'; 'SOY UN VECINO DE SESENTA AÑOS QUE LLORA' (32 and 47) ('Ivy May Be Planted at This Window [. . .] Please Climb to the Top of This Lamentation'; 'Weeping Sixty-Year-Old Neighbour Seeks . . .'). Such strategies inevitably reach back to the Lorca of *Poeta en Nueva York* (*Poet in New*

York) and *El público* (*The Public*) as well as those other male Surrealists, but Castro's writing maps the crises of sexual and gender identity using the markers of the female body in a way which frees her writing from the (male) tradition it pastiches.

Concha García's *Desdén* (1990: *Disdain*), on the other hand, while it too demarginalizes women's erotic experience and writes the female body into the text, shares many of the impulses of the *poesía pura* of Guillén, Siles, or Carnero. 'Equilibrio' ('Equilibrium') is focused on calm, absence, and sparseness:

> Los
> emblemas: uno a uno
> en el suelo.
>   (García 1990: 69)

(Emblems: one by one | onto the ground.)

These, though, are erotic as well as spiritual moments. Another of the quiet times of the collection, the poem 'Reposo' (69: 'Repose'), is that which follows a crisis in a love affair. One lover has left, with a crumpled note in her hand with the intense and enigmatic words 'te espero, soy yo' ('I'm waiting for you; it's me') written on it; the other, curled up on the bed, hears the door slam and the departing footsteps, and sighs

> 'ella se ha ido', 'sí, lo ha hecho'.
> Tiras de papelitos riegan un corto tramo
> de la calle.

('She's gone,' 'She's done it.' | Scraps of paper sprinkle a short stretch | of the street.)

Here, the three sets of four words articulated by quotation marks are ambiguously words of catharsis and defence: fixing these words in their place is all. In 'Lo escrito' (66: 'What is Written') writing is in tension between control and abandon, between the verbal and the corporeal:

> La compulsión y el estrechamiento,
> o mejor: el cerco, la baba que
> hubiese querido esparcida en mi cuerpo,
> el rato, lo largo del instante
> en que perdí los péndulos, las medidas.

(Compulsion and constraint, | or rather: enclosure, the spittle which | I would have wished spread on my body, | the moment, the length of an instant | in which I lost pendulum and proportion.)

Such contradictory pleasures—modern-day mystical recognitions of the limitations, and joys, of the corporeal world—are serious pleasures, crystallizations of living. In them is embedded a sexual politics of writing which has resonances out into the social, the everyday. Poets as diverse as Francisco Brines and García work away at the boundaries between solitude, self-involvement, and being in the world. Even the sometimes precious and often escapist poetry of the *novísimos* in its sensuality and its camp references to pop, poster art, advertising, and US culture makes specific points about being Spanish, about, as Labanyi puts it (1995*a*: 297), Spain's insertion in the global cultural market place, and the potential for freedom from sexual puritanism, and thus theorizes—poeticizes—identities in relation to the pleasures of the senses.

9.4. COMMERCIAL EROTICA

There are, of course, more plain-speaking ways of being bodily in the world of new Spanish pleasures.The publication by Cela of an *Enciclopedia del erotismo* (*Encyclopedia of Eroticism*) in 1976 signals the growing interest in the recuperation of a suppressed or ignored erotic tradition within Spain. In support of his argument that this interest did not suddenly emerge with the death of Franco, Valls lists works with a more or less veiled erotic content published by Alfaguara in the 1960s along with the novels of Biel Mesquida and anthologies of erotic poetry published in the early 1970s (1991: 29). The development of a clear commercialized erotic sector is evident in the late 1970s with the creation by the Tusquets editorial house of the collection 'La sonrisa vertical' ('The Vertical Smile') in 1978 and the prize of the same name in 1979. Its commercial success is evident, with titles in the collection selling a minimum of 7,000 copies per annum and best-sellers like the 1989 prizewinner *Las edades de Lulú* (*The Ages of Lulu*) by Almudena Grandes reaching sales figures of 100,000 copies within a year of publication (Blanco 1996: 20). The collection mixes new names like Grandes with previously banned classics of the genre such as Henry Miller and Georges Bataille. Other collections include 'Clásicos del erotismo' ('Erotic Classics') brought out by Bruguera in 1977, 'La fuente de jade' ('The Jade Fountain') by Alcor and 'Erotic&Fantasía' by Ultramar in 1988, and 'X Libris' by major publisher Plaza y Janés in 1995.[1] Catalan collections by the publishers El Llamp, La Magrana, and Pòrtic appeared in 1984 and 1988. Numerous anthologies of poetry and short stories have been brought out including *Polvo serán: Antología de la poesía erótica actual* (1988: *They Will Be Dust/Fucking: Anthology of Contemporary Erotic Poetry*) and *Relatos amorosos de hoy* (1988: *Love Stories for Today*) by the specialist publisher El Carro de Nieve, the best-selling *Cuentos eróticos* (1988: *Erotic Short Stories*) by Grijalbo which sold 15,000 copies in just six months (Barriuso 1989: 67), and *Relatos eróticos* (1991: *Erotic Tales*) by Castalia.

The genre has increasingly attracted critical attention with special issues of the literary magazines *Letras del sur* (1978), *Camp de l'arpa* (1979), and *Litoral* (1984), and conferences in Granada (1987) and Madrid (1990). Debate has centred on the apparent cornering of the market by women writers (Barriuso 1989), the quality of the erotic lexicon in Spanish, or perceived lack of it, and the attempt to differentiate between erotica and pornography (Valls 1991). This debate has been particularly marked in the case of women writers such as the poets Luisa Castro, Almudena Guzmán, Clara Janès, Ana Rossetti, and Lola Velasco, and the novelists and short-story writers Mercedes Abad, Grandes, María Jaén, and Lourdes Ortiz. In a debate about the current state of literature in Spain, the writer Fanny Rubio criticized best-sellers, by unspecified women, for not rewriting erotic paradigms but reproducing anachronistic male values for commercial gain (*Ajoblanco* 1993: 45). This is a criticism which has been levelled at the phenomenally successful *Las edades de Lulú* (Drinkwater 1995: 100). However, it can be read as a powerful critique of phallocentric (male-centred) desire, which explores the construction of female and male desire, love, and identity, in the supposed freedom of the post-Francoist era. Readers come to question, both in tandem with the protagonist's reflections and potentially counter to her moments of surrender and denial, whether they are witnessing the liberation of desire from the rigidity and reflex guilt of the Franco years, or a new configuration in which desire is still subject to more subtle patriarchal organization and staging, in a regime where economic and other unequal relationships of power inflect sexual and affective encounters.

---

[1] The factual information in this section has been adapted from Valls (1991) and Blanco (1996).

The novel opens with the simultaneous viewing and deconstruction of a pornographic film which produces a fantasy or memory of childhood sexual abuse which troublingly brings the narrator to climax, before we see her as a working woman of 30, mother of a schoolgirl and separated from the girl's father, Pablo. We then move, in a series of non-chronological flashbacks crucial to the questioning nature of the text, to the story of Lulú's relationship with Pablo, an older friend of her brother, from his seduction of her when she is 15, through his absences—during which she nurtures her fantasy image of him—to their re-encounter, marriage, and separation. After several abortive attempts, Lulú finally leaves him following a scene in which he engineers her complete surrender during a party trick doing the rounds in Madrid, in which a person agrees to be blindfolded and tied up in a bedroom. She finds herself being penetrated first vaginally and then, simultaneously by another man, anally, surrenders to both the pleasure and pain of it, but, on discovering that the second man is her brother, feels betrayed and used. Although the several instances of Lulú's voluntary surrendering of control have brought her pleasure and self-knowledge (Bermúdez 1996: 176), this instance of literally blind trust appears to set a limit for Lulú.

Both love and pleasure can be disempowering, then, and the novel explores this for men as well as women; indeed Pablo himself is 'in Lulú's power' to the extent that he needs her for his own sense of identity. It is also suggested that Pablo's regime of control is related both to repressed homoeroticism and an inability to establish emotionally intimate relationships with other men. Throughout the novel, the sadistic, dominating roles are held by the economically powerful and emotionally most distant and controlled characters, like the anonymous businessman in the final orgy. Lulú is economically dependent on Pablo and when she leaves him she gradually moves from paying for sex which feels dignified because it is socially sanctioned as powerful, to finally being paid for sex. This leads her into accepting a role in an orgy despite being warned off by her friend Ely, a transvestite and partial transsexual male prostitute. She experiences horrific pain and humiliation and is near to death when she is 'rescued' by Pablo. Yet even as he takes her to his sister, a doctor, to be healed, Lulú faces the thought that he must have known about, could even have engineered, the orgy and its outcome, to punish her for leaving him and to re-establish his control over her.

Both Pablo and Lulú's identities and their relationship are initially based on supposedly outmoded gender and sexual conventions: unequal power, the psychological or sexually fetishized infantilism of women (as bad in its own way and reminiscent of Francoist legal and social infantilization of women), and compulsory heterosexuality. In her queer reading of the novel, Bermúdez argues that Lulú goes beyond gender and sexual binaries, shifting between subject, object, and witness-voyeur positions (175), and that when she does occupy the 'male' position, it is not a mere reversal but a new configuration (172). Pablo, however, remains paternalist and heterosexist, so that the final section, in which Lulú awakes to find her broken body dressed in the custom-made baby clothes (which she describes as 'our' favourite) and responds to Pablo's arrival with an involuntary smile, is more shocking to the reader than all the preceding graphic moments. At this point we may part company with Lulú, seeing her as victim rather than author of her erotic fantasy, tracing it back to the abuse of the father in the opening section. The novel can thus be read as a socially grounded questioning of the Lolita fantasy, given respectability in Nabokov's critically acclaimed novel, as part of a wider critique of the erotic 'liberation' of the post-Francoist era. For Drinkwater (1995) much of the heavily promoted erotica by women would seem on the whole to be shackled by internalized stereotypes and clichés which are sometimes reversed but not displaced in sadomasochistic power plays in which sex is identified with genital activity and sexuality almost exclusively with heterosexuality. This focus is contested in the growing body of queer writing discussed in Chapter 10.

Further reading
Foster and Reis (1996); Valls (1991).

10
Through the Kaleidoscope

10.1. FROM ONE NATION TO MANY

The second half of the 1990s, where we end our thematic narrative of writing after the Civil War and after Franco, is a time from which those two predicating eras seem impossibly distant and distinct. These recent years are ones of constant changes and fluctuations in the forms and boundaries of imaginative writing and, possibly, in culture in general, although official cultures, for all that they are recycled as vibrant and colourful (as New Spanish/Galician/Catalan/Basque and so on), remain at base no more (and certainly no less) than art museums, Big Names, grand buildings, public image.[1] Many new texts (though countered by booming markets in good, solid reads) are characterized by a persistent questioning of identities as multiple, often contradictory images emerge of Spain (Labanyi 1995b) and Spanish subjects (whether in the sense of individuals, citizens, or cruxes of debate), as if the cultural changes of the transition to democracy, the political change, 'el Cambio', which was the PSOE's early motto, and the heady days of the *movida*s and intricately contradictory claims on *lo posmoderno* were, in some arenas anyway, mere rehearsals.

The belated recognition of cultural heterogeneity can be contrasted with the attempt by the Franco regime to project difference outside the borders of Spain or reconfigure it as anti-Spanish in the case of those perceived to be internal enemies of the state. In the case of the regions, as noted in Chapter 6, any notion of plurality was severely repressed. The transition to democracy has seen an explosion of creative activity in Catalonia, Galicia, and the Basque

---

[1] The magazine *Mondo brutto*—successfully into issue 18 in winter 1998, and in danger of institutionalization through its recent availability in the big money bookshops of Madrid—is a good opinionated place to look, from a central Castilian-cultured point of view, for on-the-spot demystifications of revered cultural figures and projects.

Country as each has engaged in a project of cultural revival. This has been done through a combination of linguistic measures—including the promotion of *euskara batua* (standard Basque) as a written language, educational programmes, and laws of linguistic normalization in Catalonia (1983) and the Basque Country (1989)—and support for cultural projects through subsidies and prizes awarded by the autonomous governments and local banks. The publishing market has enjoyed spectacular growth: in Catalonia production has risen from 800 books published in Catalan in 1976 to 4,500 in 1990 (Fernández 1995: 344); in Galicia from 78 books in Galician in 1972 to 637 in 1989 (Toro Santos 1995: 346); in the Basque Country from 95 books in Basque in 1976 to 980 in 1992 (Lasagabaster 1995: 351). In the latter case almost half of these works were translations and the Basque government has supported a major translation programme. For 1995 the figures are: 5,791 titles in Catalan, 1,148 in Galician, and 968 in Basque; 180 bilingual Castilian/Catalan editions, 164 Castilian/Basque, and 32 Castilian/Galician; 41,301 titles were published in Castilian (Villena 1997a). Translation of foreign works has also been a factor in the success of Catalan publishing houses along with the publication of popular genres such as crime fiction. Galician publishers have similarly focused on the promotion of popular literature to ensure sales. That is not to say that literary production is restricted to these genres. Whilst the proliferation of regional publications and prizes—throughout Spain—entails the risk of promoting provincialism and the fabrication of new, essentialist traditions or identities organized at a regional level, the work of writers such as Terenci Moix, Lluís Fernández, Bernardo Atxaga, Antón Reixa, and Suso de Toro radically interrogates notions of identity in texts characterized by postmodern playfulness. National recognition has again come in the form of literary prizes. The Premio Nacional de Literatura (National Literature Prize) was awarded for the first time to a novel in Basque in 1989 when it was given to Atxaga for *Obabakoak* and in 1995 to one in Catalan, Carme Riera's *Dins el darrer blau* (*Beyond the Final Blue*). *Obabakoak*, a postmodern collage of intertextual references combining Basque oral tradition with European and Near Eastern tales, was a major international success not replicated by Atxaga's following novels which turn inwards to the politics of community, the theme of *incomunicación* (solitude and lack of communication), and nationalism in the Basque Country. Although the number of literary works in Catalan, Basque, and Galician published in Castilian translations is still relatively low, nationwide recognition for at least a few big names (Atxaga, Riera, the Galician Manuel Rivas, and the Catalan Quim Monzó) is coming to be seen as normal: 'el muro de prejuicios y recelos entre las cuatro culturas españolas comienza a romperse' (Villena 1997a) ('the wall of prejudice and mistrust between the four cultures of Spain is beginning to come down').

The writers listed above do not include those who publish in Castilian such as Juan Marsé and Esther Tusquets whose work critically examines contemporary Catalan society; Marsé's *El amante bilingüe* (1990: *The Bilingual Lover*) directly addresses the relationship between Catalan speakers and 'charnegos', Castilian-speaking immigrants. Marina Mayoral and the recently deceased Gonzalo Torrente Ballester clearly engage in literary explorations of Galician identity but are paradoxically not considered Galician writers as they do not write exclusively in Galician. Within Galicia the issue of linguistic diglossia has been further complicated by the debate between those who consider Galician an Iberian language in its own right—the official Xunta policy—and the *lusistas* who emphasize linguistic parallels with Portuguese to place Galician in a Luso-Brazilian framework (Toro Santos 1995: 350). Writers who sustain the latter position do not receive official subsidies and are thus marginalized due to issues of linguistic difference from a centre which is no longer exclusively national.

Throughout Spain, the post-Franco period has been marked by literary diversification following the abolition of censorship. During the immediate transition period publishers flooded the market with hitherto unavailable works including explicit erotica and pornography, previously banned works, memoirs of oppositional figures, including the exiled writers Alberti, Ayala, and Chacel, and books about the Civil War and the immediate historic past which called into question Nationalist versions of history, including autobiographies by Juan Goytisolo, Castellet, and Barral. Under the PSOE administration Spain's cultural infrastructure was redeveloped through a combination of market economics and government subsidies on a national, regional, and local level. As a consequence of the former the publishing world has seen a simultaneous process of concentration of production in the hands of a relatively small number of large editorial houses and increased globalization following a number of multinational takeovers which resulted in Spain occupying fourth position in world book production in 1987 (Acín 1990: 107). The increased commercialization of fiction has encouraged aggressive marketing which has partly been done through promotional tours (some subsidized by the government) and the establishment of a bewildering array of literary prizes associated with publishing houses such as Planeta, which is now one of Spain's major advertisers. This intense promotion of 'lo nuevo'—in collections such as Nueva Narrative Española, Nueva Ficción, Última Narrativa, Narrativa Joven, Bajo el Signo de lo Nuevo—has led to both an upsurge in the writing of novels and an increased interest in Spanish writing both at home and abroad. The same holds, in their different milieux and mechanisms for diffusion, for poetry and drama. However, the upsurge in new literary reviews which is noted by Labanyi (1995b: 396–7) has not spawned a substantial alternative and radical infrastructure for writers; and the interventions of columnists and essayists in topical affairs seem, in the main, to be following trends laid down many years back (albeit with sharp new twists in the hands of Fernando Savater and the novelists regularly invited into the weekly glossies). In longer essays and philosophizing sociological works Endymion's Colección de Ensayo has brought back into focus still urgent issues—*asignaturas pendientes* indeed—of the middle years of the century with not only a compendium of Savater's work of the mid-1970s (small in volume, large in scale), but considered returns to María Zambrano and Jesús Ibáñez, as well as a more recent title which might easily have been on themes of the mature years of the dictatorship, Vicente Romano's *La formación de la mentalidad sumisa* (1998: *The Formation of the Submissive Mentality*, originally published in 1993), a call to break away from the manipulative manœuvres and effects of global free-market economies. To a similar, though non-politicized end, José Antonio Marina's work on the structures of emotional life—in particular *El laberinto sentimental* (1996: *The Labyrinth of the Sentiments*), into eight reprints by the end of 1998—and 'creative intelligence' picks up on North American psycho-sociology and pedagogy but also attempts to ground a New Spain in the richness of its own literary heritage.

The late 1980s and early 1990s were a time of quiet despair for many dramatists both young and old. Increased public subsidies for the theatre have been effective in modernizing the infrastructure, enabling the creation of regional centres in the Autonomous Communities (supporting a particularly lively theatrical landscape in Catalonia), and raising the profile of innovative directors such as Lluis Pasqual, José Carlos Plaza, and José Luis Gómez, and performance groups such as Els Joglars. However, there has been a strong tendency for producers and directors to use material other than texts written by contemporary playwrights—rediscovering Lorca and Valle-Inclán, reinterpreting the classics, and adapting novels and films. The cultural policies of the PSOE governments between 1982 and 1996 have been criticized again and again by authors (particularly savagely in Rodríguez Méndez 1993b) as a gravy train for the favoured few which does little in the long term to attract audiences.

Starved as they may be of public recognition, dramatists are nevertheless writing a great deal, encouraged to some extent by prizes such as the Premio Bradomín (established in 1984 for playwrights under 30), by the Centro Nacional de Nuevas Tendencias Escénicas, and by collaboration with theatre groups, often in small alternative venues. There have been signs recently of a renewal of interest in theatre based on texts by contemporary writers, as announced in *El país* in 1997: 'Los jóvenes autores de teatro devuelven la palabra a los escenarios españoles' (Villena 1997b). ('Young playwrights bring the word back to Spanish stages'). Gómez García (1996) gives details of dozens of active playwrights, some moderately well known since the 1980s—including José Luis Alonso de Santos, José Sanchis Sinisterra, Ernesto Caballero, Paloma Pedrero, Ignacio del Moral, and Pilar Pombo—and others who have emerged more recently—including Sergi Belbel, Antonio Álamo, Lluïsa Cunillé, Antonio Onetti, Luis Araujo, and Itziar Pascual. Their texts often deal with tough contemporary issues (drugs, AIDS, neo-fascist violence), usually by focusing on small-scale interactions and the possibilities of particular dramatic situations rather than the broader social and political picture. Settings are often undefined, situations enigmatic, characters' identities and motives revealed only gradually, and dialogue conversational but cryptic. Some texts explicitly announce their provisionality, offering themselves as proposals to be realized on stage, exercises for actors to explore language and movement.[2]

---

[2] Some characteristic examples are anthologized, together with interviews, in Leonard and Gabriele (1996a, 1996b).

10.2. OLD AND NEW VOICES

Whilst the removal of censorship some twenty years back did not lead to the discovery of hidden masterpieces waiting to be published, it has allowed the emergence of outstanding first works by narrative writers in their forties and fifties such as Esther Tusquets, Luis Landero, and Josefina Aldecoa—wife of Ignacio Aldecoa—who published her first novel *La enredadera* (*The Clinging Vine*) in 1984 at the age of 58. These writers are publishing alongside returned Republican exiles, successful post-war writers, established *nueva narrativa* novelists (Muñoz Molina was elected to the Real Academia Española in 1995), and young authors of the *Generación X* who have grown up or even been born after the death of Franco in a literary panorama of unprecedented diversity. In poetry, standing aside from any post-postmodern rush, Francisco Brines, building perhaps on a sub-tradition powerfully exemplified in Panero's long meditative poem 'La estancia vacía' ('The Empty Room') (first published in *Escorial* in 1944), has continued to construct his radical and beautiful spaces of 'sombrío ardor' in *El otoño de las rosas* (*The Autumn of Roses*) of 1986 and *La última costa* (*The Final Shore*) of 1995. A poem from the latter, 'Madrid, julio 1992', makes a lonely space an enabling and cathartic one and declares

> Vuelve la hora feliz. Y es que no hay nada
> sino la luz que cae en la ciudad
> antes de irse la tarde,
> el silencio en la casa y, sin pasado
> ni tampoco futuro, yo.
> . . . .
> y estoy en paz con todo lo que olvido
> y agradezco olvidar.
> En paz también con todo lo que amé
> y que quiero olvidado. (Brines 1995*a*: 40)

(The hour of happiness returns and there is nothing | but light falling on the city | before the evening goes, | silence in the house, and me, no past | no future either, there | [. . .] | and I'm at peace with all I can forget | and can be grateful to forget. | In peace, as well, with all I ever loved | and which I wished were now forgotten.)

A generation further on, Luis Antonio de Villena, on the other hand, has both returned to the exoticism of *Hymnica* in *Asuntos de delirio* (1998: *Subjects of Delirium*) and moved closer to the raucous contemporary world, in *Marginados* (1993: *The Marginalized*), whose poems use a number of voices (beggars, pushers) speaking directly to the reader (and the writer), and pick up on street slang. They are sometimes Pasolini-esque in seeking the lyrical in the sordid, but often bleakly attentive to the dictates — surprisingly — of social realism, albeit in this example given an allegorical, rather Golden Age, edge and a tinge of *tremendismo*:

> En una vieja estación abandonada — cuenta un amigo —
>   unos chavales
> apalean a un perro bajo el sol. El animal se arrastra,
>   ensangrentado,
> y muere: Imagen del mundo — cuenta — somos el can
>   escuálido
> que agoniza de daño vivo. (51)

(In an old abandoned station — a friend relates — | some boys | beat a dog with sticks under the sun. The animal drags itself along, | bleeding, | and dies. An image of the world — he tells me — we are the emaciated | cur | in the throes of death by living hurt.)

10.3. WOMEN'S VOICES?

Cross-generational activity is particularly marked in the case of women writers. Established writers such as Martín Gaite have continued to publish to widespread critical acclaim in the 1990s and the careers of those who came to prominence during the late 1970s and early 1980s in the so-called 'boom' of women's writing, such as Cristina Fernández Cubas, Rosa Montero, Lourdes Ortiz, Soledad Puértolas, and Carme Riera, have been consolidated. Critics have attempted to isolate women's writing by searching for gender-based commonalities. However, the narrative production of the 1980s and 1990s is marked by diversity of both content and form. Women writers have been successful in a wide variety of genres including detective fiction, thrillers, fantasy and science fiction, horror stories, erotica and pornographic literature, sentimental romance, the fantastic, historical novels, testimony, and autobiography. The range of narrative techniques employed is correspondingly extensive. It would seem that women writers cannot be easily categorized by thematics or style. The 'boom' served to bring them to the attention of critics and publishers. Several women, including Martín Gaite, Luisa Castro, Paloma Díaz-Mas, Adelaida García Morales, Belén Gopegui, Olga Guirao, and Clara Janés, figure in Anagrama's Narrativa Hispánica collection which sets out to promote contemporary Spanish writing. Their popularity with readers is evident as women-centred texts by female authors, such as Laura Freixas's anthology *Madres e hijas* (1996: *Mothers and Daughters*), consistently hit the best-seller lists. Perhaps even more significant is the number of male writers such as Antonio Gala, Terenci Moix, José María Merino, and Álvaro Pombo choosing to write about female protagonists (Labanyi 1999: 157).

The younger generation of women writers born from the late 1950s onwards perhaps take their rights for granted as suggested by Davies (1998: 193). However, writers such as Lucía Etxebarría confidently proclaim their feminist stance in contrast to many of the writers of the 1970s who either disavowed the feminist tag out of resistance to any form of categorization or from fear of damage to sales should they be perceived as writing for a militant minority. The promotional leaflet for Etxebarría's first novel *Amor, curiosidad, prozac y dudas* (1997: *Love, Curiosity, Prozac, and Doubts*) combines synopses of the three principal protagonists and narrators—sisters Cristina, Rosa, and Ana—with three pages of statistics related to a variety of women's issues, including stereotypical portrayals of women in advertising and the mass media, discrimination relating to literary studies and academic recognition, anorexia and bulimia, sexual discrimination in the workplace, postnatal depression, sexual abuse and rape, under the title 'la realidad supera la ficción' ('fact is stranger than fiction'). These issues are integrated into the interwoven stories of the Gaena sisters in a text which explores how models of identity—past and present—circumscribe women's lives. The uncertainty or doubts of the title are embodied in the disintegration of the Gaena family. Both the private sphere of love relationships and the public sphere of work fail to provide meaning: for the promiscuous Cristina sex is ephemeral and her work in a rave club simply a means of paying for her free time, sex is practically non-existent for the workaholic executive Rosa who works to sustain a lifestyle she has no time to enjoy, and marriage and motherhood are a smothering domestic trap for depressed housewife Ana. Each sister is summarized by Etxebarría through the categories of sex, drugs, rock and roll, work, signs of identity, and depression. Drugs and music provide a means of escape from the restrictions imposed by work and family responsibilities. Cristina submerges herself in rave culture in which techno music combines with heroin and ecstasy to erase anxieties about the self, 'Me diluyo en música, me borro, me extiendo, me transformo, me vuelvo líquida y polimorfa' (Etxebarría 1997: 35) ('I dissolve myself into the music, erase myself, extend myself, transform myself, become liquid and polymorphous'). Her older sisters are addicted to psychotropic prescription drugs, Rosa depends on the executive drug of the 1990s, Prozac, and Ana gets by on a cocktail of slimming amphetamines and tranquilizers. In contrast to Cristina's frames of cultural reference which are drawn from the youth counter-cultures of the 1990s—grunge, Nirvana, Courtney Love, Tarantino, *Basic Instinct*, Kate Moss, the Manchester sound, techno, and trance—and the 1960s—Kerouac, The Kinks, and Stanley Kubrick—Ana and Rosa are bound together by a piece of classical music, Purcell's *The Fatal Hour*. For Ana it is a cry for help which she cannot articulate verbally; she is alienated from those around her to the point that she can only express the extent of her anguish by playing Purcell down the telephone line to her sister Rosa. Rosa fails to identify her mystery caller but the music jolts her out of complacency. It acts as a mnemonic tool, resuscitating past dreams and passions which her lifestyle has anaesthetized through a consumerist work ethic. As the novel concludes, Ana's decision to divorce her husband leads Rosa and Cristina to confront their anxieties and the revelation that the sisters are not as strikingly different as socially constructed surface appearances would seem to suggest. They reject their mother Eva (Eve) to identify with the transgressive (and traditionally silenced) biblical figure of Lilith and the disruptive dark force of Darth Vader. This thematics of self-discovery and insistence on the resilience of women is repeated in her second novel, *Beatriz y los cuerpos celestes* (1998: *Beatriz and the Heavenly Bodies*). Sisterly love is developed into love between women and it is a measure of how attitudes have changed towards sexuality in Spain that this novel won the 1998 Nadal Prize.

10.4. GENERATION X: WHO AM I?

Etxebarría's novels share many of the features ascribed by critics to the narrative of an alienated generation of youth in Spain which has become known as Generation X: familiarity with mass cultural forms, preoccupation with contemporary consumerism, and detailed knowledge of drug culture. The affective relationships portrayed tend to be dysfunctional, communication breaks down between children and their parents, and sexual attachments are on the whole casual affairs, 'Las relaciones de los noventa, dicen. Efímeras. *No future*. Generation X. Hay que joderse.' (Etxebarría 1997: 39) ('Nineties relationships, they say. Ephemeral. *No future*. Generation X. You have to fuck yourself/be fucked over'). However, the optimistic tone with which *Amor, curiosidad, prozac y dudas* ends, and the belief in the possibility of self-discovery, contrasts with the apparent nihilism of much writing by her male contemporaries such as Ray Loriga whose *Héroes* (1993: *Heroes*, into its fourth economy paperback reprint in 1997) is an anarchic evocation of the restrictions on the imaginations and lives of the disadvantaged young in modern urban, jobless Spain in more than a half echo of Eduardo Haro Ibars's magnificent paean to drugs, rock music, New Romantics, old Romantics, and the glory of rebellion, *El libro de los héroes* (1985: *The Book of Heroes*). But its anarchy leaves its narrator protagonist directionless, his dreams leave him wrung out, and the open-endedness of the text is bewildering rather than empowering.

In José Ángel Mañas's *Historias del Kronen* (1994: *Stories from the Kronen Bar*) the cycle of sex, drugs, and alcohol spirals out of control towards a destructive finale in which Carlos's murderous fantasies—based around the novel *American Psycho* and the film *Henry Portrait of a Serial Killer*—and Roberto's fascination with snuff movies are enacted with tragic results. The story is focalized predominantly through Carlos, a 21-year-old student who lives off his parents. Through a blend of first person narration and direct dialogue (which is the basis of the 1994 film of *Historias del Kronen* scripted by Mañas and the director Montxo Armendáriz) the reader is immersed into Carlos's world which is primarily that of the bar and club scene in the middle-class northern suburbs of Madrid. Misogynistic and homophobic, Carlos is an unsympathetic character who becomes increasingly alienated from those around him, masturbating whilst fantasizing beating up his ex-girlfriend and obsessively rewatching the video of *Henry Portrait of a Serial Killer*. His solipsistic introversion is textually inscribed in the penultimate section he narrates in which his friends' voices are deleted and replaced by empty parentheses. He dismisses their concern at his violent actions as weakness, 'Sois todos unos débiles. ( ) En el fondo os odio a todos' (Mañas 1994: 223) ('You are all weaklings. ( ) Deep down I hate you all'). In the epilogue which follows he is displaced to the holiday resort of Santander where he blocks out everything that has happened. The narrative voice shifts to the one friend who is incapable of shutting off his emotions; in a continuous dialogue previous events are clarified as a psychiatrist encourages Roberto to stop hiding in a self-enclosed world of denial as described in the epigraph which opens and closes the novel, the song 'Giant' by The The:

. . . .
I am a stranger to myself
And nobody knows I'm here
When I looked into my face
It wasn't myself I'd seen
But who I've tried to be
. . . . . .
AND I'M CAVING IN UPON MYSELF
HOW CAN ANYONE KNOW ME
WHEN I DON'T EVEN KNOW MYSELF.

The unknowability of self is central to the novel *Nunca le des la mano a un pistolero zurdo* (1996: *Never Shake the Hand of a Left-Handed Gunfighter*) by Benjamín Prado in which the identity of the mysterious Israel is reinvented and rewritten in the three sections in which his friends Gaizka, Sara, and Blueberry recount his life to an interviewer who is identified in the final chapter of Sara's section as Benjamín Prado. In the fourth section of this self-referential text the characters and Prado come together; as narrator he not only questions the veracity of the accounts given to him but disputes the importance attached to knowing the truth. For the narrator, Israel's identity is situated in difference and deferral. This postmodern conceptualization of identity as performance or discursive construct finds expression in the literary styles deployed by the characters in their contradictory versions of events which range from Kafkaesque Gothic to Chandleresque detective fiction, from the adventures of Mark Twain to the misery and brutality of Dickens, and in the vast array of intertextual references they employ which include nineteenth-century classics of world literature, metaphysical and Surrealist poetry, children's literature, pulp detective fiction, adventure comics, contemporary narrative, classic Hollywood cinema, horror B-movies, action blockbusters, TV detective series, jazz piano, Elvis, reggae, rock, grunge, punk, and Britpop. Prado is acutely aware of the way in which language mediates experience.

10.5. RESEXING THE NATION

Something of a one-man generation, Juan Goytisolo has continued brilliantly to problematize identities through his writing, with *La cuarentena* (1991: *Quarantine*) extending the usual range of his multicultural dialogues to include, obliquely, French and North American literary responses to AIDS and, more recently, extending his range of destabilizing narrative experimentation. Homosexuality is, of course, among the best known of the many sites of contestation in Goytisolo's work (Epps 1996; Smith 1992) and he and Alberto Cardín (Smith 1997) are perhaps the two most uncompromising voices on the writing scene raised against heterosexist (and nationalist) oppressions. Neither of these two figures fits comfortably into the category 'gay' but they are central to a fast-growing body of imaginative writings on male homosexuality, alongside radical voices making use of camp and satirical humour to destabilize categories of gender and sexuality. Lluís Fernández's *Una prudente distancia* (1998: *A Prudent Distance*) wittily examines internalized homophobia and recapitulates histories of coming out and the construction of queer micro-communities. Eduardo Mendicutti and Terenci Moix have both (in addition to continuing prolific journalistic and novelistic output) used autobiography gently to explore the formation of gay (or sissy) identities—in, respectively, *El palomo cojo* (1991: *The Lame Pigeon*) and the three volumes thus far of Moix's wide-ranging Memoirs, the latest being *Extraño en el paraíso* (1998: *Stranger in Paradise*). The commercial and popular cultural categories of lesbian and gay writing have rapidly begun to form themselves in 1990s Spain. Essays by Oscar Guasch—*La sociedad rosa* (1994: *Pink Society*)— Juan Vicente Aliaga and José Miguel Cortés—*Identidad y diferencia: Sobre la cultura gay en España* (1997: *Identity and Difference: On Gay Culture in Spain*)—and, in lighter mode, Leopoldo Alas (better known as a major poet of the *posnovísmos*)—*La acera de enfrente* (1994: *On the Other Side of the Street*)—have set some parameters for this. Joining Etxebarria and Villena are (at a different level of literary achievement, but with mostly different publics) Antonio Jiménez Ariza's *La sinfonía de los veleros varados* (1996: *The Symphony of the Stranded Sail-Boats*)—one of a seminal handful of novels written in Spanish for a gay semi-popular market in the second half of the 1990s—and Armando Rabazo's *Las paredes del acuario* (1996: *The Fish-Tank Walls*) whose emphasis is on the fragmentary and provisional in sexual identity. Cristóbal Ramírez's *Sígueme* (1998: *Follow Me*), marketed as erotic writing, explores a queer and violent middle-class Barcelona youth sub-culture, a Generation Z-plus. In the booming gay and lesbian press contact ads construct micro-narratives of quest and conquest, often revealing—like these novelists—the constant fluidity of the constructions of sexualized social behaviour. A compact version of a transgressive lifestyle was to be seen in the (non-lesbian or gay) Madrid weekly *Segundamano* on 9 April 1997:

> Guapo. Cuerpazo de gimnasio, bisex
> y divertido, busca cómplice similar,
> para hacer unas risas, después de
> dejar a las novias. Convénceme con
> tu foto.

(Good-looking. Gym-honed body, bi, and fun, seeks similar mate for laughs once girlfriends are safely home. Convince me with your photo.)

While the misogyny, bodyism, and buddyism of this wishful declaration of intent attest to the individual's continuing subjection to discourses of power (and peer pressures) in the New Spain, this is a set of words and a mode of communication (a snapshot of irresponsible/carefree desire requiring a snapshot back) which was unimaginable in the Old. As the Spanish press gears up for *Milenialismo* (Millennialism), amidst a surge of New Age movements, and as Spaniards enthusiastically embrace the cyber café and experiment with identities on the Internet, new discourses proliferate, from the reclamation of graffiti by the urban *okupas* (politicized squatters) to ecological critiques of Western society,[3]

---

[3] See, for example, Luis Racionero's writing which synthesizes Oriental and Occidental cultural traditions in the pursuit of social renewal.

shaping new Spains whose fragments connect and disconnect as we turn the kaleidoscope.

Further reading

Graham and Labanyi (1995); Labanyi (1999); Leonard and Gabriele (1996*b*); McNerney and Enríquez de Salamanca (1994); Villena (1997*a*).

References

ABELLÁN, J. L. (1978). *El exilio español de 1939*. Madrid: Taurus.
—— (1980a). 'El tema de España en el pensamiento del exilio', in D. Ynduráin (ed.), *Época contempóranea 1939–1980* (vol. viii of F. Rico (gen. ed.), *Historia y crítica de la literatura española*). Barcelona: Crítica, 53–66.
—— (1980b). *Censura y creación literaria en España (1939–1976)*. Barcelona: Península.
—— (ed.) (1987). *Censura y literaturas peninsulares*. Amsterdam: Rodopi.
ACÍN, R. (1990). *Narrativa, o consumo literario (1975–1987)*. Zaragoza: Universidad de Zaragoza.
AGUIRRE, J. F., et al. (1984). *Cataluña con Franco*. Barcelona: Mare Nostrum.
Ajoblanco (1993). 'Debate literario: ¿Y ahora de qué vamos?', 53: 40–7.
ALBERTI, R. (1992). *De un momento a otro* [1942]; *El adefesio* [1944]. Madrid: Cátedra.
ALBORG, J. L. (1958). *Hora actual de la novela española*, vol. i. Madrid: Taurus.
ALONSO, S. (1988). *Guías de lectura: La verdad sobre el caso Savolta*. Madrid: Alhambra.
ÁLVAREZ, J. M. (1993). *Museo de cera*. Madrid: Visor.
ÁLVAREZ PÉREZ, A. (1964). *Enciclopedia intuitiva, sintética y práctica: Tercer grado*. Valladolid: Miñón (1st edn. 1954).
AMELL, S. (1984). *La narrativa de Juan Marsé, contador de aventis*. Madrid: Playor.
AMORÓS, A. (1977). *Sociología de una novela rosa*. Madrid: Taurus.
ANDRÉS-GALLEGO, J. et al. (1995). *Historia de España 13/3. España actual: España y el mundo (1939–1975)*. Madrid: Gredos.
ANSON, L. M., et al. (1996). *Contra el poder*. Madrid: Temas de Hoy.
ARIAS-SALGADO, G. (1958). *Política española de la Información*, vol. ii. Madrid: Ministerio de Información y Turismo.
ARRABAL, F. (1979). *Teatro completo*, vol. i. Madrid: CUPSA.
ASÍS, M. D. de (1990). *Última hora de la novela en España*. Madrid: Eudema.
BALLESTE, J. (ed.) (1955). *El artículo: 1905–1955. Antología literaria de ABC*. Madrid: Prensa Española.

BAQUERO GOYANES, M. (1992). *El cuento español: Del romanticismo al realismo*. Madrid: Consejo Superior de Investigaciones Científicas.
BARCELÓ, M. (1990). *Ciencia ficción: Guía de lectura*. Barcelona: Ediciones B Nova.
BAREA, A. (1972). *The Forging of a Rebel*, trans. I. Barea. London: Davis–Poynter.
BARRERO O PÉREZ, Ó. (1992). *Historia de la literatura española contemporánea: 1939–1990*. Madrid: Istmo.
BARRERA Y BARRO, C. (1995). *Periodismo y franquismo: De la censura a la apertura*. Barcelona: Ediciones Internacionales Universitarias.
BARRIUSO, J. (1989). 'La mejor literatura erótica en español es cosa de mujeres', *Cambio 16*, 922: 64–7.
BENEGAS, N., and MUNÁRRIZ, J. (eds.) (1997). *Ellas tienen la palabra: Dos décadas de poesía española*. Madrid: Hiperión.
BENET, J. et al. (1976). *Dionisio Ridruejo: De la falange a la oposición*. Madrid: Taurus.
BERMÚDEZ, S. (1996). 'Sexing the Bildungsroman: *Las edades de Lulú*, Pornography and the Pleasure Principle', in D. Foster and R. Reis (eds.), *Bodies and Biases: Hispanic Cultures and Literatures*. Minneapolis: University of Minnesota Press, 165–83.
BLANCO, M. L. (1996). 'En el nombre del sexo', *Cambio 16*, 1285: 20–1.
BLANCO AGUINAGA, C., RODRÍGUEZ PUÉRTOLAS, J., and ZAVALA, I. (1983). *Historia social de la literatura española (en lengua castellana)*, vol. iii, 2nd edn. Madrid: Castalia.
BORRÁS, T. (1940). *Checas de Madrid: Epopeya de los caídos*. Madrid: Escelicer.
BOUSOÑO, C. (1983). 'La poesía de Guillermo Carnero', in G. Carnero, *Ensayo de una teoría de la visión (Poesía 1966–1977)*, 2nd edn. Madrid: Hiperión.
BRINES, F. (1984). *Ensayo de una despedida (1960–1977)*. Madrid: Visor.
—— (1995a). *La última costa*. Barcelona: Tusquets.
—— (1995b). *Escritos sobre poesía española (De Pedro Salinas a Carlos Bousoño)*. Valencia: Pre-Textos.
BROOKSBANK JONES, A. (1997). *Women in Contemporary Spain*. Manchester: Manchester University Press.
BROWN, J. (ed.) (1991). *Women Writers of Contemporary Spain: Exiles in the Homeland*. London: Associated University Presses.
BUERO VALLEJO, A. (1976). *La doble historia del doctor Valmy; Mito*. Madrid: Espasa Calpe.
—— (1985). *The Sleep of Reason*, trans. M. P. Holt. San Antonio, Tex.: Trinity University Press (1st edn. 1970).
—— (1987). *The Maids of Honor*, trans. M. P. Holt. San Antonio, Tex.: Trinity University Press (1st edn. 1960).

BUERO VALLEJO, A. (1989). *La detonación/The Shot*, trans. D. Johnston. Warminster: Aris & Phillips (1st edn. 1976).

—— (1994). *Un soñador para un pueblo/A Dreamer for the People*, trans. M. Thompson. Warminster: Aris & Phillips (1st edn. 1985).

CABAL, F., and ALONSO DE SANTOS, J. L. (eds.) (1985). *Teatro español de los 80*. Madrid: Fundamentos.

CÁMARA VILLAR, G. (1984). *Nacional-catolicismo y escuela: La socialización política del franquismo (1936–1951)*. Jaén: Hesperia.

CARANDELL, L. (1968). *Los españoles*. Barcelona: Ediciones de Cultura Popular.

—— (1974). *Celtiberia Show*. Madrid: Guadiana.

CARNERO, G. (1983). *Ensayo de una teoría de la visión (Poesía 1966–1977)*, 2nd edn. Madrid: Hiperión (1st edn. 1979).

CARR, R. (1980). *Modern Spain, 1875–1980*. Oxford: Oxford University Press.

—— and FUSI AIZPURÚA, J. P. (1981). *Spain: Dictatorship to Democracy*, 2nd edn. London: Allen & Unwin (1st edn. 1979).

CASTRO, L. (1986). *Los versos del eunuco*. Madrid: Hiperión.

CELA, C. J. (1951). *La colmena*. Buenos Aires: Emece.

—— (1953). *The Hive*, trans. J. M. Cohen and A. Barea. New York: Farrar, Strauss & Young.

—— (1965). *Pascual Duarte's Family*, trans. A. Kerrigan. New York: Weidenfeld & Nicolson.

CERNUDA, L. (1984). *Las nubes, Desolación de la quimera*. Madrid: Cátedra.

CHRISTIE, R., DRINKWATER, J., and MACKLIN, J. (1995). *The Scripted Self: Textual Identities in Contemporary Spanish Narrative*. Warminster: Aris & Phillips.

Colección Visor (1998). *El último tercio del siglo (1968–1998): Antología consultada de la poesía española*. Madrid: Visor.

COLMEIRO, J. (1994). *La novela policiaca española: Teoría e historia crítica*. Barcelona: Anthropos.

Conferencia Episcopal Española (1979). *Matrimonio y familia, hoy: Documento pastoral de la Conferencia Episcopal Española (6 julio 1979)*. Madrid: PPC.

CORRALES EGEA, J. (1971). *La novela española actual (Ensayo de ordenación)*. Madrid: Edicusa.

CRUZ, J. de la (1994). 'Asuntos del corazón', *El país (Negocios)* (9 Jan.): 7.

DAVIES, C. (1991). 'Women Writers in Spain since 1900: From Political Strategy to Personal Enquiry', in H. Forsås-Scott (ed.), *Textual Liberation: European Feminist Writing in the Twentieth Century*. London: Routledge, 192–226.

—— (1994). *Contemporary Feminist Fiction in Spain: The Work of Montserrat Roig and Rosa Montero*. Oxford: Berg.
—— (1998). *Spanish Women Writing 1849–1996*. London: Athlone Press.
DEBICKI, A. (1982). *Poetry of Discovery: The Spanish Generation of 1956–71*. Lexington: University Press of Kentucky.
—— (1999). 'Poetry and Culture, 1936–1975', in D. T. Gies (ed.), *The Cambridge Companion to Modern Spanish Culture*. Cambridge: Cambridge University Press, 187–97.
DELIBES, M. (1961). *The Path*, trans. J. Haycraft. New York: Doubleday.
—— (1977). *Cinco horas con Mario*. London: Harrap.
DOMÉNECH, R. (1993). *El teatro de Buero Vallejo*, 2nd edn. Madrid: Gredos.
DRINKWATER, J. (1995). '"Esta carcél de amor": Erotic Fiction by Women in Spain in the 1980s and 1990s', *Letras femeninas*, 21: 97–111.
Ecclesia (1944). [Review of *La familia de Pascual Duarte*], 140 (18 Mar.): 17.
Edelvives (1958). *Historia de España: Primer grado*. Zaragoza: Luis Vives.
El Caso (1952). 'Ocurrió en Granada: Apuñala a su amante en presencia del juez' (7 Dec.): 7.
El español (1942). [Sección de poesía] (19 Dec.): 9.
EPPS, B. (1996). *Significant Violence: Oppression and Resistance in the Narratives of Juan Goytisolo: 1970–1990*. Oxford: Oxford University Press.
Equipo Reseña (1977). *La cultura española durante el franquismo*. Bilbao: Mensajero.
ETXEBARRÍA, L. (1997). *Amor, curiosidad, prozac y dudas*. Barcelona: Plaza & Janés.
FALCÓN, L. (1981). 'A manera de resumen del año femenino', *Poder y libertad*, 2: 5–26.
—— (1994). *Cinco obras de teatro*. Madrid: Vindicación Feminista.
FERNÁNDEZ, J. A. (1995). 'Becoming Normal: Cultural Production and Cultural Policy in Catalonia', in H. Graham and J. Labanyi (eds.), *Spanish Cultural Studies: An Introduction*. Oxford: Oxford University Press, 342–6.
FONTRADONA, O. (1995). 'Entrevista a Rosa Montero: El machismo esclaviza al hombre', *Ajoblanco*, 74: 30–5.
FOSTER, D. and REIS, R. (1996). *Bodies and Biases: Hispanic Cultures and Literatures*. Minneapolis: University of Minnesota Press.
FOXÁ, A. de (1993). *De corte a checa*. Barcelona: Planeta.
FREIXAS, L. (1979). 'La nueva moral o el machismo de vanguardia', *Vindicación feminista*, 28: 95–8.
F.T.D. (1940). *El libro de España*, 2nd edn. Zaragoza: Luis Vives.
FUENTES MOLLÁ, R. (1991). 'Novela española: Entre el testimonio y la

experiencia', in A. Ramos Gascón (ed.), *España hoy*, vol. ii: *Cultura*. Madrid: Cátedra, 109–45.
FUERTES, G. (1981). *Historia de Gloria: Amor, humor y desamor*, ed. P. González Rodas. Madrid: Cátedra.
GALLEGO MÉNDEZ, M. T. (1983). *Mujer, Falange y franquismo*. Madrid: Taurus.
GARCÍA, C. (1990). *Desdén*. Madrid: Libertarias/Prodhufi.
GARCÍA ESCUDERO, J. M. (1959). 'Un soñador para un pueblo', *Ya* (12 Dec.): 5.
—— (1960). 'Un pueblo para un soñador', *Ya* (1 Jan.): 5.
GARCÍA LORENZO, L. (1980). *Documentos sobre el teatro español contemporáneo*. Madrid: SGEL.
GARCÍA MONTERO, L. (1993). '¿Por qué no sirve para nada la poesía? (Observaciones en defensa de una poesía para los seres normales)', in L. García Montero and L. A. Muñoz Molina, *¿Por qué no es útil la literatura?*, Madrid: Hiperión, 9–60.
—— (1994). *Habitaciones separadas*. Madrid: Visor.
GARCÍA PÉREZ, A. (1976). *La rebelión de los homosexuales*. Madrid: Pecosa.
GARCÍA SERRANO, R. (1943). *La fiel infantería*. Madrid: Editora Nacional.
—— (1985). *La gran esperanza*. Barcelona: Planeta (1st edn. 1983).
GEORGE D., and LONDON, J. (1996). *Contemporary Catalan Theatre: An Introduction*. Sheffield: Anglo-Catalan Society.
GIBBONS, R. (1977). *Luis Cernuda: Selected Poems*. Berkeley and Los Angeles: University of California Press.
GIES, David T. (ed.) (1999). *The Cambridge Companion to Modern Spanish Culture*. Cambridge: Cambridge University Press.
GIL DE BIEDMA, J. (1998). *Que la vida iba en serio*. Barcelona: Plaza y Janés.
GIMFERRER, P. (1968). *Arde el mar*. Madrid: El Bardo.
GOGORZA FLETCHER, M. de (1973). *The Spanish Historical Novel (1870–1970)*. London: Tamesis.
GÓMEZ GARCÍA, M. (1980). *La cultura y los pueblos de España: Notas sobre cultura, constitución, estado y Comunidades Autónomas*. Madrid: Instituto de Estudios de Administración Local.
—— (1996). *El teatro de autor en España (1901–2000)*. Madrid: Asociación de Autores de Teatro.
GOULD LEVINE, L. (1983). 'The Censored Sex: Woman as Author and Character in Franco's Spain', in B. Miller (ed.), *Women in Hispanic Literature: Icons and Fallen Idols*. Berkeley and Los Angeles: University of California Press, 289–315.
GOYTISOLO, J. (1958). *Children of Chaos*, trans. C. Brooke-Rose. London: MacGibbon & Kee.

—— (1977). *Juan the Landless*, trans. H. R. Lane. New York: Sever Books.
—— (1981). *Makbara*, trans. H. R. Lane. New York: Sever Books.
—— (1991). *The Virtues of the Solitary Bird*, trans. H. R. Lane. London: Serpent's Tail.
—— (1997). 'In memoriam F.F.B.', in *Los contemporáneos*, ed. J. Gracia (vol. v of F. Rico (ed.), *El ensayo español*). Barcelona: Crítica, 302–8.
GRACIA, J. (ed.) (1996). *Los contemporáneos* (vol. v of F. Rico (ed.), *El ensayo español*). Barcelona: Crítica.
GRAHAM, H. (1995). 'Gender and the State: Women in the 1940s', in H. Graham and J. Labanyi (eds.), *Spanish Cultural Studies: An Introduction*. Oxford: Oxford University Press, 182–95.
—— and LABANYI, J. (eds.) (1995). *Spanish Cultural Studies: An Introduction*. Oxford: Oxford University Press.
GRUGEL, J., and REES, T. (1997). *Franco's Spain*. London: Arnold.
GULLÓN, R. (1973). 'Una región laberíntica que bien pudiera llamarse España', *Ínsula*, 29/319 (June): 3, 10.
GUZMÁN, R. de (1948). 'Tú que vas a casarte', *¡Hola!* (31 Mar.): 10.
HALSEY, M. T. and ZATLIN, P. (eds.) (1999). *Entre actos: Diálogos sobre teatro español entre siglos*. University Park, Pa.: Estreno.
HARO IBARS, E. (1986). *El polvo azul*. Madrid: Libertarias (1st edn. 1985).
HARRIS, D. (1973). *Luis Cernuda: A Study of the Poetry*. London: Tamesis Books.
HART, P. (1987). *The Spanish Sleuth: The Detective in Spanish Fiction*. London: Associated University Presses.
HERZBERGER, D. K. (1991). 'History, Apocalypse and the Triumph of Fiction in the Post-War Spanish Novel', *Revista hispánica moderna*, 44/2: 247–58.
—— (1995). *Narrating the Past: Fiction and Historiography in Post-War Spain*. Durham, NC and London: Duke University Press.
¡Hola! (1950a). [No title] (5 Feb.): 3.
—— (1950b). [No title] (15 Apr.): 3.
HOOPER, J. (1995). *The New Spaniards*. Harmondsworth: Penguin.
IGLESIAS DE USSEL, J. (1983). 'La sociología de la sexualidad en España: Notas introductorias', *Revista española de investigación sociológica*, 21: 103–33.
ILIE, P. (1980). *Literature and Inner Exile: Authoritarian Spain, 1939–1975*. Baltimore: Johns Hopkins University Press.
ILLÁN, P. (1941). 'Defensa moral de la familia', *¿Qué pasa?* (21 Aug. 1941). Madrid, [unpaginated].
IONESCO, E. (1959). 'El humor negro contra la mixtificación', *Primer acto*, 7: 63–4.
JANÉS, C. (1980). *Libro de alienaciones*. Madrid: Ayuso.
JIMÉNEZ, J. O. (1964). *Cinco poetas del tiempo*. Madrid: Insula.

JIMÉNEZ, J. O. (1998). *Diez años decisivos en la poesía española contemporánea: 1960–1970*. Madrid: RIALP.
JIMÉNEZ MARTOS, L. (ed.) (1989). *Antología general de Adonais (1969–1989)*. Madrid: Ediciones RIALP.
JORDAN, B. (1990). *Writing and Politics in Franco's Spain*. New York: Routledge.
—— (1995). 'The Emergence of a Dissident Intelligensia', in H. Graham and J. Labanyi (eds.), *Spanish Cultural Studies: An Introduction*. Oxford: Oxford University Press, 245–55.
JULIÀ, S. (1999). 'History, Politics, and Culture: 1975–1996', in D. T. Gies (ed.), *The Cambridge Companion to Modern Spanish Culture*. Cambridge: Cambridge University Press, 104–20.
JULIÁ MARTÍNEZ, E. (1944). *Se ensanchaba Castilla . . .* Madrid: Aldus.
KNIGHTS, V. (1999). 'Taking a Leap beyond Epistemological Boundaries: Spanish Fantasy, Science Fiction and Feminist Identity Politics', *Paragraph*, 22/1: 76–94.
KRONIK, J. (1981). '*Nada* y el texto asfixiado: Proyección de una estética', *Revista iberoamericana*, 47: 195–202.
LABANYI, J. (1985). *Ironía e historia en* Tiempo de silencio. Madrid: Taurus.
—— (1989). *Myth and History in the Contemporary Spanish Novel*. Cambridge: Cambridge University Press.
—— (1993). 'Introduction', in J. Labanyi (ed.), *Galdós*. London: Longman, 1–20.
—— (1995a). 'Literary Experiment and Cultural Cannibalization', in H. Graham and J. Labanyi (eds.), *Spanish Cultural Studies: An Introduction*. Oxford: Oxford University Press, 295–9.
—— (1995b). 'Postmodernism and the Problem of Cultural Identity', in H. Graham and J. Labanyi (eds.), *Spanish Cultural Studies: An Introduction*. Oxford: Oxford University Press, 396–406.
—— (1999). 'Narrative in Culture, 1975–1996', in D. T. Gies (ed.), *The Cambridge Companion to Modern Spanish Culture*. Cambridge: Cambridge University Press, 147–62.
LAÍN ENTRALGO, P. (1961). 'Spain as a Problem—Yet Again', trans. E. L. King, *Texas Quarterly*, 4: 15–20.
LASAGABASTER, J. M. (1995). 'The Promotion of Cultural Production in Basque', in H. Graham and J. Labanyi (eds.), *Spanish Cultural Studies: An Introduction*. Oxford: Oxford University Press, 351–5.
LEE SIX, A. (1990). *Juan Goytisolo: The Case for Chaos*. New Haven: Yale University Press.
LEGUINA, J. (1996). *Tu nombre envenena a mis sueños*. Barcelona: Plaza & Janés (1st edn. 1992).
LEONARD, C., and GABRIELE, J. P. (1996a). *Panorámica del teatro español actual*. Madrid: Fundamentos.

—— (1996b). *Teatro de la España demócrata: Los noventa*. Madrid: Fundamentos.
LINARES-BECERRA, C. (1989). *La extraña llamada*. Barcelona: Juventud.
LLOPIS, S. (1983). 'Elena Quiroga, la olvidada', *Cambio 16* (24 Jan.): 89.
LÓPEZ, F. (1995). *Mito y discurso en la novela femenina de posguerra en Espana*. Madrid: Pliegos.
MACKLIN, J. (1992). 'Realism Revisited: Myth, Mimesis and the *Novela Negra*', in R. Rix (ed.), *Thrillers in the Transition*. Leeds Iberian Papers. Leeds: Trinity and All Saints College, 49–73.
MCNERNEY, K., and ENRÍQUEZ DE SALAMANCA, C. (eds.) (1994). *Double Minorities of Spain: A Bio-bibliographic Guide to Women Writers of the Catalan, Galician and Basque Countries*. New York: Modern Language Association of America.
MAÑAS, J. Á. (1994). *Historias del Kronen*. Barcelona: Destino.
MARSÉ, J. (1994). *The Fallen*, trans. H. Lane. London: Quartet Encounters.
MARTÍN ELIZONDO, J. (1997). *Juana creó la noche*, in *Estreno*, 23/1: 12–22.
MARTÍNEZ CACHERO, J. M. (1997). *La novela española entre 1936 y el fin de siglo*. Madrid: Castalia.
MARTÍN GAITE, C. (1983). *The Back Room*, trans. H. R. Lane. New York: Columbia University Press.
—— (1990). *Behind the Curtains*, trans. F. M. López-Morillas. New York: Columbia University Press.
—— (1992a). *El cuarto de atrás*. Barcelona: Destinolibro (1st edn. 1978).
—— (1992b). *Desde la ventana*. Madrid: Espasa-Calpe (1st edn. 1987).
—— (1994). *Usos amorosos de la postguerra española*. Barcelona: Anagrama (1st edn. 1987).
MARTÍN PARDO, E. (1967). *Antología de la joven poesía española*. Madrid: Pájaro.
MARTÍN RECUERDA, J. (1969). 'Manifiesto de *El caraqueño*, o la deshumanización de un hombre de España', *Primer acto*, 107: 32–4.
MARTÍN-SANTOS, L. (1964). *Time of Silence*, trans G. Leeson. New York: Harcourt Brace.
—— (1989). *Tiempo de silencio*. Barcelona: Seix Barral (1st edn. 1961).
MATEO, L. (1941). 'Simancas', *Vértice*, 4/48 (Sept.): 11.
MATUTE, A. M. (1963). *School of the Sun*, trans. E. Kerrigan. New York: Pantheon Press.
—— (1988). *Primera memoria*. Barcelona: Destino (1st edn. 1960).
MIGUEL MARTÍNEZ, E. de (1979). *El teatro de Miguel Mihura*. Salamanca: Universidad.
MIHURA, M. (1962). *Obras completas*. Barcelona: AHR.
—— (1988). *Tres sombreros de copa*. Madrid: Cátedra (1st edn. 1947).

MILLÁS, J. (1996). *Tonto, MUERTO, BASTARDO e invisible*. Madrid: Alfaguara (1st edn. 1995).
MONTERO, R. (1983). *Te trataré como a una reina*. Barcelona: Seix Barral.
—— (1993). 'El misterio del deseo', *El país semanal* (31 Oct.): 16–26.
MORAL, C., and PEREDA, R. M. (eds.) (1985). *Joven poesía española*. Madrid: Cátedra.
MORAL, R. (1999). *Enciclopedia de la novela española*. Barcelona: Planeta.
MUÑOZ MOLINA, A. (1994). 'Prólogo', to Juan Carlos Onetti, *Cuentos completos*. Madrid: Alfaguara, 11–26.
NASH, M. (1991). 'Pronatalism and Motherhood in Franco's Spain', in G. Bock and P. Thane, *Maternity and Gender Policies: Women and the Rise of the European Welfare States, 1880s–1950s*. London: Routledge, 160–77.
NEUSCHÄFER, H.-J. (1994). *Adiós a la España eterna: La dialéctica de la censura. Novela, teatro y cine bajo el franquismo*. Anthropos: Barcelona (1st edn. 1991).
NIEVA, F. (1975). *Teatro furioso y teatro de farsa y calamidad*. Madrid: Akal.
O'CONNOR, P. (ed.) (1992). *Plays of the New Democratic Spain (1975–1990)*. Lanham, Md.: University Press of America.
OLIVA, C. (1989). *El teatro desde 1936*. Madrid: Alhambra.
OLMO, L. (1968). *La camisa*. Leeds: Arnold-Wheaton.
ORDÓÑEZ, E. (1980). 'The Barcelona Group: The Fiction of Alós, Moix and Tusquets', *Letras femeninas*, 6/1 (Spring): 38–49.
—— (1991). *Voices of their Own: Contemporary Spanish Narrative by Women*. Lewisburg, Pa.: Bucknell University Press.
OTXOA, J. (1989). *Centauro*. Madrid: Torremozas.
OVEJERO, A. I. (1982). 'Estructuras mítico-narrativas de *Réquiem por un campesino español*', *Anales de literatura española contemporánea*, 7/2: 215–35.
PALOMERO, M. P. (ed.) (1987). *Poetas de los 70: Antología de poesía española contemporánea*. Madrid: Hiperión.
PANERO, L. (1973). *Poesías (1928–1962)*, vol. i of *Obras completas*. Madrid: Editora Nacional.
PEDRERO, P. (1994). *Noches de amor efímero*. Madrid: SGAE.
—— (1997). *Locas de amar*. Madrid: Fundación Autor.
PEMÁN, J. M. (1939). *La santa virreina*. Madrid: Ediciones Españolas.
PÉREZ, J. (1988). *Contemporary Women Writers of Spain*. Boston: Twayne.
—— (1991). 'The Fictional World of Ana María Matute: Solitude, Injustice and Dreams', in J. Brown (ed.), *Women Writers of Contemporary Spain: Exiles in the Homeland*. London: Associated University Presses, 93–115.

PEREZ Y PÉREZ, R. (1981). *Amor y dinero*. Barcelona: Juventud (1st edn. 1951).
PERRIAM, C. (1999). 'Poetry and Culture, 1975–1996', in D. T. Gies (ed.), *The Cambridge Companion to Modern Spanish Culture*. Cambridge: Cambridge University Press, 198–207.
POMBO, Á. (1986). *Los delitos insignificantes*. Barcelona: Anagrama.
POPE, R. D. (1991). 'Mercè Rodoreda's Subtle Greatness', in J. Brown (ed.), *Women Writers of Contemporary Spain: Exiles in the Homeland*. London: Associated University Presses, 116–35.
—— (1999). 'Narrative in Culture, 1936–1975', in D. T. Gies (ed.), *The Cambridge Companion to Modern Spanish Culture*. Cambridge: Cambridge University Press, 134–46.
PÖRTL, K. (1986). *Reflexiones sobre el teatro español*. Tübingen: Niemeyer.
PRESTON, P. (1986). *The Triumph of Democracy in Spain*. London: Methuen.
—— (1993). *Franco: A Biography*. London: Harper Collins.
RAGUÉ ARIAS, M. J. (ed.) (1979). *Proceso a la familia española*, 2nd edn. Barcelona: Gedisa.
RAMOS GASCÓN, A. (1991). *España hoy*, vol. i: *Sociedad*; vol. ii: *Cultura*. Madrid: Cátedra.
RIAZA, L. (1978). *El desván de los machos y el sótano de las hembras* [1974]; *El palacio de los monos*. Madrid: Cátedra.
RIDRUEJO, D. (1981). *Cuadernos de Rusia; En la soledad del tiempo; Cancionero en ronda; Elegías*, ed. M. Penella. Madrid: Castalia.
RIERA, C. (1988). *La escuela de Barcelona: Barral, Gil de Biedma, Goytisolo: El núcleo poético de la generación de los 50*. Barcelona: Anagrama.
RILEY, E. (1976). 'Sobre el arte de Sánchez Ferlosio: Aspectos de *El Jarama*', in R. Cardona (ed.), *Novelistas españoles de postguerra*. Madrid: Taurus, 123–41.
ROBLES MORENO, D. (n.d.). 'Escritoras españolas e hispanoamericanas de ciencia ficción' [pamphlet]. Madrid: Biblioteca de Mujeres.
RODRÍGUEZ MÉNDEZ, J. M. (1968). *La tabernera y las tinajas; Los inocentes de la Moncloa*. Madrid: Taurus.
—— (1971). *Ensayo sobre el machismo español*. Barcelona: Península.
—— (1974). *La incultura teatral en España*. Barcelona: Laia.
—— (1979). *Bodas que fueron famosas del Pingajo y la Fandanga; Flor de Otoño*. Madrid: Cátedra.
—— (1982). *Los quinquis de Madriz; Historia de unos cuantos; Teresa de Ávila*. Murcia: Godoy.
—— (1987). *La 'generación realista' y la incultura teatral en España*. Bristol: University of Bristol.

RODRÍGUEZ MÉNDEZ, J. M. (1989). *Literatura española*. Murcia: Universidad de Murcia (1st edn. 1978).
—— (1993a). *El pájaro solitario*. Ávila: Diputación Provincial de Ávila.
—— (1993b). *Los despojos del teatro*. Madrid: La Avispa.
RODRÍGUEZ PUÉRTOLAS, J. (1986). *Literatura fascista española*, vol. i: *Historia*. Madrid: Akal.
—— (1987). *Literatura fascista española*, vol. ii: *Antología*. Madrid: Akal.
ROIG, M. (1981). 'Nosotras las mujeres', in M. Roig (ed.), *¿Tiempo de mujer?* Barcelona: Plaza y Janés, 45–97.
ROIG CASTELLANOS, M. (1990). *A través de la prensa: La mujer en la historia*. Madrid: Instituto de la Mujer.
ROMERO SALVADÓ, F. J. (1999). *Twentieth-Century Spain: Politics and Society in Spain, 1898–1998*. Basingstoke: Macmillan.
ROMEU ALFARO, F. (1994). *El silencio roto: Mujeres contra el franquismo*. Madrid: J.C. Producción.
ROSALES, L. (1972). *Segundo abril*. Zaragoza: Javalambre.
RUBIO, F. (1976). *Las revistas poéticas españolas (1939–1975)*. Madrid: Ediciones Turner.
—— (1989). *Retracciones y reverso*. Madrid: Endymion.
—— and FALCÓ, J.-L. (eds.) (1981). *Poesía española contemporánea (1939–1980)*. Madrid: Alhambra.
RUIBAL, J. (1977). *El hombre y la mosca*. Madrid: Fundamentos.
—— (1984). *Teatro sobre teatro*. Madrid: Cátedra.
RUIZ RAMÓN, F. (1989). *Historia del teatro español: Siglo XX*, 3rd edn. Madrid: Cátedra.
SAIZ CIDONCHA, C. (1988). *La ciencia ficción como fenómeno de comunicación de masas*. Madrid: Universidad Complutense.
SAMPERE, P. (1977). *Los muros del posfranquismo*. Madrid: Miguel Castellote.
SÁNCHEZ ARANDA, J. J., and BARRERA, C. (1992). *Historia del periodismo español*. Madrid: EUNSA.
SÁNCHEZ DRAGÓ, F. (1995). *Discurso numantino: 2ª y última salida de los ingeniosos hidalgos Gárgoris y Habidis*. Barcelona: Planeta.
SÁNCHEZ LÓPEZ, P. (1998). 'La alternativa hispanoamericana: Las primeras novelas del *boom*', *Revista hispánica moderna*, 51/1: 102–18.
SANTOS, D. (1982). *Lo mejor de ciencia ficción española*. Barcelona: Martínez Roca.
SASTRE, A. (1967). *Obras completas*, vol. i. Madrid: Aguilar.
—— (1973). *Anatomía del realismo*, 3rd edn. Barcelona: Seix Barral.
—— (1987). *Escuadra hacia la muerte; La mordaza*, 2nd edn. Madrid: Castalia (1st edn. 1957).
—— (1990). *El camarada oscuro; Tierra roja*. Donostia: Gakoa.
SAVATER F., and VILLENA, L. A. de. (1982). *Heterodoxias y contracultura*. Barcelona: Montesinos.

SCANLON, G. (1986). *La polémica feminista en la España contemporánea (1868–1974)*. Madrid: Akal.
SCHAEFFER, C. (1988). 'Conspiración, manipulación, conversión ambigua: Pascual Duarte y la utopía histórica del Nuevo Estado Español', *Anales de la literatura española contemporánea*, 13/3: 261–81.
SEMPERE, P. (1976). *Semiología del infortunio: Lenguaje e ideología de la fotonovela*. Madrid: Felmar.
SENDER, R. (1957). *Before Noon (Chronicle of Dawn; The Violent Griffin; The Villa Julieta)*, trans. W. R. Trask. Albuquerque: University of New Mexico Press.
—— (1960). *Requiem for a Spanish Peasant*, trans. E. Randall. New York: Elinor, Las Américas.
—— (1984). *Crónica del alba*. Madrid: Alianza (1st pub. 1942–66).
SERRANO DE HARO, A. (1953). *Yo soy español*, 11th edn. Madrid: Escuela Española.
SHUBERT, A. (1990). *A Social History of Modern Spain*. London: Routledge.
SIEBURTH, S. (1994). *Inventing High and Low: Literature, Mass Culture and Uneven Modernity in Spain*. Durham, NC: Duke University Press.
SILES, J. (1992). *Poesía 1969–1990*. Madrid: Visor.
—— (1994). 'Ultimísima poesía española escrita en castellano', in *La poesía nueva en el mundo hispánico*. Madrid: Visor, 7–32.
SILVER, P. (1965). *'Et in Arcadia ego': A Study of the Poetry of Luis Cernuda*. London: Tamesis Books.
—— (1972). *Luis Cernuda: El poeta en su leyenda*. Madrid: Alfaguara.
SMITH, P. J. (1992). *Laws of Desire: Questions of Homosexuality in Spanish Writing and Film 1960–1990*. Oxford: Clarendon Press.
—— (1997). 'La representación del SIDA en el estado español', in X. Buxán (ed.), *Conciencia de un singular deseo: Estudios lesbianos y gays en el estado español*. Barcelona: Laertes, 303–18.
SOPEÑA MONSALVE, A. (1994). *El florido pensil: Memoria de la escuela nacional-católica*. Barcelona: Crítica.
SPIRES, R. (1996). *Post-totalitarian Spanish Fiction*. Columbia: University of Missouri Press.
TARRIO VARELA, A. (1988). *Literatura gallega*. Madrid: Taurus.
TERRY, A. and RAFEL, J. (1983). *Introducción a la lengua y la literatura catalanas*. Barcelona: Ariel.
TORO SANTOS, X. de (1995). 'Negotiating Galician Cultural Identity', in H. Graham and J. Labanyi (eds.), *Spanish Cultural Studies: An Introduction*. Oxford: Oxford University Press, 346–51.
TORRENTE BALLESTER, G. (1963). *Don Juan*. Barcelona: Destino.
¡Tú! (1950). 'Oh, la mujer', 126 (14 Oct.): 3.
TUSELL, J. (1990). *Manual de historia de España: Siglo XX*. Madrid: Historia 16.

TUSELL, J. (1998). 'Época actual', in J.-L. Martín, C. Martínez-Shaw, and J. Tusell, *Historia de España*. Madrid: Taurus, 687–831.

TUSQUETS, E. (1979). *El amor es un juego solitario*. Barcelona: Lumen.

—— (1985). *Love is a Solitary Game*, trans. B. Penman. London: J. Calder.

—— (1990). *The Same Sea as Every Summer*, trans. M. E. W. Jones. Lincoln: University of Nebraska Press.

UGARTE, M. (1982). *Trilogy of Treason: An Intertextual Study of Juan Goytisolo*. Columbia: University of Missouri Press.

—— (1989). *Shifting Ground: Spanish Civil War Exile Literature*. Durham, NC: Duke University Press.

UMBRAL, F. (1996). 'La tribu no vota a Felipe', in L. M. Anson et al., *Contra el poder*. Madrid: Temas de Hoy, 85–97.

VALENTE, J. Á. (1980). *Punto cero (Poesía 1935–1979)*. Barcelona: Seix Barral.

—— (1992). *Material memoria (1979–1989)*. Madrid: Alianza.

VALLE, A. del (1941). 'Romances a la inmaculada', *Vértice*, Especial Navidad-Año Nuevo [no number] [Dec.]: 19–22.

—— (1992). *Antología necesaria*. Seville: Alfar.

VALLS, F. (1991). 'La literatura erótica en España entre 1975 y 1990', *Ínsula*, 530: 29–30.

VÁZQUEZ DE PARGA, S. (1980). *Los comics del franquismo*. Barcelona: Planeta.

VÁZQUEZ MONTALBÁN, M. (1981). 'Que no decaiga', *Interviú*, Extra 'El tejeratazo', 249 (19–25 Feb.): 15.

—— (1992). *Autobiografía del general Franco*. Barcelona: Planeta.

Vértice (1941). [Untitled article], 4/41 (Feb.): 32.

VILLENA, L. A. de (1980). *Para los dioses turcos*. Barcelona: Laertes.

——(1984). 'Introducción', to L. Cernuda, *Las nubes; Desolación de la quimera*, ed. L. A. de Villena. Madrid: Cátedra, 7–79.

—— (1988). *Poesía 1970–1984*. Madrid: Visor.

—— (1993). *Marginados*. Madrid: Visor.

VILLENA, M. A. (1997*a*). 'Escritores catalanes, gallegos y vascos irrumpen en el mercado editorial en castellano', *El país* (25 May): 34.

—— (1997*b*). 'Los jóvenes autores de teatro devuelven la palabra a los escenarios españoles', *El país* (27 Oct.): 36.

WELLWARTH, G. (1972). *Spanish Underground Drama*. University Park: Pennsylvania State University Press.

ZATLIN, P. (1984). 'El fulgor y la sangre: Retrato de cinco mujeres', in D. Lytra (ed.), *Aproximación crítica a Ignacio Aldecoa*. Madrid: Espasa Calpe, 109–17.

—— (1991). 'Writing against the Current: The Novels of Elena Quiroga', in J. Brown (ed.), *Women Writers of Contemporary Spain: Exiles in the Homeland*. London: Associated University Presses, 42–58.

Index

Abad, Mercedes (1961–) 205
ABC 19, 21, 113, 114
Absurd, Theatre of the 151, 185
AIDS 23, 212, 219
Acento cultural 136
Agustí, Ignacio (1913–74) 39, 144
Álamo, Antonio (1964–) 212
Alas, Leopoldo (1962–) 219
Alberti, Rafael (1902–99) 4, 77–9, 125, 179, 210
 De un momento a otro 77–8
Alcalde, Carmen (1936–) 193
Aldecoa, Ignacio (1925–69) 14
 El fulgor y la sangre 60–2
Aldecoa, Josefina R. (1926–) 213
Aleixandre, Vicente (1898–1984) 9, 23, 128, 129, 200
Alfaro, José María (1906–94) 9, 31
Aliaga, Juan Vicente (1959–) 219
Alonso, Dámaso (1898–1990) 9
Alonso de Santos, José Luis (1942–) 95, 156
Alós, Concha (1922–) 103, 165
alternative magazines 194
Álvarez, José María (1942–) 159, 182–3, 184
Andreu, Blanca (1959–) 179
Andújar, Manuel (1913–94) 40
Antolín Rato, Mariano (1943–) 171
Aparicio, Juan (1906–) 9, 32
Aranguren, José Luis L. (1909–96) 13, 107
Araujo, Alicia 104
Araújo, Luis (1956–) 212
Arbó, Sebastián J. (1902–84) 138
Arbor 11
Arrabal, Fernando (1932–) 80–1, 184
Arriba 113
Atxaga, Bernardo (pseud. of José Irazu Garmendia) (1951–) 209, 210
Aub, Max (1903–72) 4, 40, 107
Aute, Luis Eduardo (1943–) 179
autobiographical writings 210

Ayala, Francisco (1906–) 4, 40, 137, 210
Azorín (José Martínez Ruiz) (1873–1966) 9, 32

Badosa, Enrique (1927–) 129
Barceló, Elia 103
Barcelona School of poets ('Escuela de Barcelona') 159
Barea, Arturo (1897–1957) 40
Baroja, Pío (1872–1956) 146
Barral, Carlos (1928–1989) 129, 159, 210
Basque Country 45, 161
 autonomy 22
 language 5–6, 209
 literature 209–10
 nationalism 16, 22, 210
Bazar 71
Belbel, Sergi (1962–) 187
Benavente, Jacinto (1866–1954) 79
Benet, Juan (1928–1993) 62, 65, 169–70
Benet i Jornet, Josep Maria (1940–) 187
bolero 191–2
Borrás, Tomás (1891–1976) 40
Bousoño, Carlos (1923–) 34, 125, 129–30, 157, 159
Brines, Francisco (1932–) 125, 130, 157, 181, 183, 204, 213
Brossa, Joan (1919–98) 187
Buero Vallejo, Antonio (1916–) 12, 47–9, 83–6, 119–21, 151–3, 154, 156
 La doble historia del doctor Valmy 83–5
 Historia de una escalera 119–20
 Un soñador para un pueblo 48–9
Buñuel, Miguel (1924–98) 145

Cabal, Fermín (1948–) 157
Caballero Bonald, José María (1926–) 157
Calvo Serer, Rafael (1916–88) 107

Index

Calvo Sotelo, Joaquín (1905–93) 80
Campos, Jorge (pseud. of Jorge Renales Fernández) 137
Cántico group of poets 36, 181
Carande, Ramón (1887–1986) 45
Carandell, Luis 90–1
Cardín, Alberto (1948–91) 219
Carnero, Guillermo (1947–) 131–2, 180, 184
Caro Baroja, Julio (1914–95) 45
El caso 17, 138
Casona, Alejandro (1903–65) 4
Castellet, Josep María (1926–) 135–6, 210
Castro, Américo (1885–1972) 44
Castro, Luisa (1966–) 201–2, 203, 205, 215
Castroviejo, Concha (1912–) 40
Catalonia 14
  autonomy 22
  and Francoism 42
  language 5–6, 209
  literature 42, 209–10
  nationalism 16, 22
Cela, José Camilo (1916–) 5, 12, 41, 138, 169, 204
  La colmena 139–40
  La familia de Pascual Duarte 38, 74–5
Celaya, Gabriel (1911–91) 14, 46, 131, 135, 179
censorship 3–6, 14, 15–17, 118–25, 135, 156, 188
Cernuda, Luis (1902–1963) 106, 125–7, 160, 179, 200
Chacel, Rosa (1898–1994) 4, 97, 210
Church, Roman Catholic 105–6, 167
  dissent from within 106
  and education 11
  and Francoist state 3, 6, 10–11
  and religious press 11–12
  and social change 92–3
  and workers' organizations 10, 11
  see also National Catholicism
Cirlot, Juan Eduardo (1916–73) 179
Civil War, Spanish 1–4, 210
  literary accounts of 39–43, 60–1, 64, 97, 167
children, publications for 11, 30
  El Capitán Trueno 30
  Flechas y pelayos 10, 71
  El guerrero del antifaz 29, 30
Colinas, Antonio (1946–) 301

Conde, Carmen (1907–96) 182
Cortés, José Miguel (1955–) 219
'costumbrismo' 19, 36
Crémer, Victoriano (1907–) 46
Cuadernos para el diálogo 16, 113, 146, 194
Cué, Ramón 36
cultural policies 8–10, 187, 212
  regional 23, 42, 209, 210
  see also censorship
'culturalismo' 179, 182
Cunillé, Lluïsa (1961–) 212
Cunqueiro, Álvaro (1911–81) 145

Delibes, Miguel (1920–) 17, 38, 138
  Cinco horas con Mario 124–5
Destino 136, 145
detective fiction *see* narrative fiction
Diego, Gerardo (1896–97) 32, 34
Díaz-Mas, Paloma (1954–) 67, 103, 215
Diosdado, Ana (1943–) 49–50, 198
dissent:
  political 14, 111–13
  in press 113–15
D'Ors, Eugenio (1882–1954) 9
drama:
  of the 1990s 212
  anti-realist 184–5
  bourgeois 150–1, 153
  domestic 77, 79–80, 152
  escapist 150–1
  feminist 56–7, 100–02
  historical 47–57
  metatheatrical 154
  political 55–6, 85
  realist 153, 154–7
  subsidies for 211–12

Ecclesia 11, 74, 113
education, 11, 27–9, 32, 135
eighteenth century ideas 45, 48–9
empire, ideas of 8, 25–8, 33, 36
  parodied 67
erotic writing 188, 204–7, 220
Escorial 9, 34
Espadaña 45–6, 128
Espriu, Salvador (1913–1985) 42, 187
essays and essayists 19, 20–1, 23, 24, 39, 44–5, 106–7, 211
Etxebarría, Lucía (1966–) 215–6, 217
exile of intellectuals 12, 15, 125–7, 213

existentialist concerns 14, 34, 137, 164, 165, 175–6

Fabretti, Carlos 179
Falange (Falange Española Tradicionalista y de las Juntas de Ofensiva Nacional Sindicalista) 7–9
  and literary journals 9, 35
Falcón, Lidia (1935–) 56–7, 95, 100–2, 196
family:
  bourgeois 77–9
  and the Church 11, 68–70, 91–2
  critiques of 73–90, 95–6
  Falangist ideas on 70–2
  Francoist ideas on 68–9, 72–3
  and nation 72, 74–5, 83–4, 122
  and popular press 69
  in the post-Franco period 90, 91–3
fantastic literature 63–5, 178–9
  as contestatory space 102–3
Felipe, León (1884–1968) 4, 126
feminist magazines 194
Fernández, Lluís (1945–) 209, 219
Fernández Cubas, Cristina (1945–) 178
Fernández Santos, Jesús (1926–88) 14, 65, 137
  Los bravos 140–1
Ferrero, Jesús (1952–) 171
Ferres, Antonio (1924–) 137
Figuera, Ángela (1092–84) 183
'fotonovelas' 189
Foxá, Agustín, Conde de (1903–1959) 42
Fraile, Medardo (1925–) 137
Franco, Francisco:
  death of 15
  as father figure 72–3
  nature of early regime 6–12
Freixas, Laura (1958–) 194
Fuertes, Gloria (1918–1998) 158, 183

Gaceta universitaria 16, 17
Gala, Antonio (1936–) 65, 115, 215
Galicia 22
  language 5–6, 210
  literature 209–10
  nationalism 22
Gaos, José (1900–69) 44
Ganivet, Ángel (1865–1898) 32
García, Concha (1956–) 203–4

García, Consuelo (1935–) 196
García Lorca, Federico (1898–1936) 4, 37, 55, 79, 128, 179, 202, 212
García Matilla, Luis (1939–) 55–6
García Montero, Luis (1958–) 159, 160–1
García Morales, Adelaida (1945–) 176, 215
García Serrano, Rafael (1917–88) 39–40, 41–2, 131
Garcilaso 9, 33
gay and lesbian press 220
gay popular literature 220
gender 193
  and identity 165, 207, 215
  and narrative perspective 61
  and power 96–102, 197
  and science fiction 103–4
  see also women *and* women's writing
'Generación realista' (Realist Generation, of dramatists) 154–6
Generation of 1898 31, 107, 147
Generation of 1927 34, 131
Generation of 1950 (of poets) 157–8
Generations of 1970 22
Generation X 216–19
Gil Albert, Juan (1906–1994) 181
Gil de Biedma, Jaime (1929–1990) 129, 159–60, 183
Giménez Caballero, Ernesto (1899–1988) 42
Gimferrer, Pere (1945–) 131, 132–3, 180, 183–4, 201
Gironella, José María (1917–) 40
Golden Age literature:
  emulation of 34, 37, 131, 214
  as source of dissident ideas 51–2
Gómez de la Serna, Ramón (1888–1963) 144, 145
Gómez Ojea, Carmen (1945–) 67, 103
González, Ángel (1925–) 183
Gopegui, Belén (1963–) 176, 215
Goytisolo, Juan (1931–) 62, 107, 118–19, 135, 141, 143–4, 146, 164, 165, 168–9, 210, 219
Goytisolo, José Agustín (1928–99) 159
Goytisolo, Luis (1935–) 62, 145
graffiti 111–13

Grandes, Almudena (1960–) 204, 205
    Las edades de Lulú 205–7
Grosso, Alfonso (1928–95) 169
Guasch, Óscar 219
Gubern, B. Romá (1934–) 92
Guelbenzu, José María (1944–) 171
Guera, María 104
Guillén, Jorge (1893–1984) 4, 32, 160, 184
Guirao, Olga (1950–) 215
Guzmán, Almudena (1964–) 205

Haro Ibars, Eduardo (1948–88) 178–9, 217
Haro Tecglen, Eduardo (1924–) 17
Haupold Gay, Augusto 106
Hernández, Miguel (1910–42) 4
HOAC (Hermandades Obreras de Acción Católica) 16, 69
¡Hola! 69, 73
history, revisionist 44–5
homoeroticism 200, 207
homosexuality, male 219

Ibáñez, Jesús (1928–82) 23, 211
Icaza, Carmen de (1899–1979) 39, 89
Inglés, Teresa 104
Ínsula 12, 128, 136, 137, 145
'intrahistoria' 47, 52
Informaciones 114
Interviú 21
Isabel la Católica (Isabel of Castile) (as fictionalized character) 36–7, 50–1

Jaén, María (1962–) 205
Janés, Clara (1940–) 161, 205, 215
Jardiel Poncela, Enrique (1901–52) 80, 150–1
Jiménez, Juan Ramón (1881–1958) 4, 125
Jiménez Ariza, Antonio (1959–) 220
Jover, José Luis (1946–) 200–1
Juliá Martínez, Eduardo (1911–) 37–8

Kurtz, Carmen (1911–) 194

Labordeta, Miguel (1921–69) 46
Laforet, Carmen (1921–) 12, 144
    Nada 38, 86–7, 96, 138
Laín Entralgo, Pedro (1908–) 9, 13, 39, 106
Landero, Luis (1948–) 176, 177, 213

Laye 129, 135
Leguina, Joaquín (1941–):
    Tu nombre envenena mis sueños 66–7
Lera, Ángel María de (1912–84) 137
lesbian culture 199, 220
lesbian protagonists 93, 198–9, 216
'leyenda negra' ('Black Legend') 28, 67
Linares-Becerra, Concha 39, 89, 190–1
Llamazares, Julio (1955–) 177
López Mozo, Jerónimo (1942–) 55–6
López Pacheco, Jesús (1930–) 137
López Rubio, José (1903–96) 80, 150
López Salinas, Armando (1925–) 137
Loriga, Ray (1967–) 217
Luca de Tena, Juan Ignacio (1897–1975) 80
Luis, Leopoldo de (1918–) 180

Machado, Antonio (1875–1939) 4, 31, 32, 34, 47, 142, 158
Machado, Manuel (1874–1947) 32, 180
'machismo' 52–3
Madrid, Juan (1947–) 66, 174–5
Maeztu, Ramiro de (1875–1936) 25 n., 32
Mañas, José Ángel (1971–) 217–18
marketing of literature 209, 211
Marías, Javier (1951–) 171, 176
Marías, Julián (1914–) 9, 13, 18, 107
Marina, José Antonio (1939–) 211
Marquina, Eduardo (1897–1946) 36–7
Marsé, Juan (1933–) 165, 166, 171, 210
    Si te dicen que caí 166–8
Martín, Andreu (1949–) 66
Martín Descalzo, José Luis (1930–91) 137
Martín Elizondo, José (1922–) 50
Martín Gaite, Carmen (1925–) 62, 86, 88–9, 144, 165, 172, 215
    El cuarto de atrás 62–5, 98–9, 191–2
Martín Recuerda, José (1922–) 54–5, 154, 155, 156
Martín-Santos, Luis (1924–64)
    Tiempo de silencio 77, 146–9
Martínez Mesanza, Julio (1955–) 157
Martínez Mediero, Manuel (1939–) 50, 186

Martínez Sarrión, Antonio (1939–) 179, 183
Marxism 14, 129
Mateo, Lope (1898–1970) 31, 32
Mateo, Luis D. (1942–) 176
Matute, Ana María (1926–) 89, 141, 144, 165
  Primera memoria 87–8, 96
Mayoral, Marina (1942–) 210
medieval Spain:
  as ideal 29–30, 132
  values of critiqued 61
Medio, Dolores (1911–96) 89, 164–5
Mendicutti, Eduardo (1948–) 219
Mendoza, Eduardo (1943–) 172–3, 174
Menéndez y Pelayo, Marcelino (1856–1912) 32
Mengotti, Arturo 104
Merino, José María (1941–) 171, 215
Mesquida, Biel (1947–) 204
metafiction 64, 170–2, 177
  see also self-referential writing
Mihura, Miguel (1905–77) 80, 150
Millás, Juan José (1946–) 95, 116–17, 176
Miralles, Alberto (1940–) 56
Miras, Domingo (1934–) 56
'modernismo' 179, 182
Moix, Ana María (1947–) 97, 99, 159, 178, 183, 199, 200–1
Moix, Terenci (1943–) 65, 182, 209, 215, 219
Molina Foix, Vicente (1946–) 115, 171
Montero, Rosa (1951–) 93–4, 101, 102, 103, 115–16, 176, 177, 192–3, 194, 195–6
Monzó, Quim (1952–) 210
movida 23
Munárriz, Jesús (1940–)
Muñoz Molina, Antonio (1956–) 146, 171, 176, 177, 213
Muñiz, Carlos (1927–94) 56, 154, 155
myth 143, 170

narrative fiction:
  of the 1940s 38–40
  of the 1950s 163–5, *see also* realism
  of the 1960s and 1970s 17, 170–2
  of the 1980s and 1990s 95, 174–9, 208–11, 213, 214–20

detective fiction ('novela negra') 66–7, 172–5
experimental 19, 65, 148, 163, 169, 171–2
historical 67
Latin American 145–6
romantic ('novela rosa') 89, 188–91
short stories 14, 40, 104, 137, 177–8, 190, 199
testimonial 97, 177
National Catholicism 6, 10–11, 124
  critiqued 88
national identity 106–7, 147, 155
  Francoist ideas on 5, 6, 25–8, 38, 135
  questioning of 48, 51–4, 180, 208
  see also family
Neville, Edgar (1899–1967) 80
Nicol, Eduardo (1907–90) 44
Nieva, Francisco (1927–) 186
Nora, Eugenio de (1923–) 34, 46
novel, *see* narrative fiction
'novísimos' (group of poets) 20, 132, 158, 160, 181–4, 200
'nueva narrativa', *see* narrative fiction, of the 1980s and 1990s
'nueva novela española', *see* narrative fiction, of the 1960s and 1970s
'nuevo teatro' (New Theatre) 81–2, 110–11, 123, 184–7

Oliver, María Antònia (1947–) 175
Olmo, Lauro (1922–94) 76–7, 137, 154, 155
Onetti, Antonio (1962–) 212
Ortega y Gasset, José (1883–1955) 13, 32, 147
Ortiz, Lourdes (1943–) 175, 176, 205
Ory, Carlos Edmundo de (1923–) 179
Otero, Blas de (1916–79) 9, 14, 47, 128, 180
Otxoa, Julia (1953–) 134, 161–2

Panero, Leopoldo (1909–62) 9, 128, 213
Pascual, Itziar (1967–) 212
Paso, Alfonso (1921–78) 80, 119
patriarchy, challenges to 97–105
PCE (Partido Comunista Español) 21, 22
Pedrero, Paloma (1957–) 157, 197
Pedrolo, Manuel de (1918–) 187

240 Index

Pemán, José María (1898–1984) 32, 36–7, 79
Pérez Galdós, Benito (1843–1920) 136
Pérez y Pérez, Rafael (1891–1984) 39, 189–90
Pérez Reverte, Arturo (1957–) 66
Perucho, Juan (1920–) 145
poetry:
  of the 1940s 31–6
  of the 1950s and 1960s 20, 128–31, 179–84
  of the 1970s and 1980s 20, 131–4, 160, 200–2
  and communicability 128–31, 133
  of experience ('poesía de experiencia') 183
  pure ('poesía pura') 45, 125, 128–9, 182, 203
  religious 34–6, 188
  'rooted' ('poesía arraigada') 33
  and 'silence' 130–4, 158
  socially committed 20, 45–7, 129, 131, 132, 157
Pombo, Álvaro (1939–) 99, 215
Pombo, Pilar (1953–) 198
'posnovísimos' (group of poets) 132, 219
'postismo' 179, 183
postmodern traits 154, 172, 174, 176, 177, 197, 208, 218
Prado, Benjamín 218
Prados, Emilio (1899–1962) 125
press:
  conservative 114
  laws concerning 4–5, 16–17, 113
  see also censorship
prizes 42, 211, 212
PSOE (Partido Socialista Obrero Español) 114–17
Puértolas, Soledad (1947–) 176

Queizán, María Xosé (1939–) 103
Quiles, Eduardo (1940–) 186
Quiroga, Elena (1919–95) 96–7, 99, 144, 146, 163–4

Rabazo, Armando (1960–) 220
Ragué Arias, María José 91–2
Ramírez, Cristóbal 220
reading habits 23–4
realism 14, 135–9
  anti- 143–9, 173–4
  magic 144, 145–6

new 22, 174
  objectivist 143–4, 148
  psychological 19, 164
  return to in 1980s 156, 163, 175–7
  social 19, 75–7, 136–7, 140–4, 148
Reina, María Manuela (1958–) 157
Reixa, Antón (1957–) 209
Resino, Carmen (1941–) 198
Revista de Occidente 16, 146
Revista española 136
Riaza, Luis (1925–) 111, 186
Ridruejo, Dionisio (1912–75) 9, 31, 33, 34, 41, 127–8
Riera, Carme (1949–) 86, 92, 199, 210
Ríos, Fernando de los (1879–1949) 44
Ríos, Julián (1949–) 172
Rivas, Manuel (1957–) 210
Rodoreda, Mercè (1909–83) 97
Rodríguez Méndez, José María (1925–) 51–4, 154, 155, 156
  Bodas que fueron famosas del Pingajo y la Fandanga 53–4
Rodríguez, Claudio (1934–) 129, 157
Rodríguez, Josefina (1926–) 137
Roig, Montserrat (1946–91) 94, 101, 194, 196
romantic fiction, see narrative fiction
Romano, Vicente 211
Romeo, Ignacio 179
Romero, Concha (1948–) 50–1
Rosales, Luis (1910–92) 9, 35, 36, 140
Rossetti, Ana (1950–) 201, 205
Ruibal, José (1925–) 81–3, 110–11, 123, 185–6
Ruiz Iriarte, Víctor (1912–82) 150
rural life:
  and emigration to cities 18
  idealizations of 58
  literary representations of 59–62, 74, 138, 140–1, 145, 177

Sahagún, Carlos (1938–) 131
Salinas, Pedro (1891–1951) 4, 125, 132, 184
Salisachs, Mercedes (1916–) 144
Sánchez Albornoz, Claudio (1893–1984) 44
Sánchez Dragó, Fernando (1936–) 41, 114–5
Sánchez Espeso, Germán (1940–) 171
Sánchez Ferlosio, Rafael (1927–) 14

Index

El Jarama 141–3
Sanchis Sinisterra, José (1940–) 186–7
Sastre, Alfonso (1926–) 14, 55,
    108–11, 119–22, 135, 144,
    153–4, 156
  Escuadra hacia la muerte 108–11
  La mordaza, 121–2
Savater, Fernando (1947–) 23, 92,
    194, 211
science fiction 103–5, 178–9
Sección Femenina 70–2, 98
self-referential writing 63–5, 171–2,
    173, 184, 218
Sender, Ramón J. (1901–1981) 40, 57
  Crónica del alba 57–9
  Réquiem por un campesino español
    59–60
sexual morality 68, 71–2, 92, 193–5
short story, *see* narrative fiction
Siles, Jaime (1951–) 131, 133
Sirera, Rodolf (1948–) 187
Soriano, Elena (1917–) 144, 194
Sueiro, Daniel (1931–86) 137
surrealism 129, 173

'teatro independiente' (Independent
    Theatre) 123
Teixidor Martínez, Jordi (1939–) 187
Tono (pseud. of Antonio Lara)
    (1896–1978) 150
Toro, Suso de (1956–) 209
Torrente Ballester, Gonzalo (1910–99)
    34, 38, 170–1, 210
transition to democracy 20–4, 172–3,
    177
translation, literature in 209
Trapiello, Andrés (1953–) 157
'tremendismo' 74, 137–8, 139, 214
Triunfo 17, 193
¡Tú! 11, 69–70, 113
Tusquets, Esther (1936–) 90, 93, 196,
    198, 210, 213

Ullán, José Miguel (1944–) 184
Umbral, Francisco (1935–) 23, 115
Unamuno, Miguel de (1864–1936) 32,
    175
unemployment 21, 23, 155, 217

Urbina, Pedro Antonio (1936–) 171

Valente, José Ángel (1929–) 125, 129,
    133, 157, 158–9, 183
Valle, Adriano del (1895–1957) 35–6,
    188
Valle-Inclán, Ramón María del
    (1866–1936) 56, 78, 139, 185,
    212
Valverde, José María (1926–96) 34
Vázquez Montalbán, Manuel (1939–)
    17, 21, 73, 90, 173–4, 182
Velasco, Lola (1961–) 205
Vértice 9, 32–3, 35
Vicens Vives, Jaume (1910–60) 44
Vicent, Manuel (1936–) 114
Villena, Luis Antonio de (1951–) 90,
    159, 178, 194, 213
violence 30, 31, 75, 81–3, 212, 220
  domestic 76–7, 93, 100
  political 18
Vivanco, Luis Felipe (1907–75) 9, 36
Vizcaíno Casas, Fernando (1926–)
    41

women:
  and education 17
  and legal reform 17
  and political opposition 17
  restrictions on 69, 76, 89–90, 98,
    100
  role of 69–72
  and sexuality 195–9, 202–3,
    216
women's writing 64–5, 214–6
  exclusion of from literary histories
    104–5, 163–5
  on the family 86–9
  on the mother-child bond 93–4
working class protagonists 52–4,
    55–6, 57, 61, 97–8, 142–3

Zambrano, María (1904–91) 44, 107,
    211
Zubiri, Xavier (1898–1983) 13, 39
Zunzunegui, Juan Antonio de
    (1901–82) 39, 137,
    144–5